THE
NEW
SCIENCE
OF THE
PARANORMAL

© Lisa Novak

CARL LLEWELLYN WESCHCKE was Chairman of Llewellyn Worldwide, Ltd., one of the oldest and largest publishers of New Age, Metaphysical, Self-Help, and Spirituality books in the world. He held a Bachelor of Science degree in Business Administration (Babson), and studied Law (LaSalle Extension University) and completed advanced academic work toward a doctorate in Philosophy (University of Minnesota). He also held a certificate in clinical hypnosis and honorary recognitions in divinity and magical philosophy.

In addition to book publishing, he worked in the pharmaceutical industry, furniture manufacturing, and real estate management. With Llewellyn, he worked in all aspects of the business: advertising, editing, production, writing, astrological calculation, design and layout, typesetting, cover design, direct selling, bookstore management, trade sales, designing systems and procedures, printing and purchasing, warehouse and shipping, and mopping floors.

Carl was a life-long student of a broad range of Metaphysical, Spiritual, and Psychological subjects, and variously studied with the Rosicrucian Order, the Arcane School, and the Society of the Inner Light. After corresponding with Gerald Gardner and several of his associates in the late 1950s and early 1960s, he became known for holding the "Weschcke Documents," including a carbon copy of Gardner's own Book of Shadows.

He was a former Wiccan High Priest and played a leading role in the rise of Wicca and Neo-Paganism during the 1960s and 1970s. Authors Scott Cunningham and Donald Michael Kraig referred to him as "the Father of the New Age" because of his early and aggressive public sponsorship of new understanding of old occult subjects. In the fall of 1973, Weschcke helped organize the Council of American Witches and became its chairperson. Weschcke drafted *The Thirteen Principles of Belief* statement, a cornerstone of modern Wicca. This document was incorporated into the U.S. Army's handbook for chaplains.

In addition to his evolving writing pursuits, he retained ties to the Wiccan and Neo-Pagan communities through many Llewellyn authors. He was 7th Past Grandmaster of Aurum Solis, an international magical order founded in Great Britain in 1897. While Chairman of Llewellyn, he actively wrote and engaged in studies and practical research in Analytical Psychology and Parapsychology; Tarot and Divination; Quantum Theory and Cosmology; Astrology, Magick, and Kabbalah; Meditation, Hypnosis and Alternative Health; Shamanism, Tantra, Taoism, and World Spirituality; Mythology, Wicca, and Neo-Paganism; History, Geo-Politics, and Philosophy. He also authored and co-authored nine books, several e-books and audio products, and a new edition with commentary of *The Compete Magick Curriculum of the Secret Order G.∴B.∴G.∴*

Carl passed away in the fall of 2015, but his indelible contributions to the study and practice of spirituality will be remembered and honored for generations to come.

JOE H. SLATE holds a Ph.D. from the University of Alabama, with post-doctoral studies at the University of California. Dr. Slate was appointed Professor Emeritus in 1992, after having served as Professor of Psychology, Head of the Division of Behavioral Sciences, and Director of Institutional Effectiveness at Athens State University in Alabama. He is an Honorary Professor at Montevallo University and former Adjunct Professor at Forest Institute of Professional Psychology. Dr. Slate is a licensed psychologist and member of the American Psychological Association. He is listed in the National Register of Health Service Psychologists and the Prescribing Psychologist's Register.

As head of Athens State University Psychology Department and Director of Institutional Effectiveness, he established the University's parapsychology research laboratory and introduced experimental parapsychology, biofeedback, hypnosis and self-hypnosis into the instructional and research programs in the curriculum. His research includes projects for the U.S. Army Missile Research and Development Command and the Parapsychology Foundation with funding from the U.S. Army, the Parapsychology Foundation of New York and numerous private sources. He is founder of the **Parapsychology Research Institute and Foundation (PRIF)** (over 500 members) that has endowed scholarship programs in perpetuity at both Athens State University and the University of Alabama as well as undertaking research projects in dream work and mind/body health.

His official research topics have included: Rejuvenation, Health and Fitness, the Human Aura, Psychotherapy, Reincarnation, Precognition, Retro-cognition, Telepathy, Clairvoyance, Psychokinesis, Objectology, Numerology, Astral Projection, Sand Reading, Crystal Gazing, Dowsing, Dreams, the Wrinkled Sheet, Table Tipping, Discarnate Interactions, Psychic Vampirism, Hypnosis and Self-hypnosis, Age and Past-life Regression, the Afterlife, Pre-existence, the Peak Experience, Natural Resources, Learning, Problem Solving, and the Subconscious, to list but a few.

He has founded several scholarships:

Dr. Joe H. Slate Scholarship for the Arts, Athens State University.

Dr. Joe H. and Rachel Slate Scholarship, University of Alabama.

International Parapsychology Research Foundation Scholarship, Athens State University.

Note: Each scholarship exists in perpetuity and is awarded annually to students who need financial assistance.

Dr. Slate has appeared on several radio and television shows, including *Strange Universe*, the *History Channel*, and *Sightings*.

THE
NEW
SCIENCE
OF THE
PARANORMAL

*FROM THE RESEARCH LAB
TO REAL LIFE*

CARL LLEWELLYN WESCHCKE
JOE H. SLATE, PHD

Llewellyn Publications
Woodbury, Minnesota

FIRST EDITION
First Printing, 2016

Cover art: iStock.com/57954514/©ikatod
Cover design: Lisa Novak
Interior Photos: EMP Studios/Decatur, Alabama

Llewellyn Publications is a registered trademark of Llewellyn Worldwide Ltd.

Library of Congress Cataloging-in-Publication Data
Names: Weschcke, Carl Llewellyn, 1930–2015, author.
Title: The new science of the paranormal : out of the research lab to the
    real world extra-sensory perception, the out-of-body experience,
    psychokinesis, clairvoyance, mental telepathy, precognition, dowsing,
    objectology, the human aura, past-lives memories, and more! : ancient
    wisdom to modern science / Carl Llewellyn Weschcke, Joe H. Slate, PHD.
Description: FIRST EDITION. | Woodbury : Llewellyn Worldwide, Ltd, 2016. |
    Includes bibliographical references and index.
Identifiers: LCCN 2016013816 (print) | LCCN 2016015248 (ebook) | ISBN
    9780738749112 (alk. paper) | ISBN 9780738749259
Subjects: LCSH: Parapsychology.
Classification: LCC BF1031 .W4176 2016 (print) | LCC BF1031 (ebook) | DDC
    130—dc23
LC record available at https://lccn.loc.gov/2016013816

Llewellyn Worldwide Ltd. does not participate in, endorse, or have any authority or responsibility concerning private business transactions between our authors and the public.
    All mail addressed to the author is forwarded but the publisher cannot, unless specifically instructed by the author, give out an address or phone number.
    Any Internet references contained in this work are current at publication time, but the publisher cannot guarantee that a specific location will continue to be maintained. Please refer to the publisher's website for links to authors' websites and other sources.

Llewellyn Publications
A Division of Llewellyn Worldwide Ltd.
2143 Wooddale Drive
Woodbury, MN 55125-2989
www.llewellyn.com

Printed in the United States of America

OTHER BOOKS BY JOE H. SLATE

Astral Projection and Psychic Empowerment, 1998, Llewellyn

Aura Energy for Better Health and Happiness, 2002, Motilal Banarsidass

Aura Energy for Health, Healing and Balance, 1999, Llewellyn

Beyond Reincarnation, 2005, Llewellyn

Connecting to the Power of Nature, 2009, Llewellyn

Energy Psiquica, 1998, Selector

Handbuch der Aura-Energie, 1999, Bauer

Kirlian Connection, The, 1985, Athens State College

Los vampires psiquicos, Editoria Diana

Mas alla de la Reencarnacion, 2006, Llewellyn Espanol

Psychic Empowerment, 1995, Llewellyn

Psychic Empowerment for Health and Fitness, 1996, Llewellyn

Psychic Phenomena: New Principles, Techniques and Applications, 1998, McFarland

Psychic Vampires, 2002, Llewellyn

Rejuvenation, 2000, Llewellyn Espanol

Rejuvenezca, 2004, Aquilar

Self-Empowerment: Strategies for Success, 1991 Colonial Press

OTHER TITLES BY JOE H. SLATE AND
CARL LLEWELLYN WESCHCKE

All About Auras, 2011, Llewellyn

All About Tea Leaf Reading, 2012, Llewellyn

Astral Projection for Psychic Empowerment CD Companion—Past, Present and Future NOW (The Now Program), 2013, Llewellyn

Astral Projection for Psychic Empowerment—The Out-of-Body Experience, Astral Powers, and their Practical Application, 2012, Llewellyn

Clairvoyance for Psychic Empowerment—The Art and Science of "Clear Seeing" Past the Illusions of Space and Time and Self-Deception—Includes Developing Psychic Clarity and True Vision, 2013, Llewellyn

Communicating with Spirit—Long Suppressed in Western Culture and Religions, Here's How You Can Communicate with (and Benefit from) Spirits of the Departed, Spirit Guides and Helpers, Gods and Goddesses, Your Higher Self and Your Holy Guardian Angel, 2015, Llewellyn

Doors to Past Lives and Future Lives—Practical Applications of Self-Hypnosis, 2011, Llewellyn

The Llewellyn Complete Book of Psychic Empowerment—A Compendium of Tools and Techniques for Growth and Transformation—Includes Journey of a Lifetime, a Self-Directed Program of Developmental Actions to "Put it All Together, 2011, Llewellyn

PK—Moving Objects with Your Mind—The Power of Psychokinesis, 2011, Llewellyn

Psychic Empowerment for Everyone—You Have the Power, Learn How to Use It, 2009, Llewellyn

Remembering Past Lives, 2011, Llewellyn

Self-Empowerment and Your Subconscious Mind—Your Unlimited Resource for Health, Success, Long Life and Spiritual Attainment, 2010, Llewellyn

Self-Empowerment through Self-Hypnosis—Harnessing the Enormous Potential of the Mind, 2010, Llewellyn

Self-Empowerment through Self-Hypnosis Meditation CD Companion, 2011, Llewellyn

Self-Hypnosis for Success in Life, 2011, Llewellyn

Vibratory Astral Projection and Clairvoyance CD Companion: Your Next Step in Evolutional Consciousness and Psychic Empowerment—An Audio CD companion to the book, Clairvoyance for Psychic Empowerment, 2013, Llewellyn

OTHER BOOKS BY CARL LLEWELLYN WESCHCKE

The Complete Magick Curriculum of the Secret Order G∴B∴G∴—Being the Entire Study Curriculum, Magick Rituals, and Initiatory Practices of the G.B.G. (The Great Brotherhood of God), 2010, Llewellyn (with Louis T. Culling)

Dream ESP—The Secret of Prophetic Causal Dreaming to Bring About Desired Change. Derived from the Taoist I Ching, 2015, Llewellyn

This Book is dedicated to the
"Father" of 20th Century Parapsychology

J. B. Rhine

Widely recognized as the Father of Parapsychology, J. B. Rhine established the study of parapsychology as an academic discipline and developed the foundational concepts and research methodology required for it to assume scientific recognition. The results include the professionalization of parapsychology not only in the U. S. but also on a transcultural scale.

In today's diverse global community, the contemporary relevance of J. B. Rhine's early groundbreaking research stands firmly on scientific grounds. Aside from the detailed procedures and controls characterizing his lab studies, he developed the advanced analytical and statistical methods required to determine the significance of the experimental data. Beyond the lab, he inspired the application and advancement of parapsychology to include its inclusion as an academic discipline in higher education along with the establishment of professional parapsychology organizations and academic journals.

J. B. Rhine's analytical and statistical contributions to parapsychology as a science are among the seminal inspirations for not only the detailed lab studies presented in this book but for the numerous research-based applications beyond the lab.

WHAT OTHERS SAY

Upon completion of his Ph.D. at the University of Alabama, Dr. Slate joined Athens State University (then Athens College) where his instructional and administrative functions included Professor of Psychology, Chair of the Behavioral Sciences, and Director of Institutional Effectiveness. During his professional tenure at ASU, Dr. Slate conducted scores of research studies, including projects funded by the U. S. Army Missile Research and Development Command, the Parapsychology Foundation of New York, and several of private sources. His innovative research using electrophotographic technology became widely recognized as important to our understanding of the human energy system. Other important research topics included rejuvenation and longevity, health and fitness, altered states of consciousness, and a host of paranormal topics designed to explore the dynamics of various unexplained phenomena. His introduction of parapsychology into the ASU curriculum as a relevant field of study was a first for the State of Alabama.

The central focus of this book throughout is on the relevance of Dr. Slate's numerous research studies, including those conducted at ASU within the context of such instructional courses as Experimental Parapsychology, Seminar in Parapsychology, and Special Topics in Parapsychology. Other studies cited in the book were conducted under the auspices of the Parapsychology Research Institute and Foundation (PRIF), which was founded by Dr. Slate at ASU in 1970 and is now a private organization. Aside from research, a major goal of PRIF is the establishment of scholarships for students in need. A portion of the royalties from Dr. Slate's books go toward that goal.

Dr. Slate, now ASU Professor Emeritus and a licensed psychologist in private practice, is the author of numerous other books that focus on the discovery of new knowledge and its applications in daily life.

Robert K. Glenn, PhD
President

We all, to some extent, suffer from the illusion of *powerlessness*. Many of us live from day to day feeling that "something" is missing, or that we are victims of circumstances that are beyond our control, that happiness and success are improbable. We may envy others their apparent happier lives, and then blame the others, or the system, or one thing or another for our own unhappier ones. We may feel "left behind" as the train pulls out of the station with other, luckier people aboard.

From childhood on, we do often experience situations beyond our control but little about taking control ourselves. We may learn from our parents that "we just can't do anything about it." In schools we are taught basic skills and learn about the accomplishments or failures of other people, but little for making a better future. If we go on to higher education we anticipate a bright and rewarding career. Religions teach that there is a "greater power," but we find it to be of little help in our personal affairs. As young adults we look for love and romance, shared understanding and sensual enjoyment. We go to parties and play games, go to concerts and sports events, and anticipate that happiness is just around the corner. For some of us, college and advanced studies may bring mental stimulus and excitement, and the promise of good things to come. As adults, we may find meaning through independent studies or in our first "real jobs," in travel and foreign adventure, and then on into marriage and family, in advancing in our work.

But slowly things begin to dim, our sex life is merely repetitive; home, marriage and family bring chores, debt, and unexpected challenges; aging includes illness and decline; we find that our employment is unable to meet all our needs and dreams; our government is limited in providing all the things we ask of it, and the world around us becomes more threatening and we no longer even dream of a "better tomorrow."

But the "outer world" is only part of the story!

Let's instead look at "personal power" from another angle, and refer to it as "success." We all want to be successful in social and athletic endeavors, in education and training, employment and career, in marriage and parenting and having the home we desire, participating in our community, attaining financial security, enjoying health and long life, and—ultimately—in feelings of personal accomplishment, personal worth, and spiritual wholeness.

Success is really what life is all about. It's how we may be measured after we depart mortal life, going onward and *upward* to still greater opportunities in "life after death."

Success happens from the inside out! Real success is what you can take with you.

The secret to success is really no secret at all. Just ask any successful person. The "secret" is really a universal truth that belongs to each and every person on the planet. That truth is: **Success begins in the mind** and the greatest barrier to success is the illusion of helplessness and powerlessness, that you have no opportunities and no power to realize them. *But, you do!*

The good news is that you have the power—inside yourself now—to sweep illusions from your mind and use your mind for what it was intended: *to lift human consciousness to a higher level and make this world a better place for you and your children.* **You have the power!**

Success is your destiny. When you are self-empowered, you become the sole architect of your life. Why wait? **Seize your power, now!**

HOW IS THIS ACCOMPLISHED?

That's where Llewellyn's *Psychic Empowerment* books come in. Techniques and tools are available to activate your inner resources and create exciting new potentials in your life. Some techniques specifically involve <u>psychic empowerment</u> because your innate psychic powers must be developed into psychic skills to be integrated into your Conscious Wholeness.

We are not "finished products"! *Physical Adulthood is not even half your life story.* Psychic Empowerment techniques and tools directly engage your innate but mostly undeveloped and ignored Unconscious Powers and bring them into the Conscious Mind for ready application in making a better life, a life of greater Success and Happiness. With expanding Conscious Awareness of your inner powers and abilities, you advance into the development of your Super-Conscious Mind.

Starting with simple meditations and affirmation procedures, we move onward with more complex and specific empowering programs to meet your needs and your challenges, to make your life all it can be. With each step forward more opportunities become available to you. With each advancement, the Greater Cosmos opens before you.

Each technique of Personal Empowerment embodies a firm regard for the divine spark of greatness existing in everyone. With their development, you *grow towards greater Self-fulfillment.* Success and Happiness are achieved through your own efforts and not from external factors or through other people. You are the source of your own greatness, but all the parts of Self must be awakened and empowered, and then centered in your own Higher Self.

You are more than a physical being, more than an emotional being, more than a mental being—all these can be incorporated into your spiritual being. You are all these and Spirit as well—but as you center your consciousness in Spirit, you can communicate from Spirit to Spirit. Communicating at spiritual levels through the techniques presented in this book, the knowledge and wisdom of beings throughout the Cosmos are accessible to you.

Spirit is everywhere and in everything. Communicating with Spirit, you have access to all there is, to all the knowledge and wisdom there is, to other spiritual beings, and to Universal Consciousness. The Greater Cosmos welcomes your every advancement.

ACKNOWLEDGMENT

JUDITH HIPSKIND COLLINS

© Christine H. Foyle

As a senior in college, Judy worked long distance with Dr. J. B. Rhine on the thesis "ESP in the Noosphere of Teilhard de Chardin" and established a correspondence with Dr. Rhine that lasted several years. Judy worked as a teaching assistant at Indiana University while getting Master's degree, and continued with self-taught studies in paranormal fields. Taught Spanish at the University of Wisconsin at LaCrosse.

She explored ESP with experiments and learned handwriting analysis while in grade school. Judy has a life-long interest in ESP, graphology, palmistry, astrology, numerology, body language, parapsychology, meditation, mediumship, dream interpretation, symbolism and language arts. During her junior year in Madrid (Spain) she met a woman who read hands and her work inspired a study and career as a palmist.

Minneapolis Career

In 1970, she joined Llewellyn at the invitation of Carl Weschcke to help found and serve as Dean of the Gnostica School for Self-Development, which featured a curriculum of subjects ranging from astrology to yoga. The school was successful and activities included open houses, lectures, meet and greet with authors and experts from the

U.S. and England. This format expanded into several annual festivals, including the First International Aquarian Festival, in September 1971. Subsequent Festivals were known as "Gnosticons," and inspired similar Metaphysical and Pagan Conferences worldwide.

While at Llewellyn, she worked as a spokesperson for our programs and the metaphysical world, appearing on local television and radio shows, lecturing on college campuses, at theological seminaries, women's clubs and more.

She also worked as a consultant for psychologist Dr. John Geier, University of Minnesota, using knowledge of graphology, body language and hands, to work with patients in his practice, and as a lecturer at Veterans' Hospitals and for various businesses.

Judith volunteered at the Hennepin County Juvenile Detention Center, helping children to understand themselves using handwriting and palmistry. This work expanded to prisons and halfway houses in the Minneapolis area.

She began work on the first of three books published by Llewellyn Worldwide, *Palmistry, The Whole View*, 1977, followed by *The New Palmistry*, 1993, and *The Hand from A to Z*, 2005.

Judith also worked as an entertainer, reading hands at the Gnostica Retail Store, at parties and at a local Minneapolis restaurant, where a woman customer introduced her to the work of author Anaïs Nin. Established a correspondence with Anaïs Nin that led to moving to Dallas, Texas.

Dallas Career

At the invitation of Anaïs Nin, she researched and interpreted astrological charts of historical figures ranging from twelfth century monarchs, cardinals and popes to present day poets and scholars, with an emphasis on French writers. Her cousin Eduardo Sanchez spent 35 years in Europe gathering the data for these charts from a wide array of sources. This work, along with his original critical studies of Niccolo Machiavelli and the Medici family, is stored in private archives at Southern Methodist University.

While working with Eduardo Sanchez's archives, she joined a parapsychology group at Southern Methodist University run by a local Jungian analyst, graduate of the Jungian Institute in Switzerland. Dr. J. B. Rhine came to address this group one weekend, and after 10 years of correspondence, we met in person in Dallas.

Other opportunities included annual trips to London to research Celtic history and the Druids at the British Museum in London, under the sponsorship of the man in charge of the Reading Room; travel to Australia and to New Zealand, giving talks to Embassy wives in Wellington, NZ, and appearing on local television and radio shows.

Her work in Dallas focused on palmistry and led to the development of a new approach to interpreting hands through the meaning of the knuckles (see *The New Palmistry*, Llewellyn 1993). She developed a full time private clientele with individual consultations as the main focus, and also worked as an entertainer for Dallas area hotels and corporate clients.

Terre Haute Career

In 2008, Judith moved to Terre Haute, Indiana, to work on two books, the first on the world of trees and their value as a source of collected wisdom and an aid to personal growth, and the second on numerology, on the power of number patterns on a grid, to determine individual purpose and fulfillment.

In 2015, she began researching and writing *Signature Power* for Llewellyn. This book provides the basis both for analysis of the personal Signature and self-therapy through deliberate alterations of various components of the Signature.

CONTENTS

A Fourth Dimension; The Application and Development of
Paranormal Power; Scientific Validation of Paranormal Experience; Discovering the Nature and Purpose of Human Existence; The Importance of Going Beyond the Lab; PES: THE
PERSONAL EMPOWERMENT SPACE; The Totality of your
being—Past, Present, and Future; Resources to turn your Potentials into Reality; Awakening to the Power to Shape the Future; Paranormal Facilitators; The Distribution of Paranormal
Potential; The Generalization Effect; the Power of Research;
THE NEW SCIENCE OF THE PARANORMAL

Tables, Charts, and Lists

Chapter Two: Extra-Sensory Perception:
Contents include: EXTRA-SENSORY PERCEPTION DE-
FINED; The Three Major Mental Faculties of ESP; Functional
Definitions of ESP and PK more easily recognized; The PRF
Survey of College Students' ESP Experiences; TELEPATHY, THE
MOST COMMON ESP EXPERIENCE; Pre-cognition com-
monly experienced as a simple impression; Clairvoyance—A
Daily Experience for some; ACTIVATING ESP; THE DYNAMIC
EFFECT OF PRACTICE and EXPERIENCE; TELEPATHY; A
Dynamic Force; An Empowering Option; A Critical Alternative;
Animal Communication and Culture; The Power of Distributed
Practice; Meditation Exercises for Development and Applica-
tion; Clarifying Images and Powerful Symbols; Telepathy and
Mood State; Therapeutic Benefits of Positive Telepathic Messag-
ing; CLAIRVOYANCE; Experiencing the Unknown; Activating
Clairvoyance; PRECOGNITION; Awareness of Future Events;
Precognition: Fact or Fiction?; A Critical Source of Information;
Precognitive Dreaming: A Motivational Force; Inducing Precog-
nition; Conclusion

Tables, Charts, and Lists

Procedures

Chapter Three: The Out-of-Body Experience:
Reaching Beyond the Physical 57

Contents include: PROJECTING AWARENESS OUT OF THE BODY; Other Dimensional Vehicles; Vehicles for Emotion, Mind, Will, and Spirit Consciousness; The Extra-Biological Body; Case Studies of out-of-body experiences (OBEs); Emotion and the Out-of-Body State; The Higher you go, the more you have; Astral Travel During Sleep; PRE-SLEEP OBES INDUCTION PROCEDURES; The Physiology of the Out-of-body State; Induced OBEs: Analysis of Case Studies; OBEs and the Near-Death Experience; Mastering Out-of-body Skills; Many Bodies, Many Planes.\

Tables, Charts, and Lists

Procedures

Contents include: Objects as Information "Mediums"; Objects Used to "Announce" Poltergeist and Psychic Happenings; Objects Used in Spiritual Communication; Objects Used to Divine Information; Objects Used to Protect from Harm, or to Project Power; Objects Used as Magical Tools; Objects Used to Receive, Store, Transform, Transfer, and Communicate; Objectology: Using a Deep Tray of Sand to Source New Information; Objectology: Sand Reading Research in Paranormal Empowerment; Sand Reading: An Objective Resource in Paranormal Research; Sand Reading: An Objective Resource for Paranormal Information; Sand Reading: An Objective Resource into Past-Life Memories; Sand Reading: An Objective Resource for Paranormal Empowerment; Sand Reading: An Objective Resource into Stressful Conditions; Sand Reading: Hand Imprint Characteristics showing Violence; Sand Reading: Hand Imprint Characteristics in Employment Status and Gender; Sand Reading: Hand Imprint Characteristics and Career Pursuits; Sand Reading: Hand Imprint Patterns and Career Goals; Sand Reading: Potential Applications in Psychiatry; Sand Reading and Psychic Signals; Sand Reading and Numerology

Contents include: Water: A Primary Alchemical and Spiritual Element; Water: Emotional (and Astral) Empowerment; Water Gazing: Clearing the Mind for Psychic Receptivity; Water Gazing: Interaction and Enlightenment; Water Gazing and Telepathy #1; Water Gazing and the Telepathic Sending of Images; Water Gazing and Psychic Imagery; Water Gazing and Telepathy #2; Water Gazing: Telepathy, Phase I (Without Water); Water Gazing: Telepathy, Phase II; Water Gazing and Creative Writing; Water Gazing and Creative Expression in Art; Water Gazing: Effects on Memory; Water Gazing with The Triangle of

ance; Gender Differences and Pattern Stability; the Crumpled Paper Technique in the Industrial Setting

Procedures

Chapter Nine: The Next Step:

Contents include: From the Unknown to the Known, from the Lab to Real Life, and from the "Other" to YOUR OWN Personal Empowerment; Awakening "Dormant" Powers; Paranormal vs. Supernatural; Conscious and Unconscious, Two-Way Communication; Our environment is full of vibrations; Death and its Alternatives; New Age Challenges; Challenge and Response; Species and Individual Evolution and Personal Empowerment

Tables, Charts, and Lists

Chapter Ten: Psychic Development:

Contents include: Both History and Evolution are *developmental responses* to the Challenge set forth by Creation itself "in the Beginning." The first Response was *and is* the self-regulating *system of programs* we call "the Laws of Nature," and the first Law of Nature was *and is* "the Word," that always will be the *progressing* program we call "Evolution."

Ever Onward, Always Progressing; *Personal Empowerment: Command and Control; Psychic Development and Empowerment: The Next Step in Human Evolution; "Ye are Gods in the Making"; The Challenge to old, Materialist Science; The Great Leap Forward; There's more to Reality than the Physical Dimension; How we develop Clairvoyance; The New Science of the Paranormal; Quantum Theory, the "Bridge" between Physical and Esoteric Science; Vision to Solve Tomorrow's Problems Now!;*

Becoming More than You Are; Learning to "Think" long; The Importance of Personal Vision; Our Potential is Infinite

Contents include: The Power of Combined Movements—*the example of music*; "*Natural*" and "*Cultural*" *Movements*; Revolutionary and Developmental Movements; Human Response to the Challenge of Cosmic Vibrations—*planetary in dimension and causal in action*; The Extension of Physical Power and Personal Empowerment; The Next Step: Reaching Beyond Physical Limitations; The Digital Revolution and its Evolution; The Extension of Psychological and Psychic Powers for Self-Empowerment; The Spiritual Movement and "Religion" in the New Age; The Difference from Religions of the Past; Western Religions Dominated by the Old Judaic Bible; What is Overlooked and Long Forgotten; A Viable Creation Myth; The Role of Religion; Exploring the Inner Nature of Physical Reality; Modern Religions and the Role of Churches and Ministers; Will, Mind, and Self-Discipline in the New Age Movement; Quiet the Mind, Ask the Big Questions, and Listen to the Answer; The Ultimate Secret

Tables, Charts, and Lists

Procedures

Contents include: Overcome All Barriers; Varying levels of Personal Consciousness; Becoming Connected; The Self-Empowerment Potential; The Plan; Self-Dialogue: A Daily component of the Plan; Ascending the Pyramid; Global Advancement

Tables, Charts, and Lists

Procedures

PREFACE
What we want to accomplish
in writing this book

This book came into being after several years of discussion between the authors and others about what historic and modern "psychic" research has accomplished.

No longer is the "split" between materialism and spiritualty as absolute as at the beginning of the 20th Century. The role of laboratory research in showing that quite "normal" people commonly show some degree of "paranormal" ability was a major factor as is the new knowledge and increasing understanding of the psyche as a whole. Equally important is the role of quantum physics bringing awareness of the multi-layered Cosmos in which we live and have our being.

JOE WRITES ...

Controlled laboratory research is essential to our understanding of paranormal phenomena. Research not only validates the existence of the paranormal, it pushes back the borders of contemporary science and offers new ways of understanding ourselves and the universe. It reveals new possibilities for acquiring knowledge and developing our highest potentials. With the integration of paranormal insight, a new and surging force of growth energy is unleashed within. Beyond that, external dimensions of knowledge and power become readily accessible and previously unattainable goals become realistic possibilities. There exists, in fact, no end to the empowering possibilities of paranormal power beyond the lab.

The controlled studies presented in this book offer detailed research evidence of the existence of the paranormal. The laboratory studies, including those funded by the U. S. Army, the Parapsychology Foundation of New York, and the Parapsychology Research Institute and Foundation, were each conducted by the author, often with the assistance of co-investigators, in a highly controlled laboratory setting at Athens State University. The technical reports for additional studies and the developmental exercises based on them are likewise on file in the Athens State University Library Archives.

Although more research is needed to further explore the complex dynamics as well as the many practical applications of the paranormal, the evidence based on the existing body of research is clear: the paranormal potential, like intelligence, exists in everyone. It can be experienced in both direct and indirect forms. Its manifestations can range from general to highly specific. Its purposes include growth and enlightenment related to the past, present, and future. It embraces the known and the unknown as well as tangible and intangible realities. It spans the endless past and endless future alike.

While existing research offers highly convincing verification of the existence of paranormal power, the most relevant evidence remains personal experience. Only through personal experience beyond the lab can we discover the deeper meaning of our existence as endless beings of incomparable worth. That discovery is a major goal of this book.

—*Joe H. Slate, Ph.D.*
Decatur, Alabama, June 10, 2015

CARL WRITES...

In this book, Dr. Slate has shown that consistent research programs continue to validate the existence of paranormal phenomena and powers inside and beyond the controlled conditions of the laboratory while challenging us to undertake programs of psychic development and self-empowerment.

The 20th Century brought a historic integration of Eastern and Western esotericism with modern psychological theory and practice, and the 21st century has smashed through past religious and materialist barriers with new knowledge and understanding of the vast Cosmos in which we have our being and where the evolutionary drama is unfolding.

Together, we make the case for further research to help us develop and deploy these greater potentials and extended dimensions of the Whole Person, and to empower the everyday self for greater accomplishment, longer and healthier life, and well-being.

In this New Age, the *Paranormal* is becoming the new *Normal* as we more fully integrate all levels of consciousness and spirit into singular unity under our will and with our Creator Core.

Carl Llewellyn Weschcke
Woodbury, Minnesota, June 14, 2015

INTRODUCTION
THE PARANORMAL:
Taking the Next Step . . . Above, Beside, and Beyond . . . "Normal"

THE OBJECTIVE AND SUBJECTIVE MEANING OF "PARA"

"Para" is a prefix meaning "parallel to," or "to the side of," or "beside," "side by side," "beyond," or even "above" or "below," and sometimes denoting something "less than" or "not fully qualified," when attached to verb and subject words to distinguish them from "parent" or "loan-words" taken from another language. Thus a "paralegal" is less than a fully qualified lawyer but can assist one in legal matters, and with further training can become a fully qualified lawyer.

And, as the years have passed by, many "para" subjects have taken on more narrow and specific meanings while many alternative and related subjects have new "para" names.

Each "para" word takes on its own specific identify and meaning over years of usage—thus *parapsychology* has changed from being an advanced form of 19th century "psychic research" mainly studying poltergeist and the *physical* phenomena associated with Spiritualist séances into the 20th century *psychological* study of psychic phenomena as something not explainable in terms of common "materialist science."

Beside "Normal"

In the case of the word "Paranormal," we face an unusual challenge: the word has no direct association with the subjects of Psychic Research, Séance Phenomena, or Psychology for that matter. In contrast, a "Paralegal" is a person who has the professional education and certification to perform substantive legal work; a Paramedic is a trained healthcare worker; but a Parapsychologist is not a trained psychology worker, and parapsychology is not truly the study or practice of any kind of psychology. Nor is there really any kind of "paranormalist" or paranormal worker other than someone assisting in the study of paranormal phenomenon. To be facetious, a paranormal professional is not helping someone become "normal."

Yet, the word "paranormal" has established meaning, and paranormal phenomena and experiences are real and substantive, and studied by para-psychologists even though they have little to do with psychology—except for those convinced that any belief in the paranormal is an indication of mental illness! We disagree with such a conclusion.

"Feelings" prejudice "Objectivity"

We must also note other "parallel" words that have essentially the same meaning but with subtle variations largely associated with *feelings* related to their history and sometimes to the intention of the user. I've underlined certain words and word parts that introduce feelings that by themselves seem to affect perception and objectivity, i.e. what we see and how we feel about it. *Read left to right.*

TABLE OF PARALLEL WORDS		
The Para<u>normal</u>	Psychic <u>Science</u>	Para<u>psychology</u>
Esoteric	<u>Occult</u>	Metaphysics
Magical	<u>Spiritual</u>	Manifestations
<u>Phenomena</u>	Happenings	<u>Events</u>
Observations	<u>Powers</u>	Skills
<u>Abilities</u>	Training	Knowledge
Poltergeists	Ghosts	<u>Spirits</u>
<u>Spooks</u>	Psychic Energy	Thought Transfer
Telepathy	<u>ESP</u>	<u>Extra-sensory Perception</u>
Mediumship	<u>Channeling</u>	Empathy
Reading	<u>Communication</u>	<u>Astral Projection</u>
Astral Travel	Out-of-Body	<u>Traveling-in-Spirit</u>
Clairvoyance	<u>Second Sight</u>	Intuition
<u>Spirit Vision</u>	Remote Viewing	

While the above lists are of words with roughly parallel meaning (read left to right), note the subtle differences in *feelings* associated with each. These subtleties will commonly have powerful effects on how you perceive the associated subject matter. Experiment until you can view the subject without any *prejudice*, and as *objectively* as possible. The challenge is that the subtle perceptions related to the words (the chosen vocabulary) used with any subject, determines not only how you view the subject but also what the subject represents to you. In other words, *the subtleties attached to words are "part of the picture" that is the subject for you*. We will return to this matter later, but also consider that those subtle impressions and "feelings" <u>are</u> "part of the picture," adding *subjective* knowledge to the objective facts. Both are important if you can distinguish between them.

Statistical Proof in the Lab

Much of the work of J. B. Rhine and other last century parapsychologists was devoted to developing <u>statistical</u> "proof" that such phenomena as simple precognition, mental telepathy, and telekinesis performed by *ordinary* volunteers happened at <u>above chance levels</u>. In other words, the phenomena are real, but not explained. And the statistical variables were often minimal as would be expected when untrained volunteers endlessly repeated the operations under sterile and boring "laboratory conditions."

Even though parapsychology is fully recognized and officially accepted as a *science* and a subject appropriate for university study, it is often greeted with a kind of "smirk" by the scientific community and called a "pseudo-science" because (they say) it lacks a foundation in easily repeatable experiments demonstrating a psi effect on demand, nor does it provide an underlying theory to explain the *paranormal* transfer of information in terms of *normal* <u>materialist</u> science.

"Normal" and "Paranormal," Side by Side

On the other hand, the word "paranormal" implies that the world around us, as defined by materialist science, is **normal** and anything that is <u>beside</u>, <u>above</u>, <u>beyond</u>, or <u>other than</u> <u>"normal"</u> is **paranormal**. Thus, in some sense, both *normal* and *paranormal* can exist <u>side-by-side</u>, logically allowing for the possibility that Mind *can* affect Matter. Go one step further, and we have . . .

THE POWER OF BELIEF CAN CHANGE REALITY

or—at least—"reality" as you know it, i.e. the reality of your personal experience.

Ultimately, mainstream *materialist* science claims that parapsychology violates the materialist concept that "thought cannot affect matter." Well, 21st century Parapsychology and the *New Sciences of the Paranormal* demonstrate otherwise, and provide the means for anyone to gain a workable understanding and technological expertise in applying divinatory, psychic, magickal and "occult" skills to improve their lives. And, consider this: some quantum physicists do factor *intention* as a means of affecting change in matter and energy at least at the sub-atomic level parallel with the sub-conscious mind.

Does this violate both established physical science and so-called "common sense"?

Not really, but it does seem to say that forms of **non-physical realities** do exist side-by-side with *physical* reality. And, of course, religionists, mystics, shamans and visionaries of many kinds, poets and artists, futurists and prophets of all kinds, dreamers (and your nightly dreams), inventors and innovators, alchemists and magicians, adventurers and explorers here and beyond, and ordinary and extraordinary people, researchers *and scientists* searching for solutions to mysteries of all kinds have been saying variations of this forever and will continue saying it forever.

Transitioning into the New Age, NOW!

Today we are transitioning from the *comfortably familiar* ordinary world of yesterday to the more extraordinary one of today, and even as few people perceive it, we are rapidly moving on to the near miraculous hi-tech world of tomorrow—*and we do so barely sensing the changing of our reality.* We communicate around the world at near instant speeds; we witness news as it happens on the other side of the planet and into space beyond; we travel distances in hours that not long ago took days and even weeks and perhaps months; we tap into the accumulated knowledge of all time and we command extraordinary powers with movements of our fingers and a few spoken words;

and—potentially much more—including, unfortunately, **the power to destroy ourselves.**

We don't fully realize how different "things" really are from the "Old Days." Mostly we still think in terms of an ordinary, three-dimensional world, limited in time and space to the visible horizon. For most of us, *what we don't see doesn't exist.* Unless you are some kind of quantum physicist or a mystic, what you "know" probably has not changed what and how you believe. And it is change in your "Belief System" that *can* change your perceived Reality when accompanied by corresponding change in your "Knowledge System" that will empower you to live in a multidimensional world. We will discuss more of this later in the book, but do note:

IF YOU DON'T KNOW WHAT YOU ARE LOOKING FOR, YOU PROBABLY WON'T FIND IT!

Think about the implications of that statement: **Knowledge and Belief both determine how we see the world,** and the words we use *reflect and define our reality, including* differences to the objects and subjects we see and use every day.

To begin to know and believe, to understand and—in some sense—to be "born again" into this genuine *New Age,* we have first to challenge the ways we commonly look at things and think about them whenever we knowingly take <u>one step beyond the ordinary</u>. *That Next Step will open the Doors of Perception to the Cosmic Multi-Dimensional Reality just over the threshold of ordinary consciousness.* It's a step we have to <u>knowingly</u> take, and this and other "Self-Empowerment" books will help you prepare for that time.

Psychic Dimensions

We have many words (as previously listed) and many points of view for the study of the "Psychic Dimensions." We've moved from the perspectives of Western Organized Religions, Magic and Spiritualism to the personal study of Esotericism, the Occult,* and the Spiritual. We Meditate, learn Self-Hypnosis, practice Yoga, exercise Personal Discipline, give Love and Service to others, living more Spiritual Lives without always being sure what that means.

*"Occult" Contrary to myth and deliberate mis-statement, "the Occult" is not some system of evil, so-called "black magic," or a "diabolical" scheme to pervert the world's religions, but simply means *obscured, hidden (like the Moon passing in front of the Sun in an eclipse,* or some other form of *occultation* where one object temporarily obscures another by standing or passing in front of another. The terms "Occult" and "Occultism" refer to esoteric knowledge once held secret out of fear of persecution by the monolithic Catholic Church and its "Holy" Inquisition.

The New Science of the Paranormal

We move from Psychic Research to Parapsychology and to the New Science of the Paranormal. We practice forms of Divination, study the Tarot and Astrology, work Magick and the Martial Arts. We look again at the "mythic" and not-so-mythic ancient histories of Atlantis and Lemuria, of the Mayans and Aztecs of today's Mexico, the Incan religion of ancient Peru, the religions and cultures of ancient India and China, the Manichaeism, Mithraism, and Zoroastrianism of ancient Persia (now Iran), the Minoanism of ancient Crete, the Canaanite religion of ancient Jordan, the Shinto religion and culture of Japan, and that of Egypt, Greece and pre-Christian Rome, the Norse, the Druids and Celts of Pagan Europe, the Spiritist religions of Africa and Latin America, and more. *Wisdom is found wherever you look, and the more you look, the more you will see and learn, and the broader your horizons.*

Perception of non-physical realities

All of these interests, studies, and practices make a difference to our experience and perception of physical and *metaphysical* (non-physical) realities and to our overall Belief System, but we start "closer to home" as our physical world realities are slowly modified by the changes in how today's science and technology are newly re-defining the modern world in new ways. And, yet, most of us still fail to make the move over the threshold to perceive the expanded reality that is already present. *Expanding conscious awareness is vital to our transition into the New Age, and to our psychic development and Personal Empowerment.* Such growth is the logical continuation of our now *individualized* Human Evolution to Becoming More than we are both as people and persons.

Personal Empowerment

We study Psychic Phenomena and seek Psychic Empowerment and Expanded Awareness through the development of our own Psychic Powers and Skills. We don't limit our vision to that of proclaimed messengers and gurus. *Dependency of any sort is self-limiting and our goal in this New Age is self-discovery and self-understanding, leading to personal growth, development, and self- empowerment.*

We used to experience the greater Cosmic Dimensions *only* through acts of faith and mystical discipline. Now these greater dimensions are already part of the broadening horizons initiated by our open-minded studies and our daily use of "silicon-based" technologies. Too, while most *Life* on our planet is carbon based, silicon is the next most prolific "connector" and no doubt our adventures in silicon-based communications and space exploration will eventually bring us into contact with intelligent silicon-based life-forms inhabiting environments inhospitable to our own carbon-based life. As this occurs, it will lead to enormous expansions of "ordinary" awareness.

Learn this: **The Mind of Man and the Mind of God* are one and the same for Consciousness is Universal and Infinite. Our challenge as humans is to fulfill that enormous potential and opportunity to be more than we are and become co-creators of the expanding Cosmos.**

> *Note: Here is an example of how the choice of vocabulary can make a difference, and yet—in a different sense—it should not. In this instance the choice of "God" or "Creator" or "Source" or "Force" all have the same value: something created the Cosmos and all within. In the next sentence, instead of "humans," we could have said "the Children of God" and produced a different *feeling, and yet—since everything within the Cosmos is a "child" of the Creator Force or Source— specifying "humans" accomplishes our mission better than any other choice.*

Multiverse and Parallel Universes

History never repeats other than as **cyclic patterns of change**. We have moved from the distant past when our world (i.e. "field of awareness") was defined by close physical geography and limited by visible horizons, reflected in myth and shaped by belief; and on to larger worlds defined by shamanic visions, reflected in tradition and communal norms, and shaped by societal structure; then to still larger worlds even more sharply defined by thought, and more narrowly **limited by political and religious imposition**. And now, breaking the bonds of religious and political domination, we enter the Information and the Space Ages (otherwise known as the Age of Aquarius and the New Age).

In recent times, Science Fiction and now Quantum Science speak of *physical* universes parallel to our own, and yet the Ancient Wisdom and Esoteric Science—East and West—have long taught of a much Greater *Cosmos* containing not only a larger physical universe as perceived by our limited sensory awareness but still larger *metaphysical* "worlds" or *dimensions*. Today, through the work of astronomers and quantum physicists, we know that even the physical universe is far larger and more complex than commonly thought, with substance composed of particles even smaller than atoms.

And not only is our physical universe far larger and more complex than the "clockwork" vision of only a few years earlier, but the Human Person is likewise perceived as far more complex than the purely physical entity still dominating much of medical and biological science. Yet, though the subtle physical and metaphysical *dimensions* of Man and Universe remain largely unknown to materialist science, *they are the most powerful keys to our understanding and changing of every day realities.*

Multi-Dimensional Physical and Non-Physical Realities

Strangely, even the most materialist of people, scientists and religionists included, claim to believe in the non-physical concepts of Soul, Spirit, Spiritual Beings, and Creator, but still remain in denial of metaphysical dimensions of both Man and Universe.

Among other questions you might ask of yourself:

• Does a Soul or Spirit have any kind of physical dimension?

• Is Thought purely physical, and only a mechanical function of the brain?

• Is Love only biological and hormonal, simply driven by the Reproductive Urge?

- Is Courage in the face of threat to self and others only an instinct of self-defense?
- Is Foresight only a rational analysis of available facts?
- Is there nothing above or beyond *physical matter* composed of solid, fluid, and gas?

We have esoteric vocabularies to describe and give meaning to the structures of both the Greater Cosmos, inclusive of the physical and metaphysical dimensions, and the Greater Self that includes the physical body, mind, emotions, will, spirit and soul. Some of these words have become generally familiar through the 19th century popular movements of Theosophy and various other Eastern movements, the spread of Freemasonry, the Golden Dawn, Aurum Solis and other magical orders, Spiritualism and popular public séances, the Psychic Research societies, and then into the 20th century with many students studying and practicing Yoga, Tantra, systems of Meditation, the Martial Arts, and the popularization of Astrology, many forms of Divination, Channeling, and popular figures like Edgar Cayce, and then the resurgence of Pagan magical movements, and more.

We are increasingly familiar with words and concepts like *Astral Plane and Body, the Etheric Double, Out-of-Body, Mental and Causal Bodies, Chakras, Kundalini, Prana, Astral and Mental Projection, Alternative States of Consciousness, Clairvoyance, Scrying, Dowsing,* and others, but still too little to bring them into a cohesive and understandable system for everyone.

We have the words, but generally lack the structure to give them substance. To give meaning we need to place them in the dual context of "Man and Universe" (Greater Self and Greater Cosmos). And we further need to relate this *esoteric* Cosmos to the new perceptions of Quantum Physics, and the *esoteric* Self to new discoveries of psychology and physiology and metaphysical terminology.

The "Esoteric" is not something weird and separate from reality but is omnipresent and personal. We need the greater vision of Wholeness in order to meet the challenges we all face in terms of Global Climate Change, near Universal Pollution and Environmental Hazards, the potentials of a World Religious War and Economic Collapse, Epidemics,

Political and Corporate Corruption (particularly in areas of Banking and Finance), etc. It's the old problem of "Church on Sunday and Work on Monday" with work presumed to be at odds with the "spirituality" of Sunday. *It doesn't have to be that way but it will be until we enhance our vision and see reality as it really is.*

Just as said earlier," The Mind of Man and the Mind of God are one and the same for Consciousness is Universal and Infinite," so is Man and Universe one and the same. Our bodies are of earth substance enlivened by the universal consciousness. Yet Man's body and soul function in different but parallel ways. Esoterics distinguish between the two by speaking of "non-physical planes" and "subtle bodies." We have a physical body on the physical plane, and that body has a physically derived consciousness. But that "body-consciousness" is neither mind nor soul. Side by side with the physical body is the *Astral body* (also called a "vehicle") on the astral plane. In addition there is a Mental body on the mental plane, and more bodies and planes parallel to and "above" those.

But it is also in error to think that Body and Soul, Planes and Bodies, Physical and Astral are any more separate from one another than are Books from a Library. Just as *normal* and *paranormal* exist side-by-side, all these planes, bodies, things, entities, forms, functions, and categories likewise exist in parallel, above and below, and all together, and—indeed—Mind can affect Matter and Matter does affect Mind. All is inter-related but in differing degrees as circumstances, desire, attention and intention, happenings, and so much more affect each and every thing and every being.

That may sound like overload, but the "laws" of each plane and body organize life and function, while human will, desire and intention powerfully affect personal reality, and even that of other people, places and things. A trained and disciplined Will is very powerful—in fact Will is the means to focus the ultimate creative power that shapes the Universe—but we are confident that few living humans anywhere are capable of that. Yet, it is our destiny as eventual co-creators.

Planes and Bodies

Our studies of the Paranormal, both inside and beyond the Lab, combine objective and subjective experience of both physical and metaphysical realities, giving new perceptions and new and expanded meanings to everyday life.

Our perceptions have grown from physical to include astral, mental, causal and spiritual, and beyond to yet higher and broader dimensions that have always been with us but beyond the focus of our present awareness. Our goal now includes *making Conscious selective contents of the Unconscious at Will.* Focus begins the process of self-control of Emotions (the Astral dimension), of Decision Making (the Mental) under Will (the Causal).

Words such as Soul, Higher Self, Spirit, Psyche, Inner Self, the *Atman,* the Whole Personality, Causal Self, *Chiah, Neshamah,* Higher Manas, Higher Ego, Holy Guardian Angel, Spiritual Soul, Intuitional Self, *Buddhi,* Higher Causal Self, Super Conscious Mind, and many more in all languages and cultures have been used variously with little definition other than a presumed meaning of "other than physical consciousness," and "that which survives physical death," and "that which is immortal."

In modern psychological and esoteric terminology these same words and related concepts have been associated with the Personal Unconscious, the Collective Unconscious, the Archetypal Mind, the Subtle Bodies making up the complex structure of the whole person, and more.

For our purposes here, we see a basic psychological model that parallels a similar esoteric model as follows:

The Psychological and Esoteric Model of the Whole Person	
TABLE OF THREE LEVELS OF SELF-CONSCIOUSNESS	
PSYHOLOGICAL MODEL	ESOTERIC MODEL
Lower Self, aka Sub-Conscious Mind	Astral Body and Consciousness (Self)
Middle Self, aka Conscious Mind	Mental Body and Consciousness (Self)
Higher Self, aka Super- Conscious Mind	Causal Body and Consciousness (Self)

In both models, at each level, there is more complexity than shown. Generally, and in relation to their multiple functions, each level in both models is further divided into seven sub-levels. Our focus is on the highest sub-level of Level 3, simply called the Higher Self and the Causal Self. Essentially, they are the same, but because our focus in this book is on Psychic Development and Personal Empowerment, we will target the Mental and Causal Selves.

The Causal Self is not the Soul, nor is it the Spirit, but is the highest aspect of <u>personal</u> consciousness in *the incarnating personality*. Understand that *the Soul, itself, does not incarnate,* but abstracts the life lessons from the incarnated personality through the Causal Self, which then "dies" along with that personality. The Soul then creates a new "Causal Seed" with the abstracted memories of many life times and a new life plan which generates a new incarnating personality, step-by-step, following the Esoteric Model into physical incarnation from which new levels of psychological consciousness develop as the physical body grows and matures to work side-by-side with the esoteric selves through a new life time. It is the fulfillment of this process that fully transfers "command and control" of the entire personality from the reactive emotional-centered Lower Self and the more-or-less brain-centered mental Middle Self to the Spirit-centered Causal Higher Self.

UNDERSTANDING THE WHOLE AND ITS PARTS

We are, individually and collectively, both a part of the whole and a summation of its parts. As physical bodies we are an organic collection of parts, and so is the physical world we live within. What we do individually and collectively affects the whole world, and yet, individually, we are no more than a speck of dirt in the cemetery. Yet, what meaning does the world have without us? Is a book merely an assemblage of words on pages collected into chapters and bound together between two covers? No, each word, each comma and each period come together to form sentences that are parts of paragraphs that say important things giving even more important meaning to chapters and onward to make the whole book that is the author's contribution towards the SELF-improvement of many readers who grow by taking the Next Step in personal development.

At the same time, the "collective" becomes more than the summation of its parts and aids individuals to again become more than they were, and onward again and again. The whole of Universal, Planetary, and Individual Evolution is a synthesis of particles becoming parts of Wholes building on more parts and wholes to become greater wholes to becoming greater and greater objects, parts, wholes, communities, planets, systems, and more. And individuals grow to become more, expanding in awareness and conscious powers, ever onward, ever upward.

Look at the chart below showing Bodies and Planes side-by-side, interacting, integrating, growing, producing, developing; individuals growing and innovating, fulfilling new potentials beyond what was before, becoming more and more of all they can be. We grow and evolve by acting, by doing, by seeking, by seeing, by searching, by reaching.

We take what we learn, in Life or Laboratory, develop it and apply it, improving Self and Life, growing from Lower to Higher, expanding Awareness and Consciousness to be more inclusive, enlarging our comprehension, and controlling rather than reacting.

Study the chart from bottom to top, understanding each column and each level as a plane or field of manifestation. The first two columns are those of most immediate interest. In essence, the first is a field of Cosmic creation and activity, whereas the second is the field of Human form and development. At each level there is constant interaction—a flowing back and forth between Cosmic Reality and Challenge and Human Will and Capacity. This shows the Path of Action and Evolution.

Next, turn your attention to the third and fifth columns to see the functional resources opening up with each step of the evolutionary development process. The more conscious effort you put into the developmental process, the easier and faster your progress. No matter how *easy* and how *fast,* it's still calls for deliberate WORK on your part—but, remember that such "Work" is known as "the Great Work" and is that which provides meaning and enjoyment to your life.

It is this **Personal Empowerment** that we seek to provide in all our books. It's a careful combination of text, references to real life cases and stories, programs and procedures, selected illustrations, and developed charts and tables all working together for your **Personal Empowerment.**

Seven Planes and Seven Bodies Chart

It may be helpful to readers to conceptually study the content of the first four main columns extending from left to right on pages 14 and 15 respectfully as "manifestations" of:
1 – Shiva, Vishnu, Brahma;
2 – Ain, Ain Soph, Ain Soph Aur;
3 – Father, Son, Holy Ghost ;
4 – Nothing, the Infinite, the Absolute;

* Bladon's standard Theosophical terms

** The nature of the seven sub-planes— solid, liquid, gaseous, etc.—repeats in every plane in the nature of that plane's own substance.

Solar Scale		Esoteric Planes*	Esoteric Bodies	Esoteric Body's Functions and Powers
7:7 7:6 7:5 7:4	Universal Consciousness	7 Upper Divine Plane	Spirit-Self Upper Divine Body	Manifestation Self The Universal I AM
7:3 7:2 7:1		Lower Divine Plane *Adi*	Lower Divine Body	Spiritual Will
6:7 6:6 6:5 6:4 6:3 6:2 6:1		6 *Anupadaka*, or Monadic Plane 8 dimensions	Monad Monadic Body	Divine Perception
5:7 5:6 5:5 5:4		5 Upper *Spiritual Plane— 7 dimensions	Atman	Spirit
5:3 5:2 5:1	Universal Consciousness	5 Lower *Spiritual Plane *Atma*	Lower Spiritual Body	Collective Unconscious
4:7 4:6 4:5 4:4 4:3 4:2 4:1	Universal Consciousness	4 Buddhic, or Intuitional Plane 6 dimensions World of Love and Bliss *Buddhi*	Buddhi or Intuitional Body Spiritual Soul	Intuition Spiritual Consciousness Understanding and Judgment
3:7 3:6 3:5		3 Causal Plane World of Knowledge Causal Substance Elemental Essence 1	Higher Manas or Causal Body—the Higher Ego The Thinker	Abstraction Clear and Unifying Awareness Objective Thinking
3:4 3:3 3:2 3:1	Universal Consciousness	3 Mental Plane— 5 dimensions World of Thought Mental Substance Elemental Essence 2	Lower Manas or Mental Body—the Conscious Mind Concrete Thinker (Egyptian KHU)	Perception Universal thinking Subjective thinking Thought forms
2:7 2:6 2:5 2:4 2:3 2:2 2:1	Universal Consciousness	2 Astral Plane— 4 Dimensions AKA Emotional Plane Kama World of Reaction Astral Substance Elemental Essence 3	Astral Body Emotional Body Dream Body The Animal Soul (Egyptian BA)	Sensation Emotional (or Astral) Substance for Thought Forms Directly relates to the Subconscious Mind— memories, etc.
1:7 1:6 1:5 1:4	Universal Consciousness	1 Upper Physical Etheric Plane World of Life Force Etheric Substance	Etheric Double Energy Body	Receives and distributes prana via the chakras and meridians. Energy Healing
1:3 1:2 1:1		1 Lower Physical Plane: 3 dimensions World of Action Physical Substance	Physical Body Action Body	Action

Esoteric Sub-planes	Consciousness Flows	Consciousness Structure and Interrelationships
Atomic** Atomic** Atomic**	The Human Being is the unity of 5 bodies: Physical, Etheric, Astral, Mental and Causal. Each consciousness Is evolving independently to be absorbed into Monad.	<u>Divine Atom</u> SPIRIT The Highest, Divine Self <u>Divine Molecule</u> Three Primary Forces: Fohat—Masculine Energy, Prana—Vitality, and Kundalini—Feminine Energy exist on all planes and in all the bodies. Monadic Atom MONAD ↕
 Atomic** Atomic** Cultured Our true home Philosophic Philanthropic Spirituality Law and Relation-ship	There is constant interaction between the 3 lower bodies and the Causal Body which abstracts the experiences and memories into permanent "lessons."	<u>Spiritual Atom</u> **Atman, Buddhi and Manas** Compose the Soul or Higher EGO which serves as the vehicle for Spirit, the Immortal Self and True Individuality <u>Spiritual Molecule</u> <u>Intuitional Atom</u> The Monad is formed by Atman and Buddhi. The Monad manifests through the Causal Body as The Higher EGO which manifests the Personal Ego or Personality <u>Mental Atom</u> The Causal Body is the *Immortal Self* incarnating a portion of Self as the Personality. ↕
Atomic** Positive Emotions Negative Emotions (Spirit World) (Summerland) (Underworld) Atomic** Subatomic Super Etheric Etheric Gaseous Liquid Solid	Experiences and memories from previous incarnations flow from the Subconscious to the Causal Body where they are abstracted and permanently retained.	<u>Mental Molecule</u> PERSONALITY or Personal ego The Mortal Self consisting of the trinity of the Causal, Mental and Astral bodies manifests through the Physical/Etheric body. <u>Astral Atom</u> Super-Conscious Conscious Self Intellect and Mind ↕ Feeling Emotion Sensation ↕ <u>Physical Atom</u> Subconscious Mind ↕ Autonomic System

Mind over Matter

As a kind of "Mind over Matter" summary to this Introduction, we add a few words from an early 20th Century self-help classic, *As a Man Thinketh,* by James Allen, taking its theme from Proverbs 23:7 of the King James Bible. A few quotations here say a lot.

"Man is made or unmade by himself."

"The body is the servant of the mind. It obeys the operations of the mind, whether they be deliberately chosen or automatically expressed."

"Composer, sculptor, painter, poet, prophet, sage, these are the makers of the after-world, the architects of heaven. The world is beautiful because they have lived; without them, laboring humanity would perish."

"The dreamers are the saviors of the world. As the visible world is sustained by the invisible, so men, through all their trials . . . are nourished by the beautiful visions of their solitary dreamers."

And so, reader, we say "Dream on" but work to make your dreams real.

CHAPTER ONE
Taking the Paranormal Beyond the Lab

It is much easier to be critical than to be correct.
(British politician and Prime Minister,
Benjamin Disraeli, January 24, 1860)

PERSONAL EMPOWERMENT IS ESSENTIAL IN TODAY'S WORLD

Becoming *personally* empowered is essential to our functional existence in the world today as self-initiative, self-responsibility, and self-development are increasingly the foundational keys to personal security, career achievement, good health and longer life, *AND for twenty-first century scientific, technological, economic, and cultural progress.*

A New Age

Why is this necessary? Simply because we are in a New Age in which old ways are fast being replaced and new technologies, new economics, new relationships, new cultural and global challenges, and new, new, new everything that affects our daily lives and even more so for our children and coming generations.

And we are changing as the vibrational energies of the New Age affect us physically and mentally, opening new psychic and spiritual doors bringing a new level of awareness. We increase all our opportunities (and challenges) both individually and universally as we expand conscious awareness to include those higher dimensions traditionally known as "Paranormal". Today we are no longer limited to a specifically materialist concept of Man and Cosmos but acknowledge Mind as more than the physical brain and the physical dimension as more than pure matter empowered by clockwork mechanisms.

Lab Research Opened Doors

Twentieth century parapsychology was not a direct continuation of nineteenth century psychic research. Instead of focusing mostly on spiritualist séance phenomena precipitated by "extraordinary" people, often with the intent of exposing presumed mediumistic fakery, the twentieth century statistical research initiated by J. B. Rhine at Duke University demonstrated that, even under emotionally sterile laboratory conditions and long, repetitive "ESP Card" readings, coin tosses, dice rolls, etc. by "ordinary" people, *ESP is real.*

Moving on into the, Joe H. Slate at Athens State University focused on the development of specific paranormal techniques, demonstrating their validity under supervised Laboratory conditions, and then taking them beyond the Lab in successful "everyday applications" by ordinary people as well as those trained in paranormal skills.

Revolution and Evolution, over a few short decades

Like anything else, acceptance and familiarity turn the unusual and previously unfamiliar into everyday "reality." The *New Science of the Paranormal* has brought about an extraordinary "revolution" in a few short generations during which purely innate and undeveloped psychic powers have evolved into readily developed psychic skills and practical abilities.

A Sixth Sense, A Fourth Dimension

There's more to this story than *meets the eye!* Only a few of us were born artists, but nearly everyone can sketch a recognizable facsimile of an object. With that foreknowledge, we can learn to draw better pictures whether or not we want to become skilled artists. We become more broadly skilled and culturally diverse people through broader education opportunities than even before in human history.

Throughout history there have always been a few exceptional individuals born with fairly well developed skills, perhaps carried over from previous lives—natural clairvoyants, wonderful story tellers, more successful hunters, many great artists, builders, herbal and energy healers, etc. as well as people born physically stronger than most others, born leaders, born explorers, born thinkers, and more.

Variety is important to the evolutionary process. Often the few have taught others, but developing an illustrator into an artist does not involve developing a new sense, while becoming a *natural* psychic does. It necessitates raising our sensory vibratory capacity and making a place for it in our "middle" consciousness where the other five senses function in realization of our normal mental operations.

Putting it another way, psychic skills requires the *evolution* of a <u>Sixth</u> <u>Sense</u> beyond the familiar five, and *realization* of a <u>Fourth Dimension</u> beyond the familiar three. This, too, requires the raising of our sensory vibratory capacity to perceive a dimension that has always been there but only experienced in altered states of consciousness, states that are now becoming normal.

In order to fully perceive and participate in new realities, it is your expanded belief and perception that will enable you to develop your innate powers into usable skills. In other words, this is a case when "Seeing is Believing" is reversed to *Believing enables Seeing.*

The Application and Development of Paranormal Power

Through the discovery and application of paranormal power, we accelerate that process and achieve otherwise unobtainable personal and communal goals.

Once paranormally empowered, we can draw back the curtains of deliberate obfuscation and cultural prejudice and step into a new world of opportunities. We can engage new sources of power and create responsible pathways that reach beyond the commonly perceived limits of conventional knowledge. We can activate empowering interactions within the deepest levels of the subconscious mind. Equally as important, we can discover ways to seamlessly engage the highest planes and dimensions of power as sources of new growth and knowledge. We can experience in minute detail the totality of our personal existence, to include our pre-existence, past lifetimes, and the afterlife. On a wider scale, we can become empowered to contribute to the well-being of others while helping to promote positive international relations and global advancement.

Scientific Validation of Paranormal Experience

Although personal experiences in daily life can provide convincing evidence of the paranormal power available to everyone, controlled research conducted in the experimental laboratory setting can offer compelling scientific validation and replicative understanding of that power.

Cutting edge paranormal research not only identifies the wide range of potential paranormal powers existing within each of us, it probes the external sources of paranormal power and ways of accessing them. By activating the sources of paranormal power both within and beyond the self, new forms and directions of paranormal research can establish effective ways of developing the inner potential for paranormal empowerment and using it to achieve a seemingly unlimited range of goals, from personal to global and beyond, as we will later see.

Discovering the Nature and Purpose of Human Existence

Aside from validating paranormal power, controlled research in the lab setting can help meet the basic human need to discover new knowledge. It can provide enlightenment concerning the nature and purpose of our existence—past, present, and future. It can provide explanations of the unexplained by identifying the underlying components and complex dynamics of a given paranormal phenomenon. These results, once applied, can promote success in achieving otherwise unattainable goals. Laboratory research thus becomes a functional gateway that adds both meaning and power to life.

Complementing research *inside* the lab setting is a wide range of research methods and techniques appropriate for use *outside* the lab. Among these are surveys, personal reports, systematic observations, computer simulations, structured group exercises, archival research, field experiments, self-report inventories, interviews, physiological monitoring, and case studies, all of which can be applied to further investigate multiple paranormal phenomena. Taken together, these research methods can reveal realities that reach far beyond conventional perceptions.

The Importance of Going Beyond the Lab

The research presented throughout this book recognizes not only the need for new knowledge but active participation in the process of generating it. The lab studies, along with a variety of research efforts outside the lab, were designed to expand our understanding of paranormal phenomena and our capacity to personally experience them. It is hoped that this book will replace fixed skepticism and denial with inventive thinking and innovative applications to make the multiple powers of the paranormal available to everyone.

This *New Science of the Paranormal* can become a defining characteristic of "the New Age." It is the Next Step beyond the three dimensions of physical space and time to the perception of the fourth and fifth dimensions of the psychic and spiritual worlds.

PES: THE PERSONAL EMPOWERMENT SPACE
The Totality of your being—Past, Present and Future

A major goal of paranormal research is the discovery of the so-called *Personal Empowerment Space (PES)*, which is a secure, personal (Conscious) space that includes the totality of your being—past, present, and future. It characterizes the bi-directional endlessness of your existence as having neither beginning nor ending. It is through this unique personal space that you can consciously discover the power within your own being as well as the power beyond. Through that personal space, you can experience first-hand the inexhaustible possibilities of true paranormal power. All the resources you need to actualize your potentials and achieve your highest goals become readily available to you.

LIST OF EXAMPLE RESOURCES
TO TURN YOUR POTENTIALS INTO REALITY

Here are a few examples:

- Expand your awareness of the inner and outer sources of personal growth and power.
- Experience the spirit dimension and discover ways of accessing its empowering resources, including personal guides and growth specialists as well as higher planes and dimensions of power.
- Advanced spiritual beings, including discarnates and spirit guides with special innate or acquired skills applicable to the spiritual advancement of others.
- Overcome barriers to your growth by building self-esteem and positive perceptions of personal worth.
- Discover the subconscious sources of self-empowerment.
- Accelerate learning and improve memory.
- Facilitate better health and fitness.
- Promote rejuvenation and longevity.
- Reverse the mental and physical effects of aging.
- Build successful relationships.
- Replace self-defeat with positive expectations of success.
- Achieve career success.
- Disengage the negative, vicious cycle of failure and replace it with the cycle of success
- Break unwanted habits.
- Discover the reality and nature of life after death.
- Expand awareness of your pre-existence and past lifetimes.
- Discover the relevance of past-life experiences on present-life growth.
- Discover the bi-directional endless nature of your existence.
- Develop your capacity to access new knowledge and power.

- Develop your ESP and PK powers.
- Activate your creative thinking skills and overcoming habitual, self-imposed limitations.
- Replace fixed skepticism with liberated thinking.
- Dissolve habitual limitations and growth barriers.
- Build positive expectations.
- Master effective problem-solving skills.
- Achieve financial success.
- Contribute to the well-being of others.
- Make the world a better place.

Are these All possible? Yes, They Are! Can I (the reader) Achieve the Goal? Yes, You Can! Say it to yourself: Yes, I Can! Personal Affirmation is itself a source of Empowerment, both Personal and Paranormal— ultimately they are one and the same.

These are only a few of the many possibilities of paranormal power available to everyone. The multifunctional role of paranormal power in promoting both personal and global advancement beyond the lab is the hallmark of paranormal empowerment. It characterizes both the process and the product of paranormal power.

Paranormal experiences are becoming so common that many of us consider them a normal part of daily life. Like reasoning, creativity, intuition, and a host of other mental functions, the paranormal experience does not always lend itself to direct observation and experimental control. Nevertheless, serious experimental probes of the paranormal have not only yielded useful concepts and explanations, they have also uncovered a host of workable techniques for developing our paranormal potentials. Our studies, some of which are currently underway, have consistently shown that many of the spontaneous paranormal phenomena observed in "real" life are readily evident in the lab setting and receptive to step-by-step procedures designed to activate them.

The discovery of paranormal power clearly has many rewards, including awareness of the paranormal as an essential growth resource. Among the major challenges we face today are (1) the personal discovery of the paranormal power underlying our existence and (2) the mastery of techniques that effectively apply it. The escalating interest in paranormal power in such diverse areas as health and fitness, career success, research and development, psychotherapy, philosophy, and global advancement is due, at least in part, to the growing awareness of its potential benefits to both the individual and the world.

The evolving body of applications related to paranormal power, both personal and global, offers clear evidence of its multifunctional potential. With bold new concepts and innovative methodologies now available to everyone, paranormal power becomes increasingly essential to the pursuit of new knowledge and better quality of life.

Awakening to the Power to Shape the Future

A major goal of paranormal empowerment is the liberation and constructive application of dormant powers, including those with potential to shape the future. As an evolving science, paranormal empowerment strips away conventional constrictions and exposes hidden dimensions of power. It conceives as possible that which was previously believed impossible, not only for the present but the future as well. *By liberating dormant mental energies and hidden potentials, it shapes totally new perceptions and opens new channels of power with unprecedented possibilities.*

Paranormal Facilitators

Paranormal empowerment as a dynamic growth process rather than a fixed state is facilitated by certain essential conditions that are conducive to performance both in the experimental lab setting and beyond.

These Paranormal Facilitators include:

1. A positive self-concept, including a strong sense of personal worth and well-being.

2. Recognition and acceptance of one's paranormal potentials.

3. Appreciation of the value of paranormal power.

4. Self-confidence and a success orientation.

5. Flexibility and a willingness to explore.

The Distribution of Paranormal Potential

The *objective* study of paranormal power can dispel many of the *myths and "stories"* surrounding the topic, including the belief that very few individuals possess paranormal powers. Although certain individuals, often called "advanced beings" or "gifted psychics", may appear to be extraordinarily empowered, everyone to some degree possesses paranormal potential. Not unlike intelligence, the distribution of paranormal potential within the general population seems to occur in a so-called "normal curve" ranging from minimal to exceptional with a majority possessing an average degree of paranormal power. Although no test has been developed to accurately measure innate paranormal potential, it seems plausible that individuals with frequent spontaneous or involuntary paranormal experiences are more likely to be endowed with higher paranormal potential than those whose spontaneous experiences are less frequent. It is important to note, however, that the degree of receptiveness to the paranormal experience can be a critical influencing factor, with a high degree of acceptance facilitating the development of the paranormal potential. While more research is needed to develop instruments that accurately measure both potential and achievement levels of paranormal power, the observed distribution of performance in the controlled lab setting on paranormal tasks for randomly selected populations is profound. No longer can we think of paranormal potential as an *either/or* condition.

Another myth concerning paranormal power holds that paranormal experiences occur only in a spontaneous or involuntary manner. Although many paranormal experiences are spontaneous in nature, our research consistently demonstrated the controllable and often measurable nature of paranormal events. The distribution of paranormal powers among individuals, however, is typically fluid rather than fixed.

Fortunately, effective techniques and procedures are now available to stimulate paranormal development and to activate specific paranormal faculties. Although spontaneous paranormal experiences have been known to play an important role in human development, only recently have the learned techniques based on controlled laboratory studies become recognized as essential to paranormal development.

The Generalization Effect

Paranormal development does not occur in a vacuum. Our lab studies repeatedly showed that focused practice of one form of psychic ability typically promoted the development of other psychic potentials, a phenomenon called the *generalization effect*. For instance, practice in telepathy typically improves performance in both clairvoyance and precognition. Even more remarkably, practice exercises involving any given paranormal faculty often improves performance involving a myriad of other apparently unrelated faculties, including problem solving, memory, reasoning, and creativity, to list but a few. Even athletic skills showed marked improvement following practice exercises in ESP, a finding that was attributed to improvements in the underlying mental functions associated with the particular skill. Marked improvements in concentration and coordination along with endurance were particularly evident following practice exercises in ESP.

The Power of Research

Research is essential to the discovery, development, and application of paranormal power. Controlled research and objective observations can verify the existence of the paranormal, uncover its dynamics, and facilitate its development. Investigative research can discover, document, analyze, and advance paranormal knowledge. As Marcus Aurelius* noted, "Nothing has such power to broaden the mind as the ability to investigate systematically and truly all that comes under thy observation in life." (*Meditations*, Chapter II)

> *Marcus Aurelius (April 26, 121 CE to March 17, 180) was a famed Stoic philosopher who also served as Emperor of Rome from 161 to 180 CE.

A major focus throughout this book is on the effective application of paranormal power based on investigative research. Among the cited studies are projects sponsored by the Parapsychology Research Foundation established in 1970 at Athens State University; the U. S. Army Missile Research and Development Command of Huntsville, AL; the Parapsychology Foundation of New York; and numerous private sources. The technical research reports, which are referenced throughout this book by Technical Report (TR) Number, are on file and available for inspection at the Athens State University Library Archives, Athens, AL 35611. While certain of the research studies are presented in considerable detail, our emphasis remains throughout the book on paranormal empowerment in life beyond the lab.

THE NEW SCIENCE OF THE PARANORMAL
Throughout this book, we generally refer to the "New Science of the Paranormal" rather than the standard and more familiar *academic* term of "Parapsychology" to distinguish the long overdue move from the mostly statistical analysis of repetitive phenomena performed by students and "non-professional" volunteer under isolated laboratory conditions to the more modern study of demonstrable phenomena by both professionals and under real life "field" conditions and careful study of spontaneous paranormal events.

Our goal in this book is to take what we have learned through scientific study in the lab and apply it to gain understanding of traditional practices in the real world beyond the lab in the development of mind-directed psychic technology for everyone.

To a large extent the modern study of the paranormal practices and events relates to the "real" world, and parapsychology is more concerned with phenomenon in isolation from the real world. It can even be said that the study of the paranormal starts with "believers" while parapsychology starts with "non-believers."

CHAPTER TWO
Extra-Sensory Perception:
Expanding the Limits of Awareness

For I dipt into the future, far as human eye could see,
Saw the Vision of the world, and all the wonder that would be.
—Alfred, Lord Tennyson, *Locksley Hall*

EXTRA-SENSORY PERCEPTION DEFINED

Extra-Sensory Perception (ESP), possibly the most common and identifiable form of paranormal power, can be simply defined as:

The knowledge of, or response to, events, conditions, and/ or situations independent of *known* sensory mechanisms or processes.

The emphasis here is on "known" since it is highly conceivable that many sensory mechanisms and processes exist but are yet to be scientifically recognized and accepted into the common vernacular.

The Three Major Mental Faculties of ESP

These three psychic faculties of Extra-Sensory Perception are the most widely recognized forms of ESP today. In the 19th century, the most common experience of the Paranormal was associated with the Spiritualist Séance. The particular difference we want to point out is that such Spirit Communication generally involved a "professional" working with a group, whereas these three are common to individual experiences. Note there is no need for group support or various kinds of equipment.

1. Telepathy: the psychic sending and receiving of thoughts as well as emotions and mood states;

2. Clairvoyance: the psychic perception of existing objects, conditions, and/or events; and

3. Precognition: the psychic awareness of the future.

Functional Definitions of ESP and PK more easily recognized

Psychokinesis (PK), defined as the psychic ability to influence objects, events, or processes, is not considered a form of ESP since it is explained primarily as an *intervention phenomenon** rather than a form of psychic perception. Our studies of ESP and PK in the controlled laboratory setting, however, consistently reflected the widespread manifestation of both phenomena among research participants of wide-ranging age and background characteristics.

> *Intervention phenomenon: An intervening occurrence that influences processes and/or outcomes.

Interestingly, self-report survey studies of personal paranormal experiences consistently revealed a much higher frequency of reported experiences among participants when *functional definitions* were used instead of paranormal labels, such as ESP and PK. That approach, which clearly identifies the definition of the paranormal concept but without the use of identifying labels, was used in a survey of ESP experiences among undergraduate college students (TR 1) enrolled at Athens State University (then College). Conducted by the Parapsychology Research Foundation (PRF), the survey was administered during student registration in a college auditorium setting. Participating in the study was a total of 500 volunteer students consisting of 210 men and 290 women, with an age range of 17 through 32 years.

The PRF Survey of College Students' ESP Experiences

Shown in Figure 1 on the next page is the survey form with the number of responses inserted for each survey item. In order to promote thoughtful, unbiased responses among participants, the questionnaire used descriptions and examples rather than the usual paranormal terms: ESP, telepathy, precognition, clairvoyance, and PK.

Figure 1
BEHAVIOR ASSESSMENT SURVEY FORM
(With Survey Results)

The Parapsychology Research Foundation (PRF) is conducting a survey of certain behavior patterns and opinions among upper level college students. You are invited to participate by completing the following questions. Thank you for your cooperation.

Name (Optional):_____.

Gender: ( ) Male ( ) Female

Date of Birth: (_____)

Student Classification: ( ) Junior ( ) Senior ( ) Other

1. In my opinion, human beings have certain mental capacities beyond those presently recognized by conventional science.

    468 Yes

    12 No

    20 Undecided

2. I have had at least one experience of knowing, for no apparent reason, what another person was thinking.

    460 Yes

    17 No

    23 Undecided

3. My experiences of knowing, for no apparent reason, what another person was thinking occur:

    11 Everyday

    87 Almost everyday

    280 Only occasionally

    96 Very infrequently

    17 Never

    9 Undecided

4. I have had at least one experience of knowing, for no apparent reason, what was about to happen or what was going to happen in the near future.

    427 Yes

    43 No

    20 Undecided

5. My experiences of knowing, for no apparent reason, what was about to happen or what was going to happen in the near future occur:

> 3 Everyday
>
> 63 Quite frequently though not daily
>
> 174 Only Occasionally
>
> 236 Very infrequently
>
> 24 Never

6. My experiences of knowing, for no apparent reason, what was about to happen or what was going to happen in the near future were most likely to occur as:

> 384 A simple impression
>
> 76 A dream experience
>
> 37 A mental image, though not a dream
>
> 3 None of the above.

7. I have had the experience of knowing about situations or events occurring elsewhere, such as an accident at a distance as it occurred or the contents of a test before I looked at it, for no apparent reason.

> 283 Yes
>
> 172 No
>
> 45 Undecided

8. My experiences of knowing, for no apparent reason, about situations or events happening elsewhere occur:

> 8 Every day
>
> 41 Quite frequently though not daily
>
> 132 Only Occasionally
>
> 146 Very infrequently
>
> 99 Never
>
> 74 Undecided

TELEPATHY, THE MOST COMMON ESP EXPERIENCE

In this survey, a vast majority of students (468 of the 500 respondents) concluded that *human behavior is often characterized by certain capacities beyond those presently recognized by conventional science.* Telepathy was the most frequently reported ESP experience, with 460 of the 500 respondents reporting having experienced that phenomenon.

Pre-cognition commonly experienced as a simple impression

The second most frequently reported experience was precognition, with 427 of the respondents reporting having experienced that phenomenon, primarily as a simple impression. Seventy-six of the respondents reported having experienced precognitive dreaming. It is possible, however, that many precognitive dreams remain unrecognized until after the occurrence of the predicted event. In some instances, *déjà vu* may result from subliminal association of an event with its antecedent precognitive dream, which hypothetically could remain in subconscious form.

Clairvoyance—A Daily Experience for some

Of the 500 respondents, 283 reported having experienced clairvoyance, with 8 respondents reporting the phenomenon as an everyday occurrence.

A limitation of this study was the environment in which it was conducted: a student registration situation in a college auditorium setting. Although the environment was reasonably quiet and controlled, the stresses associated with registration could have influenced the results of the study. As already noted, the questionnaire did not include paranormal terms; however the paranormal concepts were clarified in the STEMs* of the survey items. Arguably, the results of the survey could have been markedly different had paranormal terms been used or had other definitions or examples been given.

*STEM is an acronym referring to the academic disciplines of science, technology, engineering, and mathematics, all necessarily integrated in modern educational programs no matter the subject major. All are fundamental to the objective awareness and mental discipline of modern life as distinct from the elements of faith and acceptance common to the subjectivity of the recent past.

A two-year later replication of this survey with a different student population showed highly similar results (TR 1a). As in the previous survey, telepathy was the most frequently reported ESP experience with precognition the second most frequently reported.

ACTIVATING ESP

In the absence of extra-sensory awareness, we become caged beings, confined by limiting borders of the purely physical dimension and out of touch with the greater reality. Whether spontaneous or deliberately induced, ESP not only expands the borders of awareness, it opens totally new pathways for personal growth and success. Fortunately, research based ESP programs are now available to activate dormant ESP potentials and promote their development.

Activating Various Forms of Extra-Sensory-Perception

Among the most effective procedures for activating various forms of ESP is the "Extra-sensory Activation Procedure" (EAP). Developed in our labs, EAP is based on the premise that ESP is a multifunctional phenomenon with several interrelated components. As a broad-spectrum procedure, EAP activates relevant Extra-sensory faculties and focuses them on designated goals ranging from general to highly specific. It recognizes information of ESP origin as direct knowledge in its purest form. The procedure has shown effectiveness when applied to such specific goals as telepathic sending and receiving, precognitively identifying future happenings, and clairvoyantly viewing distant realities.

Here's the procedure, which requires approximately 30 minutes in a quiet setting free of distractions:

ESP ACTIVATION PROCEDURE

Preliminary Note: In all paranormal work, the careful, precise, and concise formulation of *outgoing* Goals, Questions, Stated Affirmations, and Visualized Imagery is important to your success. At the same time, the extended awareness and open receptivity to *incoming* impressions is equally important. Think of yourself planting a garden: the seed you plant is small and precise; the resulting tree can grow to great size with branches spreading wide and serving many purposes, including the reproduction of many seeds for many more trees.

Step 1. *Goal Setting:* As you settle back into a comfortable seated or reclining position, **formulate your ESP goal,** stating it in positive terms and affirm your commitment to it.*

> *Commitment. You are sending a message to your Deep Inner Self to make whatever contacts are necessary via non-material *Inner Dimensions* to accomplish an important mission on your behalf. Treat this work seriously. *Frivolity* can backfire!

Step 2. *Prepare the Body:* With your eyes closed, clear your mind* of active thought and focus your full attention on your breathing. Take in a deep breath, and while exhaling slowly, develop a rhythmic breathing pattern as relaxation spreads throughout your body.

> *Clear your Mind. You are preparing the "channel" to communicate your important message. Focusing upon your breathing is the most proven *voluntary* technique to relax the body and clear the mind to communicate with the Deep Inner Self.

Step 3. *Affirm and Visualize:* Again, **state your ESP goal and visualize it as an unfolding reality.*** Such visual aids as a mental screen upon which relevant images appear are especially effective for goals related to precognition and clairvoyance. Images of a bird in flight are particularly effective for sending and receiving telepathic messages. **Allow plenty of time for the mental images to unfold.**

> *Unfolding Reality. You are asking for a change of reality, no matter what your message is. By visualizing a bird in flight or some similar image, you are seeing change to induce change.

Step 4. *Open and Receive:* Extended Receptiveness. **Allow additional insight to unfold, excluding any unrelated to your stated goals**. Interactions* with higher sources of knowledge, including other dimensions and growth specialist often unfold at this step.

*Interactions. By communicating your precise goal or concise question to the Inner World you are calling upon the appropriate Inner (or "Secret") Agents to <u>act</u> on your behalf. All change is precipitated from inner to outer, or—depending on your perspective and chosen vocabulary—downward from the Astral to the Physical Dimension.

Step 5. Affirm and Act:* Concluding Affirmation. In your own words, state your commitment to responsibly apply the knowledge obtained through this program, and affirm your commitment to develop your ESP potentials.

*Affirm and Act. To Affirm, in your own words, starts the process of bringing that changed Inner Reality to manifest in the Outer World. To Act brings it into concrete reality in the Outer Manifest World.

Step 6. Record and Review: Document your use of this exercise in your ESP Journal.*

*Documenting your work—*action, result,* and *conclusion*—is vitally important to the success of each application, experiment, and observation in all scientific work, and even more so in all personal developmental work. Write it down, review it later—perhaps several times—make further comments and later summaries. Clearly identify the programs and procedures you are undertaking, and keep each major subject activity in a separate file or binder, These become a record of your inner life development. This action itself—so easily neglected—is the foundation of your growth and *advancement!*

As a practice procedure designed to activate various forms of ESP related to specific goals, this program is among the most effective known for promoting extra-sensory awareness on a "need to know" basis. Spontaneous enlightenment unrelated to stated goals often emerges in Step 4 during interactions with other dimensions of power.*

*"Need to Know" and "Spontaneous Enlightenment" are two important results of your increasing interactions with the much larger Inner World. Aside from the programs introduced in this book, your daily presence through meditation and active inner awareness invites recognition of your needs for growth and knowledge.

THE DYNAMIC EFFECT OF PRACTICE and EXPERIENCE

In the development of our psychic abilities, there seems to be no substitute for practice and experience. Our research (TR-2c) showed that repeated practice of ESP, whether inside or outside the lab, awakened dormant ESP potentials while increasing the frequency and accuracy of ESP. Our studies also found that the presence of others as either participants or observers often facilitated performance. A common characteristic of group practice in the controlled clairvoyance situation, however, is the possibility of *empathic telepathy** in which a group member who experiences clairvoyance of the experiment material may spontaneously send that information telepathically to other members of the group. That same dynamic can occur in group practice exercises in precognition in which precognitive impressions of one group member can be sent telepathically to others, thus "contaminating" the precognitive effects. Although the intervention of other forms of ESP can occur in any group exercise, our studies found that group practice designed to promote the development of specific psychic abilities remains highly effective in facilitating psychic performance both within and outside the controlled practice setting.

*Empathic Telepathy: Spontaneous, unintended telepathy based on consciously perceived need.

Another possibility is that the intentional effort to exercise paranormal powers itself brings about an altered and "higher" state of consciousness that not only awakens a person's own dormant ESP potential but also *vibrationally* raises that of others in an immediate group.

Further reflecting the extensive benefits of practice in paranormal development, a time–extended study of 40 undergraduate students at Athens State University found that the grade point average (GPA) for each student increased progressively (with but two exceptions) following the completion of a course titled "Seminar in Parapsychology" which focused on developmental practice exercises. The two exceptions were for students who had already achieved and continued to maintain a perfect GPA.

TELEPATHY
A Dynamic Force

Thinking is an energy phenomenon with interactive patterns that include both thought and emotion components. The product of thinking, the formulated thought, is a complex constellation of information, perceptions, and emotions. It can be expressed both verbally and non-verbally as well as independently of conventional communication channels.

In many instances, telepathy may be the preferred method of communication. It provides a personal and unobtrusive communication channel in which an almost unlimited range of messages can be effectively conveyed. It can transfer totally new information, complement a verbal communication, and clarify ambiguous communications. Ideas, concepts, emotions, and perceptions, which do not lend themselves to direct verbal or written communication, possibly due to language barriers, may be effectively transmitted telepathically.

There is another factor to consider: Telepathic Sensitivity. We are mentally sensitive to those of our immediate family and our close associates. And that sensitivity is mutual—there is a general awareness of thought and feeling between those in close relationships. We need, therefore, to be sensitive to our own thoughts and feelings towards others. Be Nice!

Telepathy not only transmits the desired message, it can also locate the target receiver. That so-called *paging function* of telepathy may be among its most valuable features, especially in situations involving urgency or danger. Although telepathy typically occurs in everyday life situations as a common feature of daily communications, it can center around extraordinary situations in which other means of communication are unavailable.

Although telepathy is often experienced as the mental transference of bits and pieces of information, it can convey highly complex messages with combinations of thoughts and emotions. For instance, a message of a celebrative event is often accompanied with emotions of joy, while a message of a tragic event is often accompanied with emotions of sadness. In both instances, the emotions can be experienced by the receiver independently of the thought message.

We speculate as to the "mechanism" involved in the non-local transference of information, and even more with the added complexity of emotions and the abstract nature of images and symbols. The natural conclusion is that "consciousness" is not materialistically limited but extends through all dimensions of the Cosmos, and can be accessed through a match-up of vibratory rates and "identity" codes that are largely matched to desire and intention.

Adding to the complexity of telepathic interactions are certain mechanisms, often of subconscious origin, that disguise the communication by either condensing or fragmenting the message through the use of symbols and imagery. Although these mechanisms can be challenging to the receiver, they tend to diminish resistance and facilitate acceptance of the message. While the use of these disguises is not uncommon, the typical telepathic communication appears to be clear, concise, and purposeful.

An Empowering Option

In the controlled lab setting, objectivity and rigorous controls are essential to the validity and replicability of the ESP research effort. Among experimental subjects, however, a strong acceptance of paranormal phenomena and expectations of success on the experimental exercises are associated with successful performance. Similarly, persons in general outside the laboratory who report frequent paranormal experiences, including telepathy, are more likely to be believers in psychic phenomena and confident of their own psychic abilities. They tend to value telepathy in its capacity to transfer totally new information, clarify ambiguous communications, and complement a verbal communication.

A Critical Alternative

Telepathic channels are always available—the only required variables are two minds. When other communication channels are unavailable, telepathy can become a critical alternative. But even when other channels are available, telepathy can be a highly efficient option, especially when the location of the target receiver is unknown. This important *paging function* of telepathy may very well be among its most important application.

Animal Communication and Culture

It can be applied toward locating not only missing persons but animal companions as well. In the highly controlled lab setting, animals have often demonstrated ESP powers, characteristics that reflect the inherent nature of animals as beings of worth. Supportive of the view that recognizes the value of animals are the numerous cultural observations that found the best indicator of a given culture's advancement level is the nature of its treatment of animals: *The more advanced the culture, the more humane its treatment of animals.*

The Power of Distributed Practice

Aside from past experiences and positive acceptance of telepathy, participation in various practice exercises has shown remarkable effectiveness in promoting the development of ESP skills. *Distributed practice in which the exercises are relatively brief and rest periods are frequent tends to accelerate development of telepathic skills,* including sending and receiving. Distributed practice using either Zener ESP Cards* or standard playing cards in both individual and group situations has shown effectiveness in the development of not only telepathy but also clairvoyance and precognition.

> *Developed by psychologist Karl Zener (1903–1964) to conduct ESP experiments with his colleague, J. B. Rhine (1895–1980). A Zener deck consists of 25 cards repeating 5 distinct symbols—a hollow Circle, equal armed Cross, 3 wavy Lines, a hollow Square, and a hollow 5-pointed Star.

Meditation Exercises for Development and Application

Not unlike other paranormal phenomena, telepathic sending and receiving are highly receptive to meditation exercises that focus on the development and positive application of paranormal skills. Among the most effective sending methods are those that generate physical relaxation and a positive mental state. For sending, the use of mental imagery that includes motion such as a bird in flight or a banner in the wind with a written message or symbol upon it can significantly increase effectiveness. For either sending or receiving, visualizing a mental screen upon which relevant images are depicted can likewise be effective, especially in sending symbolic messages.

Clarifying Images and Powerful Symbols

In telepathy, appropriate symbols or images of objects can represent ideas, feelings, or happenings. A mental image transmitted telepathically can convey more complex and comprehensive information than verbal communications. In telepathy, a meaningful picture can indeed be worth a thousand words. When accompanying verbal communications, relevant telepathy utilizing imagery can enhance the clarity and effectiveness of the communication.

Controlled lab research suggests that even the sending of sensations, including aromas, is possible through telepathy. Our lab studies found that the telepathic sending of images of lilacs induced in the telepathic receiver the aroma of lilacs. Similarly, telepathic images of gardenias induced the aroma of gardenias in the receiving subject, including groups of students in a classroom setting. Experiencing the differences between these two aromas through telepathy paled in comparison to conventional communication efforts to describe them.

Telepathy and Mood State

It is important to note that communication, whether psychic or non-psychic, never occurs in a purely cognitive vacuum. Mood state, including a wide range of feelings, emotions, and attitudes, appears to be a critical component of our interactions with others, including individuals and groups. That principle suggests the capacity of telepathy to induce changes in the mood state in the receiving subject while also influencing the social interaction between the sender and receiver.

To investigate the effects of telepathic messages on mood state, both during and following the ESP interaction, the Parapsychology Research Foundation designed a laboratory study (TR-4 Telepathy and Mood

State) that used a subjective pre- and post-test self-rating of mood state to determine the immediate and after effects of a positive and neutral telepathic communication on the mood state of receiving subjects. For ethical reasons, we did not investigate in this study the effects of negative telepathic communications.

The subjects of the study were college student volunteers consisting of 20 telepathic receivers (11 females and 9 males) drawn from the general student population and 10 telepathic senders (5 females and 5 males) who were enrolled in a senior level course in experimental parapsychology. All senders had training and experience in telepathic sending and receiving strategies. None of the 20 receivers had formal training in telepathy, and none had participated in previous parapsychology research.

The experiment was conducted in a quiet laboratory setting with moveable desks situated in pairs facing each other. A screen was erected between the sender and receiver for each of the telepathic exercises. From the population of 20 receivers, 10 were randomly designated as the experimental group and the remaining 10 were designated as the control group. Members of the control group, upon entering the laboratory, were administered a 5-point Mood State Self-rating Scale (Figure 1) of their present mood state with a rating of one indicating an elated, optimistic state and a rating of 5 indicating a depressed, pessimistic state. Here's the Scale:

Figure 2
MOOD STATE SELF-RATING SCALE
Please rate your present mood state on the following 5-point scale:

Elated, Optimistic (__)(__)(__)(__)(__)Depressed, Pessimistic
                        1   2   3   4   5

Upon completion of the scale, each control subject was randomly assigned a telepathic partner who, upon being seated across from the assigned subject, advised the telepathic partner as follows: "Over the next two minutes, I will attempt to send you a certain telepathic message. Your task is to simply allow yourself to be receptive to the message." The telepathic message for the control group consisted of the following: "The season is autumn. The weather is mild. The trees are aglow with color." Upon completion of the 2-minute period, the Mood State Self-rating Scale was again administered to each control subject.

The experimental group then entered the laboratory and, like the control group, completed the Mood State Self-rating Scale. Each participant was then randomly assigned a telepathic sending partner. While seated across from the partner and concealed by a screen, the sender attempted to send, for a period of two minutes, the following message: "You are beginning to feel better and better about yourself. Your future is bright and promising. You are happy and content." Upon expiration of the two-minute sending period, each experimental subject was again administered the mood state rating scale.

Comparisons of the pre- and post-test ratings of mood state revealed a typically elevated mood state for the experimental subjects; whereas the control group's mood state typically remained unchanged or was only mildly affected. Closer inspection showed the post-test rating results remained unchanged for seven of the ten control subjects. For one control subject, it increased toward the depressed, pessimistic position by one point, and for two of the control subjects, it moved by one point toward the elated, optimistic position. For the experimental group, the post-test results indicated changes toward the positive direction for eight of the ten subjects with the remaining two showing no change.

The statistical analysis (correlated t on before/after designed with matched control group) showed a significant difference in the effects of telepathy on improving self-ratings of mood states (t=2.89, reject Ho; significant at p<.05).*

*For the statistical studies presented throughout this book, the results of statistical analysis enclosed in parenthesis following the discussion of research findings in the narrative offer an objective scientific basis for the conclusions drawn. The t-test as used here is applied to determine whether the mean of a given population significantly differs from that of another.

Therapeutic Benefits of Positive Telepathic Messaging
This study suggests possibilities for telepathy that reach far beyond the mere transfer of information in the controlled lab setting. Among them are valuable therapeutic benefits and more positive interpersonal relationships through telepathic messages that generate a more positive mood state. While more research on the empowering benefits of positive telepathy is needed, it seems plausible that both sender and receiver would benefit from positive telepathic interactions, whether in a controlled lab setting or in life situations beyond the lab, including psychotherapy settings.

THE *SEND* METHOD TO COMMUNICATE and EMPOWER
The SEND Method is a telepathic approach based on the concept that communication is a complex process with multiple verbal and non-verbal expressions of ideas, thoughts, impressions, and feelings, all of which can be expressed telepathically. *The research-based method focuses on the empowering nature of telepathy not only to communicate but also to empower.* It is especially effective in sending relevant imagery and symbolic messages. Here's the 4-step procedure:

S—**Specify** your telepathic objective, to include the specific message and telepathic receiver

E—Envision your message as an **energized "thought form"** * that can include relevant imagery and symbols.

> ***Thought Form:** 1) An astral image created by concentrated thought intended to accomplish a specified objective. When reinforced with emotion and charged with etheric energy, it will become physically manifest. 2) A spontaneous image created in the imagination that is charged with emotional energy. Either is perceived by a clairvoyant and is felt by ordinary people with some degree of psychic sensitivity. A carefully constructed mental image that is charged with emotional energy can become a manipulative tool used in product marketing, political action, and religious domination.

N—Navigate the message along the pathway to the desired destination.

D—Deliver the message to the desired destination by taking in a deep breath and exhaling slowly as the telepathic receiver is visualized.

This procedure is flexible and can be easily modified to meet personal preferences and goals. Although more research is needed to determine its usefulness as a group strategy, there is considerable evidence to suggest its effectiveness when used to promote positive group interactions and success in achieving group goals.

CLAIRVOYANCE
Experiencing the Unknown

Clairvoyance as the ESP of existing conditions, objects, and/or events is one of the most complex and advanced forms of paranormal phenomena. *Unlike telepathy, it functions independently of another mind, thus providing a potentially unlimited field of expanded awareness.* It can focus awareness on distant realities, including physical and non-physical alike. It can probe the non-physical realm, including higher dimensions of advanced knowledge and power. Beyond these, it can uncover concepts yet to be discovered by conventional science.

Clairvoyance accepts the premise that all knowledge currently known existed in some form before it became known. Learning is, in fact, often defined as the discovery of knowledge, a concept that recognizes the existence of knowledge *before* it was discovered. None would dispute the fact that *knowledge, once acquired, is power.* It would follow that knowledge, before it is acquired, existed in a power or potential power form. Clairvoyance may be among our most effective methods for acquiring that knowledge and thus accessing its power.

The dynamics of clairvoyant interactions

From a psychic empowerment perspective, the dynamics of clairvoyant interactions with sources of new knowledge can be summarized as follows:

1. Knowledge exists as a manifestation of energy. It includes that which is known, that which is unknown, and conceivably that which is presently beyond the human capacity to know.

2. Personal existence, like knowledge, is a manifestation of energy.

3. Energy manifestations are endowed with the capacity to interact.

4. Clairvoyance results from the interaction of the human energy system with other sources of knowledge.

5. Once acquired, knowledge of clairvoyant origin is empowering. It can advance both personal and global progress.

Clairvoyance and Situational Factors

Over the years, a major concern among researchers has been the relationship, if any, between ESP performance in the laboratory and ESP experiences outside the laboratory. In view of that concern, a laboratory study (TR-2) was conducted at Athens State University by the Parapsychology Research Foundation to investigate the effects of situational factors on clairvoyance in a laboratory setting and the relevance of those factors in predicting ESP behavior beyond the laboratory. The study revealed a strong, positive relationship between performance in the laboratory and the reported frequency of ESP outside the laboratory when mundane realism (i.e., the experimental laboratory conditions were perceived by the experimental subject as similar to real-life situations) was high. An even stronger relationship was found when the laboratory task was high in both mundane and experimental realism (i.e., the participant perceived the experiment itself as convincing).

Twenty college students enrolled in Experimental Psychology at Athens State University participated in the two phase study. Ten participants (5 men and 5 women) were randomly assigned to Phase I and ten additional subjects (also 5 men and 5 women) were assigned to Phase II, which was a replication of Phase I. The study was conducted in a controlled laboratory setting over a three-day period in which three experiments were performed for each of the two phases. The first experiment was designed to be high in experimental realism but low in mundane realism. The second experiment was designed to be high in mundane realism but low in experimental realism, and the third experiment was designed to be high in both mundane and experimental realism. For each task, the subject was allowed one minute to respond.

Prior to the first experimental task, all participants stated their frequency of personal psychic experience outside the laboratory on a five-point rating scale with a rating of one signifying "very frequent" and a rating of five signifying "very seldom".

In the first task designed to be high in experimental realism, each participant was required to clairvoyantly locate a key placed under one of five small boxes on a table in the laboratory. The location of the key was known only to the research assistant who had placed it under the box and was absent during the experimental task. A second research assistant who sat at the table across from the subject presented the following instructions to each experimental subject:

"You are a traveler from outer space who has landed on earth. You have misplaced your ignition key in one of five shipping compartments represented by one of the five boxes on the table before you. But there is a problem. You have only one trial in which to locate the key, and then return to your home planet. When you open one compartment, the others will automatically lock permanently. It is thus critically important that you locate the key on the first try. You have one minute to find the key."

Following this first task, as well as the two that followed, the participants rated the exercise for both experimental realism and mundane realism on a five-point scale, with a rating of one signifying "very highly convincing" and a rating of 5 signifying "not convincing".

In the second task, which was designed to be high in mundane realism, the participants were again given the task of locating a key; but for this experiment, they were instructed:

> "Under one of the five boxes placed before you, there is a key. Your task is to identify the location of the key in a single trial. You have one minute to find the key."

For the third task designed to be high in both experimental and mundane realism, the participants were instructed as follows:

> "You are a dormitory student, and you have lost the key to your room. The key is under one of the five boxes before you. Your task is, on a single trial, to locate the key. You have one minute to find the key."

For Phase I, the highest performance was found to be for experiment three in which both experimental and mundane realism were rated as high. For that experiment, 6 of the 10 participants correctly located the key. These results remained unchanged for Phase II of the study.

This study further found a strong relationship between ESP performance in the laboratory and frequency of ESP experience outside the laboratory.

Statistical analysis of the participants' ratings for experimental and mundane realism of the three experiments in both phases of the study revealed significant differences. In Phase I, the ratings of experimental realism were significantly greater than the ratings for mundane realism in Experiment 1. (t=8.125, reject Ho; significant at p<.01)

In Experiment 2 of the same phase, mundane realism was found to significantly greater than experimental realism (t=6.86, reject Ho; significant at p<.01). In Experiment 3, Phase I, a significant difference was again found between experimental realism and mundane realism, with mundane realism being greater (t=3.08, reject Ho; significant at p<.01); however the t value was approximately half the value of t for Experiment 2 and only slightly more than a third of the value of t for Experiment 1.

In Phase II of the study, a replication of Phase I, analysis of the realism ratings revealed similar results. In Experiment 1, a significant difference was found between experimental realism and mundane realism, with experimental realism being greater (t=6.86, reject Ho: significant at p<.01). In Experiment 2, mundane realism was significantly greater than experimental realism (t=7.81. reject Ho,; significant at p<.01). In Experiment 3, no significant difference was found between mundane and experimental realism ratings (t=1.24, accept Ho; not significant), a finding suggesting that the experiment contained both experimental and mundane realism.

Inspection of the data indicated that clairvoyance performance was greatest for Experiment 3 in both phases of the study. As noted, Experiment 3 attempted to combine both experimental realism and mundane realism. Clairvoyance performance was poorest for Experiment 1 (both phases) in which mundane realism was low, although experimental realism was high.

Based on these findings, we could cautiously conclude that as mundane realism increases in the experimental situation, performance on clairvoyance tasks should likewise increase. As both experimental and mundane realism increase, clairvoyance performance would be expected to increase to an even greater degree.

Analysis of the data further showed that the participants' ratings of frequency of psychic experience outside the laboratory were greater for those participants in both phases of the study who performed well in the laboratory, especially for Experiment 3. A statistically significant correlation was found between the total number of correct responses for participants and their reported frequency of psychic experiences outside the laboratory (r=.82, reject Ho; significant at p<.01).

In summary, the more realistic the laboratory clairvoyance task, the more likely the research effort will adequately measure the clairvoyance skill as well as predict clairvoyance performance outside the laboratory. While more study is needed, we could cautiously assume that lab performance on other forms of paranormal phenomena would likewise be influence by the realistic nature of the experiment.

Activating Clairvoyance

In view of the findings of this project, a follow-up study (TR-2b) was designed to identify other factors that are conducive to clairvoyance, both in the lab setting and beyond. The study identified the following essential conditions: (1) a positive self-concept and sense of personal worth and well-being ; (2) Recognition and appreciation of one's ESP potentials; (3) confidence in one's ability to perform on ESP tasks in the lab setting; (4) a success orientation; (5) flexibility and a willingness to experiment; and finally, (6) *practice, practice, practice.*

CLAIRVOYANCE ACTIVATION PROCEDURE

Among the most effective exercises designed to promote clairvoyant perception is the Clairvoyant Activation Procedure (CAP). For this procedure, practice in appropriate visualization effectively sets the stage for clairvoyance to occur in either fixed or active form. Central to the effectiveness of the procedure are mental images of both fixed and moving objects, which appear to exercise the mental and physical components of clairvoyance. Fixed clairvoyant images suggest an established situation resistant to change, whereas moving images suggest conditions that are highly receptive to intervention. Here's the procedure, which requires approximately 30 minutes in a comfortable setting free of distractions:

1. View a picture, a scene, or an object, paying particular attention to details.

2. With your eyes closed, recreate the view, again giving special attention to such details as color, shape, texture, and movement.

3. Check the accuracy of your imagery by again viewing the picture, scene, or object.

4. Repeat the above steps.

5. With your eyes closed, allow a new image to appear—a tree, building, person, landscape, or any image spontaneously emerging. Notice such details as color, shapes, and movements characteristic of the image. Give special attention to the emotions and physical sensations associated with the image

6. Allow clairvoyant impressions to emerge by flowing with the image and allowing it to be experienced at a deeper level of awareness.

7. Document the exercise in your ESP journal.

Even limited practice of the above exercise can markedly increase the frequency of clairvoyant experiences. Combining other clairvoyant practice exercises, such as guessing the hour before checking the time, pulling a book from a shelf and guessing its total number of pages, and practicing with cards can markedly increase the number of spontaneous clairvoyant experiences. Adding to the rewards of this procedure is the sheer enjoyment of developing clairvoyant skills. Even clairvoyant mistakes can be both amusing and motivating as illustrated by a student whose clairvoyant impression of a book with 322 pages was 223 pages, a possible illustration of *clairvoyant reversal.* Although the development of psychic abilities can require serious effort, clairvoyant reversal illustrates a lighter side of the paranormal.

PRECOGNITON
Awareness of Future Events
Precognition as the awareness of future events not based alone on existing conditions can range from clear, specific extra-sensory messages to imprecise impressions lacking detailed information. The conditions related to *precognition can include a myriad of information channels such as dreams, impressions, images, symbols, and emotions as well as such highly indirect channels as lapses of memory, slips of the tongue, and even*

antithesis or the extreme opposite of the future event. Possibly the most complex precognitive mechanism is the subconscious expression of double meaning or *double entendre.* Such highly indirect expressions seem to be designed to convey information through an attention demanding but non-threatening channel.

Precognition: Fact or Fiction?

In January 2012, the Parapsychology Research Foundation gathered precognitive data from its membership in an effort to determine the accuracy and relevance of the precognitive experience. Participating in the study (TR-82: Precognition: Fact or Fiction) was a group of 50 volunteers who were active members of the Foundation. Each of the participants of the study submitted individual psychic predictions on January 15, 2012 for a full year. A total of 402 predictions were submitted, 342 of which had been verified by January 15, 2014.

Following is a summary of the 342 predictions, which were validated as accurate by the end of the two-year period:

Summary of 342 Validated Predictions

1. Seventy-two percent of the predictions related to events associated with oneself, a relative, a close associate, or a friend.
2. Fourteen percent of the predictions related to events of national or international significance.
3. Twelve percent of the events related to apparently insignificant events.
4. Thirty-eight percent of the incidents were categorized as neutral, 42% as negative, and 20% as positive.
5. Eighty-one percent of the predictions were seen as preventative or preparatory in nature.
6. Five percent of the predicted events were viewed as a confirmation of the appropriateness of a previous decision.
7. Sixty-two percent of the events were seen as motivational in purpose.

8. Seventy percent of the events were seen as enriching in purpose.

9. Fourteen percent of the events were seen as providing information needed to solve a pressing problem.

The results of this study suggested that precognition, rather than fictional, is typically factual and purposeful in nature. Here are some categories of purposes suggested by this study:

Purposes and Benefits of Precognition

1. Preparation. Precognition can provide important preparation for the predicted event.

2. Prevention. Precognition can suggest strategies for avoiding or preventing undesired situations or consequences.

3. Confirmation. The predicted event, once fulfilled, can confirm the wisdom or correctness of a previous decision. Many major personal and career decisions are fraught with uncertainty and apprehension. Relevant precognitions can be a source of reassurance and support.

4. Motivation. Precognitive awareness of future success can promote success expectancy, build self-confidence, and give the winning edge to goal-striving behavior.

5. Enrichment. A broad perspective that spans not only the past and present but the future as well can be a source of deeper insight and understanding of the relatedness of events and the continuity of life experiences.

6. Problem Solving. Precognition is frequently a problem-solving activity with the prediction providing optimal solutions and suggesting more effective problem-solving strategies.

A Critical Source of Information

According to this study, precognition can be a critical source of information with multiple purposes and empowering possibilities. Whether spontaneous or voluntarily induced, it appears to be consistently goal directed. It can be experienced directly as a clear, detailed message or more subtly as an impression directly proportional to a future event. Striking examples of precognition included the Jeane Dixon's prediction of John F. Kennedy's assignation; Clark Gable's uncharacteristically depressed, agitated mood state prior to the accidental death of Carole Lombard; and the host of reports of elated mood states frequently experienced by gamblers as winning signals. By their own claims, professional gamblers often express a sixth sense of knowing when "lady luck" is about to strike.

Precognitive Dreaming: A Motivational Force

Dreams appear to be among the most common precognitive channels, possibly due to the dreams use of both direct and indirect precognitive mechanisms. In the direct mode, the future is presented in clear, explicit forms while in the indirect mode it is presented in complex ambiguous forms that include the use of symbolism and antithesis. In symbolism, the dream is typically condensed, often in an imaginative but highly meaningful way. For instance, a dream of climbing a mountain may symbolize success in overcoming adversity. In antithesis, the precognitive message represents the opposite of the predicted event. For instance, a dream of financial loss may represent future financial gain. In both instances, the dream experience increased persistence and promoted success in achieving the desired goal.

In a remarkable instance of the capacity of precognitive dreaming to predict a career decision, a psychology professor reported a lucid dream that occurred frequently during his several years of graduate study. The recurring dream became a *tableau vivant* firmly etched in his memory: a third floor office window opening upon a giant tulip tree with an amicable squirrel scurrying among its branches. Upon completion of his graduate studies and assuming a college teaching position, he saw the precognitive dream unfold into reality. The view from the third floor office he was to occupy for several years was identical to the recurring dream in every detail, down to the friendly squirrel scurrying among the branches of the tulip tree. The precognitive dream, by his report, gave reassurance of the wisdom of his decision to accept the teaching position. (That professor, incidentally, is the co-author of this book.)

Inducing Precognition

While spontaneous manifestations of precognition are common and often profound, certain practice exercises have shown remarkable effectiveness in activating specific precognitive perceptions while promoting development of precognition as a paranormal faculty. Among the most effective programs are dream induction techniques that utilize suggestion during the pre-sleep stage. The pre-sleep auto suggestions are presented either immediately before falling asleep or in the earliest phase of sleep called hypnogogic sleep. The suggestions are typically more effective when presented in a simple, positive form that does not interrupt the normal sleep and dreaming cycle. Examples include such suggestions as: *I am open to the messages of my dreams. I will recognize my precognitive dreams, and I will help them to occur. I will understand my dream messages, and I will benefit from them.* Our lab studies repeatedly showed that dream induction programs designed to stimulate a specific dream function were likewise effective in spontaneously activating other dream experiences as needed. *Given the dream channel, it seems that the extra-sensory part of our being knows which ESP faculty to activate.*

A concern expressed among certain behavioral scientists is whether paranormal power, once acquired, could be used in a harmful, malevolent way. Fortunately, there seems to be an inherent built-in mechanism that prevents the negative use of paranormal power. Among the striking examples is the so-called *boomerang effect*, which interrupts negative telepathic messages and returns them to the sender who, consequently, experiences the message's negative effect. In contrast to the boomerang effect, positive telepathic interactions tend to be empowering to the sender and receiver alike. They can add both quality and meaning to life.

Conclusion

As human beings, our existence in the universe demands awareness, exploration, and interaction. Because of its capacity to transcend the limits of sensory experience, ESP is among our most valuable resources for meeting those demands. Through ESP, we can discover new sources of power and meaning, both within ourselves and beyond.

CHAPTER THREE
The Out-of-Body Experence:
Reaching Beyond the Physical

PROJECTING AWARENESS OUT OF THE BODY

The out-of-body state, also known as astral projection or soul travel, is typically defined as:

> **"A state of awareness in which the locus of perception shifts to a conscious state of being in a spatial location outside the physical body, and—even more challenging—*beyond physical time and space!*"**

As this book is directed both to the "science-oriented" parapsychology reader and the more general reader of paranormal-related subjects, we want to clarify that this alternative state of consciousness that is commonly known as the "Astral Body" which, while existing holistically as one dimensional *vehicle* among several—including and beyond the *materialist-limited* physical body, is exactly that—a "state of consciousness."

Other Dimensional Vehicles

But, these several states of consciousness (or "dimensional vehicles") do function through transitional units of subtle non-biological energy and substance as our means of action and experience at different levels of consciousness defined by intention.

Vehicles for Emotion, Mind, Will, and Spirit Consciousness

The Astral Body is also called "the "Emotional Vehicle," while the Mental Body serves as a vehicle for Mind, the Causal Body as vehicle for Will, and yet higher (vibrationally speaking) vehicles likewise serve for action and expression of other levels of consciousness and spirit. (Please see end of chapter for a simple chart showing the Seven Levels of the Human Structure.)

The Extra-Biological Body

Out-of-body experiences (OBEs) assume a duality of human nature and the existence of an astral or extrabiological body with the capacity of disengaging the biological body and link awareness to distant spatial realities. In both OBEs and certain near-death experiences (NDEs) in which OBEs are believed to occur, the disengagement is transient and limited whereas in the discarnate state, it is complete, at least until re-embodiment or reincarnation occurs. The nature of the out-of-body state and certain (NDEs) points to the perpetual existence of personal identity and conscious being. There is, incidentally, a growing body of evidence that animals, likewise, experience the out-of-body state along with increased awareness of distant realities.

In the following discussion we will examine several studies designed to explore the essential nature of the out-of-body experience and its evidenced-based relevance to our existence as spiritual beings. The studies cited in this chapter, as were other studies presented in this book, were conducted at Athens State University under the auspice of the Parapsychology Research Institute and Foundation (PRIF).

Case Studies of out-of-body experiences (OBEs)

Much of what we know about OBEs is based on case studies of individuals who report having experienced the phenomenon. This study (TR-5: Case Studies of Out-of-body Experiences) was based on the premise that the case study approach in the study of OBEs could be useful in determining the essential characteristics of the altered state and developing effective induction strategies.

The Parapsychology Research Foundation, in addition to conducting scores of controlled laboratory experiments on the topic, has maintained case files of reported out-of-body experiences (OBEs) over several years. Although many of the 283 subjects included in this study reported more than one out-of-body experience, only one instance from each case file was selected at random for inclusion in this study. The 283 cases consisted of 152 females and 131 males. Their ages ranged from 17 to 51 years.

COMMON CHARACTERISTICS OF OBES

This study analyzed each reported instance and attempted to identify some of the *common characteristics of OBEs. Here are the results:*

1. Of the 283 cases analyzed, all indicated that *cognitive functions continued normally in the out-of-body state. Over half (211 cases) indicated positive emotions associated with the experience.* Common among them were serenity, well-being, and peace of mind. A total of 27 subjects reported negative emotions accompanying the experience to include varying degrees of anxiety and fear of losing control.

2. Psychomotor performance in which objects or matter were influenced was reported by over one-third (103) of the cases.

3. Many instances of sensory experience were noted among the cases. All of the 283 subjects reported the sensation of sight, 21 subjects reported taste, 18 subjects reported smell, 142 subjects reported weightlessness, 192 subjects reported hearing, and 119 subjects reported touch.

4. No gender differences were noted in the ability of subjects to enter the out-of-body state.

5. A total of 42 participants reported awareness of a guiding presence during the out-of-body state. In 13 instances, the presence was visible to the subject.

6. Meaningful interactions with others were occasionally reported as having occurred during the out-of-body state. Among the 283 cases, 22 subjects reported interactions with others who were not in the out-of-body state at the time; whereas 11 subjects reported interactions with others who were also in the out-of-body state. Forty-one subjects reported interactions with deceased relatives or friends.

7. The frequency of spontaneous OBEs was greater among subjects who reported the ability to induce at will the out-of-body state.

8. Out of the 283 subjects, 264 viewed OBEs as significant sources of insight and knowledge. In 12 instances, the OBE was believed to be of important motivational value or instrumental in preventing serious injury or death.

9. None of the 283 subjects considered OBEs as being without value. With the exception of 2 subjects, all believed OBEs validated the existence of the soul and conscious survival of bodily death.

10. All 283 subjects reported certain unique, identifying characteristics of OBEs which set them apart from any other altered states.

11. A total of 227 subjects experienced their astral body as an exact replication of the physical body, though not necessarily clothed in ordinary attire.

12. All subjects experienced the out-of-body state as a state of consciousness with cognitive and emotional functions intact.

13. Perceptual awareness was described as significantly heightened by 197 of the subjects. They described colors as more brilliant, surroundings more distinct, and sounds clearer.

14. Material barriers were non-existent for all subjects. They could walk through a closed door or defy gravity and exit a room through the ceiling. They could soar over terrain and in some instances glide among the stars. Viewing the universe from above, and in some instances, spontaneously viewing other distant universes. a phenomenon called *multiversal perception,* was experience by 12 of the participants.

15. The circumstances surrounding the spontaneous OBE were varied. While most of the subjects (211) reported a calm state of relaxation or serenity, 23 reported a state of emotional distress, 7 reported that they were seriously ill or near death immediately before the experience, and 2 of them believed that they had actually experienced death briefly during the OBE.

Emotions and the Out-of-Body State

It was frequently noted among the subjects of this study that one's emotional state could either promote or inhibit the out-of-body state. Often, OBEs seem to occur during intense mood states, such as grief, fear, and elation. In several instances, the experience occurred during the so-called "peak experience" or heightened state of awareness. While moderate pain seemed often to inhibit the out-of-body state, intense pain in some instances seemed to facilitate it. One subject who reported numerous spontaneous OBEs pointed out that the spontaneous out-of-body state could be facilitated in some instances by the subconscious as a defense against potentially overwhelming situations, such as life-threatening injury or near death.

It should be noted that the astral dimension is often referred to as "the Emotional World" and characterized by emotional power and energy. "E-MOTION" is *Energy-in-Motion*. Ecstatic States, Magickal Rituals, and Powerful Religious Rituals are all highly energized and often characterized by physical movement—Dancing, Swaying, Rapid Rotation, Fast Drumming—often leading to Out-Of-Body experiences. Even techniques involving a stilled and relaxed physical body may involve the rapid up and down movement of internal energies.

The Higher you go, the more you have

Please also realize that the "higher (vibrationally speaking) you go" in paranormal, spiritual, and magical technologies, the greater the variety of techniques that work. In other words, don't presume that only "this or that" technique will work or is to be preferred over others. *Intention* is the major key to accomplishing any goal firmly stated, visualized, and seen as moving to the desired result.

The Out-of-Body Experience and Sensory Functions

The out-of-body state, if viewed as a phenomenon in which the astral or extra-biological body is temporarily disengaged from the biological body, raises questions concerning the nature of certain sensory functions in that state. This study (TR-6: The Out-of-body Experience and

Sensory Functions) was designed to investigate the sensation of smell during the out-of-body state.

The subjects for the study were 20 undergraduate student volunteers (10 males and 10 females) who had participated in a seminar designed to develop skill in entering the out-of-body state. All reported having the ability, to some degree, to enter the out-of-body state at will. The age range of the subjects was 22 through 29 years.

The study was conducted in a carefully controlled experimental setting. The experimental set-up consisted of 10 open pint containers, 9 of which were filled with water and one with ethyl alcohol, placed 3 feet apart on a table in the laboratory. The placement of the containers in numbered positions was determined by a laboratory technician who was absent for the OBE exercise and who alone knew the location of the ethyl alcohol container.

In a comfortable room adjacent to the laboratory, each subject entered the self-induced out-of-body state. Prior to induction, each subject was instructed to use the out-of-body state as a vehicle to enter the adjacent laboratory and identify through the sense of smell the open container of ethyl alcohol. Upon return to the normal state, the subjects recorded their responses on a record form. Following each trial, the 10 containers, all identical in appearance, were randomly rearranged by the laboratory technician. The trials were repeated daily over a five-day period for the 20 subjects.

On the first trial, 7 of the 20 subjects, while in the induced out-of-body state, correctly identified the location of the container of ethyl alcohol. On the second trial (day 2), the number of correct responses increased to 8, and on the third trial (day 3), the number of correct responses increased to 9 where it remained for the fourth trial (day 4). On the fifth and final trial (day 5), 10 of the subjects correctly identified the location of the ethyl alcohol container. Four of the 20 subjects correctly identified the container on all five trials; whereas 6 of the 20 subjects were unsuccessful on all trials.

In follow-on interviews, the successful subjects typically expressed strong confidence in their ability to enter the out-of-body state at will, and all reported the capacity to view the laboratory situation and sense the odor of ethyl alcohol while in that state. The unsuccessful subjects expressed less confidence in their ability to achieve the desired out-of-body state, and they were uncertain of their capacity to sense the odor of ethyl alcohol. Subjects who were successful on all trials or who were unsuccessful on only one trial reported complete success in achieving the out-of-body state; whereas the subjects who were unsuccessful on all trials reported uncertainty or doubt.

For this study, an overall accuracy rate of 43% was observed. The probability of a correct response was .10.

The findings of this study are of at least three-fold importance. First, the capacity to perceive smell does seem to continue in the out-of-body state as an extra-sensory phenomenon; second, strong confidence in one's ability to enter the out-of-body state seems to facilitate the phenomenon; practice seems to improve out-of-body performance, at least on this designated task.

Astral Travel During Sleep

In an effort to develop a procedure that uses sleep as a vehicle to promote astral travel, we devised a study (TR-7: Astral Travel During Sleep) that examined the characteristics of frequent astral travelers and the strategies used by them.

Fifteen college students (9 males and 6 females), all reporting a high frequency of out-of-body travel during sleep, volunteered for the study. The subjects, whose ages ranged from 21 through 29 years, were interviewed to determine the strategies they used and to identify relevant personal traits. Here's a summary of the interview results:

OUT-OF-BODY TRAVEL DURING SLEEP FACTORS

1. All subjects expressed confidence in their ability to travel out-of-body to selected destinations, whether during sleep or in the normal wakeful state.

2. All subjects recognized the critical importance of a tranquil mental state prior to sleep, along with motivation to travel out-of-body. Worry, anxiety, and apprehension, they believed, were counterproductive to travel.

3. They recognized the importance of a clear intent to travel out-of-body as a prerequisite for productive travel. While the exact destination of travel was not always specified, they formulated travel plans that were related to prevalent issues or concerns.

4. They were highly receptive to interactions with other planes or dimensions. One participant in the study recounted astral travel to another plane in which she interacted with a ministering guide who facilitated her recovery from a serious illness. Another participant experienced a joyous reunion with her deceased brother who had died in a small plane crash.

5. They considered the out-of-body state as distinctly unlike other altered states, including the normal dream state, meditation, and hypnosis.

6. In the drowsy, preparatory stage for travel, all the subjects affirmed their intent to travel out of body and their ability to direct the out-of-body experience. Examples included: *I'm now free to leave my body. I can go wherever I wish. I'm fully protected as I travel. I'll return to my body at will.* For specific destination travel, images of the destination were usually formed and integrated into the induction process.

7. In the drowsy, initial stage of sleep, all participants believed they had some control in initiating the out-of-body experience. Physical relaxation, slowed breathing, and imagery of the astral body bearing consciousness gently disengaging the physical body and rising above it were common. Among their descriptions of the process were "freeing oneself", "letting go like a balloon in the breeze", "defying gravity", "almost dying or seeing my body below as if it were dead", and letting oneself be "lifted up" or "borne aloft as if by an unseen attraction".

8. Although return to the physical body was usually spontaneous, it could be deliberately initiated by intent alone.

The results of this study suggested that deliberate intervention during the drowsy state preceding sleep could facilitate out-of-body travel and, in some instances, direct it to specified destinations.

PRE-SLEEP OBES INDUCTION PROCEDURES

The sleep state seems particularly conducive to out-of-body travel. In fact, one view of OBEs holds that sleep itself is an out-of-body state with the non-biological double or astral body being projected over the physical body for the duration of sleep while it remains connected to the physical body by a "silver cord".

Whether sleep itself is an out-of-body state or simply an altered state conducive to OBEs, it seems plausible that appropriate pre-sleep strategies could facilitate the out-of-body state, and possibly out-of-body travel to selected destinations during sleep. To explore that possibility, a study (TR-8: Pre-sleep OBEs Induction Procedures) was designed in which certain pre-sleep procedures were applied to promote out-of-body travel.

The subjects of the study were 10 volunteers (5 males and 5 females), all college students whose ages ranged from 19 through 24 years. All subjects had completed a course in parapsychology that included instruction in out-of-body travel and dream intervention strategies.

The 10 participants of the study were instructed to present a simple autosuggestion immediately before falling asleep that out-of-body travel would occur as they slept. The suggestion consisted of the following: "As I sleep, I will be free to leave my body and travel wherever I wish." Images of a specific destination were then formed, and additional autosuggestions directing travel to that destination were presented.

Immediately upon awakening, participants of the study recorded in a journal the details of their dreams and any apparent out-of-body travel experience. They then evaluated their OBEs against their destination goals.

Analysis of the results of the study indicated that all subjects believed they had succeeded in entering the out-of-body state during sleep, with 7 of the 10 subjects reporting success in out-of-body travel to a desired destination. In one instance, the female subject reported travel to a distant city to visit a friend whom she had not seen in several years. During the visit, she noted yellow appliances, white tie-back curtains, and a fresh arrangement of red tulips on the table in her friend's newly decorated kitchen. A phone conversation with her friend the following morning validated the details of the out-of-body visit.

Another participant of the study, a male subject, reported an out-of-body visit with the deceased Albert Einstein who lectured and filled a chalkboard with complicated formulas and calculations. Upon awakening, the student immediately recorded Einstein's lecture conclusions as follows:

> As you can readily see from our calculations, the form of time as we know it in this place is symptomatically caused by the dominant energy of this plane known as light, and can be non-existent or different on other planes determined by the dominant and sub-dominant energy forms.

This limited investigation suggests that, with more concentrated study and refinement of induction strategies, astral travel during sleep could become a recognized source of important knowledge and a valued tool for learning.

The Physiology of the Out-of-body State

Casual observations of the out-of-body state in the laboratory setting suggest a slowed physiological state and either diminished or extinguished biological responsiveness to sensory stimulation. With the exception of simple reflex actions, motor performance seems to cease.

This laboratory study (TR-9: The Physiology of the Out-of-body State) was designed to determine more precisely the physiological changes that accompany the out-of-body state. Ten college students volunteered to participate in the study, which was conducted in a controlled biofeedback laboratory setting. The subjects (5 males and 5 females) ranged in age from 19 to 23 years. Each subject had completed a parapsychology course in which they had been trained in the techniques of out-of-body travel. All subjects reported that they could, at will, enter the out-of-body state.

The apparatus required for the experiment consisted of the Davicon M-44 for obtaining electromyographic (EMG) measurements, the Cyborg J-42 for obtaining thermal measurements of the right index finger-tip area, the Edmond Scientific 508 for obtaining galvanic skin response (GSR) measurements, the Edmond Scientific Brain Wave Monitor for obtaining brain wave activity, and a mercurial sphygmomanometer (Edmond Scientific No. 72,101) for measuring blood pressure.

With the exception of a biofeedback technician who recorded changes in physiology, the subject who was resting comfortably on a couch was alone in the laboratory during the experimental session of 40 minutes. At the beginning of each session, and at 10 minute intervals throughout the session, physiological measurements were obtained by the biofeedback technician. Following the experimental session, the subjects were interviewed to determine their assessments of the session.

In the post-session interviews, all 10 subjects reported success in entering the out-of-body state. The physiological measurements obtained indicated almost instant changes, which continued for the duration of the session in every parameter. Here are the results:

Physiological Changes during OBE Sleep

- Changes in EEG for all subjects suggested the alpha state.
- Finger temperature increased for all subjects by an average of 6 degrees Fahrenheit with a range of 4 to 8 degrees increase for the 10 subjects.
- Pulse rate for the 10 subjects decreased by an average of 12%.
- Respiratory rate decreased by an average of 20%. (The respiratory rate for one subject of the study decreased from 19 to 6 per minute.)

• For systolic blood pressure, the average decrease was 8 with only minor variations in diastolic pressure.

While this study revealed changes in physiology similar to those characteristic of relaxation, they occurred more rapidly in the out-of-body state where they remained for the duration of the state.

Induced OBEs: Analysis of Case Studies

The purpose of this study (TR-10: Induced OBEs: Analysis of Case Studies) was twofold: First, to determine the personal characteristics associated with successful out-of-body travel, and second, to determine the specific techniques used by the subjects.

A total of 18 subjects (10 females and 8 males) who reported the ability to induce out-of-body travel at will volunteered for the study. Thirteen of the subjects were college students and 5 were drawn from the career setting. The subjects were instructed to write a two-part narrative describing themselves and the techniques they used for inducing OBEs. The participants were instructed to give particular attention to the following:

1. Describe yourself and your present life situation, to include your physical condition and mental state.
2. What do you consider to be among the most important benefits of the out-of-body experience?
3. Describe specifically the techniques you use to induce the out-of-body state.
4. What are the situational or personal factors that facilitate the out-of-body state?

Analysis of the case reports found that the subjects typically viewed themselves as competent and in control of their lives. They described their physical state as healthy and their psychological state as positive. Among the terms used were physically fit, well-adjusted, self-reliant, secure, confident, motivated, and effective in adapting to life's demands. Whether students or career persons, they described their performance as above average.

The reported benefits of OBEs emphasized the enrichment potentials of the experience. OBEs were seen as relaxing, a source of insight, and effective in reducing stress. They were described as personally gratifying and spiritually relevant. Seven of the subjects reported that the solution to personal and career problems often emerged during OBEs. All of the 18 subjects reported that OBEs provide a broader view of the nature of one's existence.

Analysis of the induction strategies used by the 18 subjects uncovered several common factors. Various forms of mental imagery and visualization were used by all subjects. Relaxation procedures to include such techniques as slowed breathing, body scan, and muscle relaxation were also common among all subjects before the self-induced out-of-body state. Four of the subjects reported skill in using a particular cue—typically a mental image or a series of images—to induce the out-of-body state. Images of brightness and sensations of motion and spatial distance upon entering the out-of-body state were reported by 8 of the 15 subjects. All subjects reported that practice in meditation improved their ability to travel out-of-body.

The subjects of this study emphasized the importance of a positive mood state, self-confidence, a healthy self-image, awareness of one's psychic powers, and a state of personal well-being as vital in developing one's out-of-body skills.

OBEs and the Near-Death Experience
This study (TR-11: OBEs and the Near-death Experience) examined the case reports of near-death experiences (NDEs) and out-of-body experiences (OBEs) collected from 18 volunteer subjects who were students at Athens State College (now University). Although the near-death experience itself can be seen as an out-of-body experience, OBEs for the most part do not involve near-death.

Nine of the 18 subjects reported having experienced near-death. Four of the 9 NDEs subjects also reported having experienced at least one OBE. The remaining 9 subjects reported having experienced at least one OBE but in the absence of near-death.

Analysis of the 18 cases revealed certain strong similarities along with distinct differences between the OBEs and NDEs as follows:

SIMILARITIES BETWEEN OBE and NDE

1. All subjects reported that the experience, whether OBE or NDE, was profoundly meaningful. One subject reported that his NDE resulted in a career change and a dramatic shift in his belief system. Another subject reported that her OBE empowered her to end an abusive relationship, which had thwarted her growth for several years. All subjects reported that the experience, whether OBE or NDE, confirmed survival of bodily death.

2. All subjects viewed their experiences, whether NDEs or OBEs, as spiritually relevant. Four NDE subjects and three OBE subjects reported visits with spiritual entities from the other side, including beings believed to be ministering guides. Two NDE subjects reported visits with departed relatives.

3. Sensory experiences, particular sight and sound, were reported as common by all subjects. Neither OBEs nor NDEs included sensations of pain or discomfort.

4. OBEs and NDEs were characterized by a serene state of mind rather than mental distress.

Differences:

1. NDEs were described as highly intense with enduring significance, possibly due to the life-threatening situations involved. OBEs were seen as more commonplace, but nevertheless profoundly relevant.

2. All of the NDE subjects but only two of the OBE subjects believed they had engaged the spiritual realm. Four NDE subjects reported having seen heaven and recognizing departed relatives in a luminous, garden-like setting.

3. A sense of slow motion was reported among 6 NDE subjects but only three OBE subjects.

4. Interactions with a personage of profound spiritual significance were reported by seven NDE subjects but only two OBE subjects.

5. A glowing presence described as angel-like was seen by four NDE subjects but only one OBE subject.

All the subjects in this study considered OBEs and NDEs as among their most profound past experiences. They concluded unanimously that both NDEs and OBEs reveal the endless, indestructible nature of our being.

Mastering Out-of-body Skills

Although the effectiveness of specific techniques for initiating the out-of-body state will vary among individuals, the more highly successful self-induction approaches will typically evolve in the context of considerable experimentation and practice, either individually or within groups. Among the characteristics that typify the most effective self-induction approaches are progressive relaxation, appropriate mental imagery, and increased sensory awareness. The following program called the **OBEs Self-induction Procedure** developed in our labs at Athens State University provides a composite of techniques organized in an approach that provides a basic structure within which modifications can be readily made.

THE OBES SELF-INDUCTION PROCEDURE

Essential to the success of the procedure is a state of security and control as noted in Phase II. Here's the 4-phase procedure:

Phase I. Preliminaries. A period of approximately 30 minutes should be allowed for the exercise during which no distractions occur. A comfortable semi prone or reclining position is recommended.

Phase II. Physical Relaxation. A state of deep physical relaxation should be induced with particular attention focused on breathing and relaxation of specific muscle groups. Use such autosuggestions as, *I am peaceful and secure; my body is becoming more and more relaxed; my muscles are loose and limp; I am secure, at peace with the world; and I am at complete control of my mind and body* are combined with mental images of certain objects moving very slowly, such as a sail boat, billowy clouds, or floating balloons.

Phase III: The Out-of-Body State. Continue the auto-suggestions with mental imagery as the out-of-body state induction procedure continues. In this phase, slow the procedure to allow the out-of-body event to occur unhurriedly and to permit the unfoldment of clear mental images. To induce the out-of-body state, the following auto-suggestions are slowly presented and with appropriate imagery: *I am now prepared to leave my body. In doing so, I will remain secure and in complete control. I am now surrounded by radiant, protective imagery. I am free to go wherever I wish. As I drift slowly away, I can see my body, relaxed and secure at a distance. I will return to my body with comfort and ease whenever I decide to do so.*

Phase IV: The Return. The out-of-body state is concluded by the simple intent to return to the physical body.

Considerable practice is usually required to master effective OBE self-induction skills. With mastery of those skills, however, the frequency of spontaneous, productive OBEs almost always increases.

Conclusion

The evidence is clear: The out of body experience is an essential part of our existence as mental, physical, and spiritual beings. OBEs are critical to our spiritual evolement: they offer not only evidence of our spiritual nature, but enlightenment and growth available from no other source.

Through the out-of-body experience, you can become fully liberated from the constraints of mind and body. You can become empowered to experience first-hand the essential nature of your being as an evolving soul. You can experience totally new realities, including the spiritual realm with its abundance of growth resources. You can interact with your personal guides who can empower you to overcome growth blockages, solve pressing problems, and generate totally new growth opportunities. Through the out-of-body experience, you will discover your destiny for greatness.

Many Bodies, Many Planes

There's more to Cosmic Reality than just the physical "World" and the physical "Body" even when we include the Astral Body and the "Plane" or Level experienced Out-of-Body. Even the Dream State and the creative power of the human imagination should begin the process of expanding awareness beyond that of the familiar Five Physical Senses.

Materialist science *assumes* that what we may think to be non-physical or extra-physical is only *illusion* caused by electrical and chemical stimulus to certain areas of the brain without considering that these same "altered perceptions" may be actual windows and doorways into expanded awareness revealing actual realities that only can be explored and understood as part of a larger picture inclusive of more than the physical dimension.

In the table below we provide a very simple outline of both sides of the picture that are often referred to as "Inner" and "Outer." The point being that *our* reality is inclusive of both "what is" and "what we perceive," and what we perceive is limited to the senses of that body (vehicle) of consciousness through which we are active. We are more than we think we are, but we don't know we are until we develop that level of awareness and related sense of perception. We must grow to become more than we are and all we can be.

The Lesson of the Out-of-Body Experience is that most of us reading this book are still a bundle of potentials, and it's our job to develop those potentials. We need to learn about those potentials and accept their reality, and then explore and practice techniques to awaken and develop them.

TABLE OF THE SEVEN PLANES OF THE SOLAR SYSTEM
and SEVEN LEVELS OF THE HUMAN STRUCTURE

Three Dimensions

Physical Plane		**Five Senses**
Solid	)	**Physical Body**: vehicle of thought,
Liquid	)	feeling, awareness,
Gaseous	)	and action in the physical world.
Etheric	)	**Etheric Double**: connecting link between
Super-Etheric	)	the inner and outer man, and container
Sub-atomic	)	of vital energy (*prana*) received physically
Atomic	)	from the sun and super-physically from
	)	the spiritual sun.

Four Dimensions

Astral Plane:		**Six Senses**
	)	**Astral Body**: vehicle of desire, emotion.
(Seven	)	
sub-planes)		

Five Dimensions

Mental Plane:	*Rupa*		**Seven Senses**
(Lower four		)	**Mental Body**: vehicle of the formal mind, and
sub-planes)		)	instrument of concrete thought.
Arupa		)	**Causal Body**, or higher mental body: vehicle of
(Higher three		)	Will, the abstract mind of the threefold Spiritual
sub-planes)		)	Self, the Augoides or Ego.

<u>Six Dimensions</u>

Buddhic Plane   )   **Buddhic Body**: vehicle of spiritual intuitiveness.

)   Soul

<u>Seven Dimensions</u>

Atomic Plane   )   **Atomic Body**: vehicle of the spiritual will.

(aka Nirvanic)   )   Spirit

<u>Eight Dimensions</u>

Monadic Plane   )   **Monad**: the Dweller in the Innermost.

(aka   )
Paranirvanic)

<u>Nine Dimensions</u>

Adi (aka   )   **Divine Spark**
Manapara-
nirvanic)

Note: The names for the Seven Planes the Seven Levels are not universally adhered to, but the overall concept of the invisible structure of Man and Universe is important to understanding the potentials of Astral Projection and the Out-of-Body Experience.

Note also that this chart can be interpreted both from "Bottom-to-Top," i.e. the *evolutionary* process from the physical level to the Divine, and from "Top-to-Bottom," the *devolutionary* (or *incarnational*) process. But, <u>understanding</u> the difference between the two is vastly complicated.

CHAPTER FOUR
Objectology and Sand Reading:
The Hand's Message

The substance of psychic phenomena does not always lend itself to direct observation and quantification. Consequently, indirect means are often sought to gain access to elusive sources of extra-sensory information and organize it into meaningful, objective form.

Objects as Information "Mediums"
It should be noted that <u>certain</u> *inanimate objects* have a long history of serving as a "medium" for both spontaneous paranormal phenomena and intentional activities. These range, on the one hand, from poltergeist happenings and forms of spirit communication to divinatory devices and ritual transformers and transmitters.

Objects Used to "Announce" Poltergeist and Psychic Happenings
Some of the common objects relating to poltergeist happening are doors and windows opening and closing, grandfather clocks stopping or starting, bells and chimes ringing, and other phenomena that seem to say little more than "I'm (or something is) here!"

Objects Used in Spiritual Communication
In addition to these usages are those involved in actual spiritual communication, such as Table-tipping, the Ouija™® and other "talking boards," a Swinging Pendulum over a circle of letters and numbers, Spirit Trumpets to magnify spirit voices and sounds, and pen and paper in automatic writing.

Objects Used to Divine Information
In more direct forms of divination, we have the use of various cards inscribed with Tarot images, rune letters, I Ching hexagrams as well the use of rolling dice, coin tosses, picking straws, etc. Also, we have the use of forked and swinging rods, pendulums weighted with samples in dowsing work not only for water but often for minerals as

specified by the attached sample, pendulums and the flattened hand moving over maps to locate lost objects, missing persons and pet animals, and for detecting health problems.

Objects Used to Protect from Harm, or to Project Power

Another use of objects is as Amulets and Talismans, and also as Sacred Objects and Magical Tools. Amulets, worn on the body to protect one against harm, are traditionally natural objects such as gems, crystals, and herb packets with long established correspondences specific to the need. Talismans are most often carefully crafted objects of chosen materials and designs associated with appropriate correspondences and carried, worn, or used to project such powers as Luck, Success, Health, etc. In addition to their associated powers they usually are ritually *charged* to enhance those powers specifically for the person involved.

Objects Used as Magical Tools

Both Sacred Objects and Magical Tools are likewise carefully crafted and ritually charged to project or invoke particular powers in religious or magical rituals. The Chalice is a traditional sacred object that receives, transforms, and transfers power, while the Wand is a magical tool that conducts and directs power. The major characteristic of all these objects is that of appropriate symbolism, either of historic association or/and long established astrological, mythic, and Kabbalistic empowerment.

Certainly some readers will associate Sand Reading with the ancient divinatory practice of Geomancy. Yet, other than the use of sand or earth, the two function in vastly different ways. Sand Reading primarily receives and stores current "impressions" while Geomancy develops and communicates future "expressions."

Objects Used to Receive, Store, Transform, Transfer, and Communicate

But, here's the point about this long discussion involving the psychic use of inanimate objects: they have a long history of receiving, storing, sometimes transforming, transferring, and communicating energy as information or power. In this long history, the cumulative knowledge and lore has evolved into a science concerning the appropriate materials for intentional usage of a particular substance or object. Sand is <u>Silicon</u>, the fundamental substance of the Information Age. It's use in Sand Reading to receive, hold, and transfer knowledge is scientifically sound.

Figure 3. Sand Tray. An open tray of sand is prepared for use in sand reading.

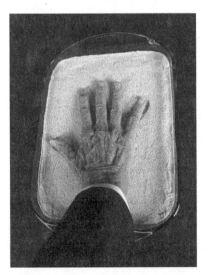

Figure 4. Hand Placement. The hand (palm side down) is placed on the surface of the sand.

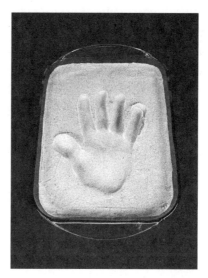

Figure 5. The Resultant Hand Imprint.

Objectology: Using a Deep Tray of Sand to Source New Information

Objectology, the study of the psychic significance of inanimate objects and their unique applications as sources for new knowledge, has shown outstanding promise in achieving that important goal. One of the most effective examples of objectology is *sand reading* in which the hand imprint in a tray of sand is used as a focal point to stimulate the psychic process, including precognition and clairvoyance. One of the major goals of our research was to examine the hand imprint as a source of information *independent of its metaphysical applications.*

In sand reading, an open tray of sand is placed before the subject who is instructed to simply make an imprint of either hand by pressing the hand, palm side down, upon the smooth surface of the sand. The tray must be large enough to accommodate the full hand, including its spread position, with palm-side down. The sand is usually moistened slightly so as to retain an accurate imprint, which can include one's own hand or that of others. Before a hand imprint is obtained, the edge of an index card is drawn across the sand to smooth its surface.

Objectology: Sand Reading Research in Paranormal Empowerment

The hand imprint is used as an important information source as well as a focal point to stimulate a wide range of psychic mechanisms. It can interface various energy systems, stimulate specific psychic functions, and interact with energies impinging upon or channeling through the hand imprint. In its capacity to stimulate a host of psychic faculties, the activation of paranormal functions during sand reading is typical. The results can include not only self-empowerment but the empowerment of others as well.

Sand Reading: An Objective Resource in Paranormal Research

A major goal of paranormal research related to sand reading is twofold: First, to examine the hand imprint as an objective source of information and, second, to explore its metaphysical applications. Early on, our controlled lab research related to sand reading provided compelling evidence of the significance of the technique as a source of psychic insight and personal empowerment.

Sand Reading: An Objective Resource for Paranormal Information

Knowledge related to the findings of lab research into sand reading can provide an objective basis for a variety of paranormal functions. For instance, a hand imprint as a focal point that scientifically signals stress often clairvoyantly identifies the sources of stress along with the most effective coping measure. Similarly, a hand imprint that objectively indicates low aspirations often identifies psychically the hidden causes while stimulating motivation and achievement. Given objective scientific relevance, observations of an imprint that indicates imbalance often activates the psychic functions required to generate equilibrium. Furthermore, sharing with the subject the known meanings of a specific imprint characteristic often generates a positive interaction that facilitates resolution.

Sand Reading: An Objective Resource into Past-Life Memories

Repeatedly, our research found that even the subconscious past-life sources of current-life barriers can became evident through sand reading. By simply focusing on the hand imprint, past-life details related to such present-life conditions as phobias, conflicts, obsessions, and depression can become spontaneously evident with profound therapeutic benefits. Enlightenment based on lab research is thus transformed into paranormal power that reaches far beyond the lab.

Sand Reading: An Objective Resource for Paranormal Empowerment

Because the findings of relevant research can provide a scientific basis for paranormal empowerment beyond the lab, our focus throughout this chapter is on sand reading research and its relevance to the development of paranormal potentials. Given the scientific findings of sand reading related to stress, violence, career pursuits, and psychiatry, to mention but a few, sand reading becomes more than an impressionistic technique with limited applications. It objectively assumes paranormal relevance that facilitates paranormal empowerment with far-reaching implications, including but not limited to problem-solving, self-enlightenment, stress management, and career success.

Sand Reading: An Objective Resource into Stressful Conditions

This study (TR-12: Sand Reading and Stress) was designed to investigate the effects of situational stress on the hand imprint pattern. The study explored the relationship between hand imprint characteristics and stressful versus non-stressful conditions. Because waiting to take an academic examination is known to be a potential stressful situation, that circumstance was designated as the stressful condition. The non-stressful condition was designated as the situation immediately following the examination.

The experimental population for this study consisted of 16 females and 2 males, all enrolled in a senior college level course in social psychology. An experimental pre- and post-test situation was arranged in which each subject made a hand imprint in a square tray of slightly moist sand (18" x 18" by 3" deep) just before taking the final examination for the course. A second imprint was obtained from each subject upon completing the examination. The two sets of imprints were obtained by a research assistant in a quiet office adjacent to the classroom in which the examination was administered. The only hand imprint characteristic considered for this study was whether the fingers were in a spread or closed position. All imprints were obtained under standard sand-reading conditions in which the subject was seated at a table across from the research assistant with a tray of sand conveniently situated on the table between the subject and the assistant. For both pre- and post-test sand readings, the subject was instructed as follows:

> This is a study exploring the way people make imprints of their hand in sand. Simply place your hand, palm side down, on the sand and make an imprint of your hand in the sand. Please go ahead.

The sets of imprints for each subject were evaluated by an objective rater who was not otherwise involved in the experiment. Comparisons of the hand imprints revealed that the fingers were typically in a closed position before testing; whereas after testing, they tended to be spread apart. A total of 12 of the 18 participants made hand imprints with the fingers in the closed position before testing whereas only three made imprints in that position following testing.

Statistical analysis of the data revealed a significant difference between the pre-test and post-test positions of the fingers (x square=5, reject Ho; significant at p<.05), thus indicating that the pre-test condition, which theoretically was precipitative of greater stress, was associated with hand imprints characterized by a closed position of fingers.

The findings of this study suggested that sand reading has potential as an instrument for use in detecting stress associated with situational factors.

Sand Reading: Hand Imprint Characteristics showing Violence

This study (TR 13: Violence and Imprint Characteristics in Sand Reading) was designed to investigate the effectiveness of sand reading as a strategy for assessing violence by comparing the hand imprints of violent versus non-violent offenders in a prison inmate population.

The study was conducted in a prison setting where hand imprints in sand were obtained from 14 volunteer male inmates in a small, quiet consulting room. The violent offender group consisting of 7 males had a history of such acts as assault and attempted murder. The non-violent offender group, also consisting of 7 males, had a history of such acts as larceny and possession of an illegal substance. The age range of the subjects was 21 to 42 years for the violent offenders and 20 to 30 years for the non-violent offenders.

Standard sand reading conditions and procedures were utilized for the study. The only materials required were 14 trays of moist sand (size 18" x 18" by 3" deep), one for each subject, a table upon which the tray was placed, and two chairs, one for the technician who obtained the hand imprints and one for the subject. A blind procedure was used in which the technician was not informed regarding the violent or non-violent classification of the subject.

The subjects of the study were individually escorted into a prison consulting room by a prison guard who remained present (standing at the door) for the hand imprint procedure. The subject was greeted by the examiner, and upon being seated at the table across from the examiner, instructed as follows:

> Thank you for volunteering for this study. We are conducting a study of the way people make imprints of their hand in sand. All you need to do is simply place your hand, palm side down, on the sand and make an imprint of your hand in the sand. Please go ahead and make an imprint of your hand in the sand.

Upon completion of the procedure, the subject was thanked and ushered from the room by the prison escort. The trays of sand, each with an imprint, were saved and used for ranking by two independent raters who were not present for the experimental procedures and who did not know the identities of the hand imprints. The only criterion for ranking was simply depth of the imprint on the following 5-point scale:

Figure 6
Depth Rating (Check position on scale):

Deep |_____|_____|_____|_____|_____|Shallow

     1   2   3   4   5

The results of the rankings showed a strong agreement between the two raters with the violent offenders typically receiving higher ratings on depth of hand imprint. Statistical analysis of the data revealed a significant difference between the depth of imprints for the violent versus non-violent subjects ($t=4.55$, reject Ho; significant at $p<.01$, at reliability with a confidence interval of + or -1).

Based on this study, greater depth of hand imprints in sand reading does seem to suggest a greater tendency toward violent behavior.

Sand Reading: Hand Imprint Characteristics in Employment Status and Gender

In an effort to determine whether employment status and gender are related to hand imprint characteristics, this study (TR- 14: Employment Status, Gender, and Hand Imprint Characteristics in Sand Reading) analyzed a series of hand imprints formed in a tray of sand by employed and unemployed male and female subjects.

The subjects of the study were 16 volunteers (8 males and 8 females), all high-school dropouts who were enrolled in an evening program designed to prepare them for a high-school equivalency test. Four of the males and 3 of the females reported that they were unemployed. The age range of the subjects was 20 to 28 years, with a median age of 25.

The hand imprints were individually obtained during the third week of the preparatory course. Standard procedures were followed in obtaining the hand imprints. A set of 16 trays of moist sand (18" x 18" by 3" deep), one for each subject, was used for recording imprints in a quiet office adjoining the classroom. Each subject, seated across from the examiner, was instructed as follows:

Thank you for volunteering for this study. We are conducting a study of the way people make imprints of their hand in sand. All you need to do is simply place your hand, palm side down, on the sand and make an imprint of your hand in the sand. Please go ahead and make an imprint of your hand in the sand.

Each of the 16 trays was identified only by a number assigned to the subject and was then ranked independently by two raters, both psychology majors who had studied sand reading. They were instructed simply to rank the trays on depth of hand imprint on the following 5-point scale:

Figure 7

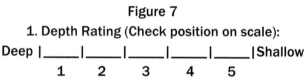

1. Depth Rating (Check position on scale):
Deep |_____|_____|_____|_____|_____|Shallow
       1   2   3   4   5

The results of this study indicated that males typically pressed the hand at greater depth in the sand than females; however unemployed males made imprints of less depth. Employment status among females did not appear to influence the depth of the imprints.

Statistical analysis revealed a significant difference between depth of hand imprints for males versus females (t=3.92, reject Ho; significant at p<.01 at reliability with a confidence interval of +or-1).

Sand Reading: Hand Imprint Characteristics and Career Pursuits

The purpose of this study (TR 15: Career Pursuits and Hand Imprint Characteristics) was designed to investigate the relationship between vocational pursuits and the characteristics of hand imprints formed in a tray of sand. The study investigated the imprint characteristics of 5 plumbers and 5 dentists drawn from the world of work in an effort to determine the differences in hand imprint patterns between these two groups.

The dentists and plumbers were first contacted by phone for an appointment and the sand reading imprints using trays of moist sand were obtained at their work sites, again using standard sand reading procedures. The instructions presented to each subject were as follows:

Thank you for volunteering for this study. We are conducting a study of the way people make imprints of their hand in sand. All you need to do is simply place your hand, palm side down, on the sand and make an imprint of your hand in the sand. Please go ahead and make an imprint of your hand in the sand.

The hand imprints were evaluated and recorded by the laboratory technician on the Hand Imprint Orientation and Rating Scale which included ratings of depth, finger position, hand orientation, space between fingers, and any unusual imprint characteristic. Here's the scale.

Figure 8
Hand Imprint Orientation and Rating Scale

1. Depth Rating (Check position on scale):

Deep |_____|_____|_____|_____|_____|Shallow
      1   2   3   4   5

2. Finger Position (Check One): _____Open _____Closed

3. Hand Orientation in Container:
    A. Horizontal (Check One): ___Left ___Center ___Right
    B. Vertical (Check One): ___Top ___Center ___Bottom

4. Space Between Fingers (Check distance on scale):

Maximum Space|___|___|___|___|___|No Space
           1   2   3   4   5

5. Unusual hand imprint characteristics: _____

_____

_____

_____

_____

Results of the study indicated that certain hand imprint characteristics of plumbers and dentists tended to differentiate those vocational groups. Dentists tended to show greater variation in hand orientations including the left, right, and middle placement positions when compared to plumbers. Plumbers, without exception, oriented the hand to the middle position. Regarding the vertical placement of the hand imprint in the tray, dentists typically placed their hand near the bottom of the tray; whereas plumbers typically placed their hand near the center of the tray. No dentist and only one plumber placed the hand near the top of the tray.

Dentists, on average, showed greater depth of the little finger imprint; whereas plumbers typically showed greater depth of the thumb. One dentist and one plumber showed relatively even depth for all fingers.

Without exception, dentists showed no unusual depth in the outer areas of the hand; whereas three of the five plumbers showed unusual depth in the outer hand areas, a finding that could be due to differences in hand muscle characteristics of plumbers, with plumbers showing greater muscular development in their hands than dentists.

Dentists, with only one exception, showed less space between their fingers in the hand imprints.

The results of this limited study raise the possibility that vocational interest and career pursuit may be related to certain hand imprint characteristics in sand reading. These results, however, were based on a very limited research population and visual analysis only.

Sand Reading: Hand Imprint Patterns and Career Goals

The purpose of this study (TR 16: Career Goals and Hand Imprint Patterns in Sand Reading) was to explore the relationship between certain career variables and sand reading. More specifically, the study attempted to determine whether certain hand imprint patterns in sand were related to career goals and selected personal traits.

Twenty subjects (8 males and 12 females), all drawn from the college student population, volunteered for the study. The age range of the subjects was 19 through 27 years, with a median age of 22.

Prior to the sand reading exercise, each subject was administered the Career Questionnaire to assess career goals and aspirations. The questionnaire was specifically structured for the project to determine whether career goals had been clarified and whether the subject was actively working toward them. Here's the questionnaire.

Figure 9
Career questionnaire

NAME: _____

DATE OF BIRTH: _____

STUDENT CLASSIFICATION: _____

MAJOR:_____

1. Are you presently employed? ___Yes ___No

2. If yes, are you planning a career change? ___Yes ___No

3. What are your long range career goals? _____

_____

_____

4. Are you actively pursuing or planning toward certain long-range career goals? _____Yes _____No

Upon completing the questionnaire, each subject was individually administered the sand reading exercise under standard sand-reading conditions. Sand reading instructions were presented as follows:

> Thank you for volunteering for this study. We are conducting a study of the way people make imprints of their hand in sand. All you need to do is simply place your hand, palm side down, on the sand and make an imprint of your hand in the sand. Please go ahead and make an imprint of your hand in the sand.

The subject's imprint was analyzed by a laboratory technician who recorded the orientation of the hand using the following guide.

Figure 10
Hand Orientation in Container:

A. Horizontal (Check One): ___Left ___Center ___Right

B. Vertical (Check One): ___Top ___Center ___Bottom

This study found that subjects who had clarified their career goals and who had definite career plans tended to orient the hand toward the upper right region of the sand tray. Subjects who had not clarified their career goals or who were not actively pursuing them were more likely to place the hand in the lower left region of the tray.

Sand Reading: Potential Applications in Psychiatry

One of the most challenging applications of sand reading involves its potential use in the psychiatric setting. In that context, the technique could have possible value in promoting a positive therapeutic relationship between therapist and patient. Another area of possible value concerns the technique's diagnostic potential. This study TR-17: Sand Reading in Psychiatry) was deigned to investigate the relationship between hand imprint characteristics and certain diagnostic classifications of patients in a psychiatric hospital setting.

The subjects of the study were 20 psychiatric inpatients selected for inclusion by the hospital's staff that had been instructed to select patients representing various diagnostic classifications. Arrangements were made to obtain the sand readings individually for each patient in a private consulting room at the facility. Standard sand reading procedures were followed, and the results were recorded on the Hand Imprint Orientation and Rating Scale as follows:

Figure 11
Hand Imprint Orientation and Rating Scale

1. Depth Rating (Check position on scale):

       Deep |_____|_____|_____|_____|_____|Shallow
            1   2   3   4   5

2. Finger Position (Check One): _____Open _____Closed

3. Hand Orientation in Container:
    A. Horizontal (Check One): ___Left ___Center ___Right
    B. Vertical (Check One): ___Top ___Center ___Bottom

4. Space Between Fingers (Check distance on scale):

    Maximum Space|_____|_____|_____|_____|_____|No Space
                   1   2   3   4   5

5. Unusual hand imprint characteristics: _____

_____

_____

_____

_____

Upon entering the consulting room, each patient was greeted by the researcher and instructed as follows:

> Thank you for volunteering for this study. We are conducting a study of the way people make imprints of their hand in sand. All you need to do is simply place your hand, palm side down, on the sand and make an imprint of your hand in the sand. Please go ahead and make an imprint of your hand in the sand.

Diagnostic categories included undifferentiated schizophrenia (1), alcohol dependence (5), anxiety disorder (4), paranoid schizophrenia (4), major depression (3), bipolar disorder (2), and cocaine dependence (1).

An unusual hand orientation feature noted among the 4 paranoid schizophrenic patients were a non-perpendicular imprint, with 2 hand imprints slanted to the right and 2 slated to the left. Of the 20 subjects, only the 4 slanted orientations were centrally located—the remaining 16 were located at the left of the tray, a feature that could suggest frustration and a tendency toward regression. Ten of the 20 subjects placed their hand at the bottom of the tray, a feature that could suggest low aspirations.

Without exception, the depressed as well as anxiety patients produced shallow imprints with little space between the fingers. Three of the 4 anxiety patients expressed dissatisfaction with their first imprint and requested a second trial.

The cocaine dependent and 4 of the 5 alcoholic dependent subjects oriented their hand to the left and at the bottom of the tray.

While the results of this experiment must be considered tentative, they do seem to suggest interesting possibilities for the use of sand reading in the clinical setting.

Sand Reading and Psychic Signals

During sand reading, certain signals of paranormal significance often emerge. For instance, imprints in which the thumb digs into the sand are associated with a highly practical orientation along with outdoor interests along with the pursuits of skilled or semiskilled occupations. An imprint in which the little finger shows greater depths is associated with esthetic, artistic, and philosophical interests along with pursuit of professional careers. Individuals who experience dissatisfaction with their first imprint and consequently request a second trial are often dissatisfied with their current life situation. Individuals who are hesitant to make an imprint in the sand are often cautious and insecure. Individuals who are secure, open to change, and actively striving for personal goals often place their hand to the right of the tray, whereas individuals who have experienced recent failure and are resistant to change often place their hand to the lower left of the tray. Placement of the hand to the lower right of the tray typically signifies persistence, even when faced with recurrent failure. Attempts to dig the hand deeply into the sand are associated with rejection, insecurity, and suspicion of others.

Sand Reading and Numerology

Around 550 B. C., Pythagoras reduced the universal numerals to figures 1 through 9 and asserted, "The world is built on the power of numbers." Two thousand years later, Cornelius Agrippa theorized that numbers possessed significance beyond the expression of quality. Consistent with that view, contemporary numerology holds that every name and date has its vibratory number with certain significance. As a universal number with vibratory significance, the number *one* represents purpose and action whereas the number *two* signifies antithesis and balance. The number *three* represents versatility and talent, *four* represents solidity and steadiness, *five* signifies adventure, *six* represents dependability, *seven* represents mystery and knowledge, *eight* stands for success, and *nine* signifies universal achievement.

Sand reading provides a unique condition for the application of numerology. The subject of sand reading, having formed an imprint of the hand in sand, is instructed to select a number ranging from 1 through 9 inclusively, and then to write the number anywhere in the sand but without overlapping the hand imprint. The number is seen as a representation of the individual's native vibratory symbol.

Aside from their universal meanings, numbers inscribed in sand reading are believed to reveal certain specific characteristics of the individual as follows:

- One: Strong achievement drive, self reliance, and independence.
- Two: Flexibility, indecisiveness, and inconsistency.
- Three: Self-confidence, intelligence, and talent.
- Four: Persistence, practicality, and trustworthiness.
- Five: Restlessness, impulsivity, friendliness, and diversity.
- Six: Competency, honesty, optimism, and leadership.
- Seven: Psychic and analytic abilities, philosophical interests, and impracticality.
- Eight: Forcefulness, competitiveness, materialistic interests, and indulgence.
- Nine: Holistic personality, persuasiveness, and humanitarian interests.

Although zero is not included in the range of numbers presented, it is occasionally selected by the subject. When written in the sand, it represents loneliness, emptiness, fear, and a general sense of inadequacy.

Conclusion

In sand reading, a simple tray of sand becomes a unique resource for both the discovery of new knowledge and the activation of psychic sources of power. Developmental in nature, sand reading is receptive to practice and experience. Its research basis adds validation to its application as a unique resource with multiple functions. Enlightenment and personal advancement including paranormal empowerment are within the scope of this unique procedure.

CHAPTER FIVE
Objectology and Water Gazing:
Feelings Count

Water: A Primary Alchemical and Spiritual Element

Water—without it, the earth would be a barren, desolate place void of beauty and appeal. But with it, the earth becomes a dynamic place for life and growth, from the lowliest of beings to the most advanced forms. As a source of power, water sustains and empowers our existence on the planet. Aside from that, water is a resource that adds joy and meaning to life, from such water-related recreational activities as swimming, diving, sailing, and skiing. Beyond these, simply viewing a sea at sunset or a magnificent moon-lit cove can inspire, attune, and balance the mind, body, and spirit. Our studies showed that tossing a specially programmed quartz crystal into the water, preferably a stream, appeared to significantly amplify its programmed energies and empower us with success in achieving even the most difficult of personal goals. (Slate, Joe H.: Connecting to the Power of Nature, Llewellyn, 2009).

Figure 12. Water Gazing. A spherical bowl of water is situated to permit a slightly downward gaze.

Know, too, that Water is one of the five primary Spiritual Elements: Earth, Water, Fire, Air, plus Spirit. In Western Alchemy there are just four Primary Elements: Earth, Water, Air, and Fire. In either system, it is the four primary elements that make up the World as we see it. In the Eastern Spiritual system, those four are seen as having their own origin from Spirit. *The Four are essential to the World of Manifestation, while Five is the number given to Man as Spirit becomes his conscious resource.* Each element has a fundamental role to play.

Water: Emotional (and Astral) Empowerment

Water, essential to all Life, is also the element associated with emotion, with the astral body and astral plane, and with psychic powers. It is astral/emotional energy and substance that is the major resource for magical and religious ritual. *Water is the vehicle of Life*, the birthplace of life on Earth, and essential to its continuity.

The surface of water reflects whatever is seen above it. Water, placed in a clear glass bowl becomes an Object used in psychic reading.

Water Gazing: Clearing the Mind for Psychic Receptivity

Given these instances of the power of interacting with water, it would appear reasonable that simply gazing into a body of water could clear the mind of clutter and connect us to the highest sources of power, both within and beyond oneself. Water Gazing is a specially structured procedure specifically designed to achieve that important goal.

Developed in our labs at Athens State University, Water Gazing is a specially structured procedure in which a spherical bowl of water, like a fish bowl, is used to promote a focused and relaxed state of heightened receptiveness to psychic impressions. Similar to the crystal ball as used in crystal gazing, the bowl of water is usually positioned on a table to facilitate a comfortable, slightly downward gaze.

Water Gazing: Interaction and Enlightenment

Profoundly meaningful interactions with both inner and outer sources of enlightenment and power are common during the water gazing experience. Telepathy, clairvoyance, precognition, and other forms of paranormal phenomena including meaningful interactions with spirit guides frequently occur during water gazing.

Water Gazing and Telepathy #1

This study (TR-18: Water Gazing and Telepathy) was designed to investigate the capacity of water gazing to facilitate telepathy. The two-phase study was conducted in a laboratory setting with a group of 20 participants drawn from the college student population. Ten of the 20 subjects were randomly designated as telepathic senders and the remaining 10 were designated as receivers. Phase I of the study utilized water gazing; in Phase II, the bowl of water was removed. Each phase of the study consisted of three trials of 5 minutes each in which the sending group attempted to send the color of a card.

In Phase I of the project, the 10 senders were seated across from and facing the 10 receivers with a table situated between the two groups. On the table, a spherical bowl of water was centrally positioned so as to facilitate a comfortable gaze. The sending and receiving groups were instructed to use water gazing to communicate one of three colors—green, yellow, or red—on each of three trials. The sending group then selected one of three colored cards mounted on a piece of cardboard, with the card viewed only by the sending group. The card was then removed from the laboratory and both sending and receiving groups were instructed to focus on the bowl of water, with the senders attempting to communicate the correct color to the receivers.

Following a focusing period of one minute, subjects in the receiving group were instructed to record their responses. The second card was then presented and finally the third, with the same instructions and procedures as for the first card.

A total of 23 correct colors out of a possible total of 30 were recorded by the receiving group for the three trials.

Phase II of the study was then introduced to determine the effectiveness of the same sending and receiving groups in communicating impressions of color in the absence of water gazing. All other conditions and procedures were held constant as for Phase I.

In the absence of the bowl and water gazing, the total number of correct responses dropped from 23 in Phase I to 15 in Phase II.

Statistical analysis revealed a significant difference between the results of Phase I and Phase II (x square=4.26, reject Ho; significant at $p<.05$), a finding that indicated water gazing did indeed improve performance in group telepathy.

Water Gazing and the Telepathic Sending of Images

This two-phase study (TR-19: Water Gazing and the Psychic Sending of Images) was designed to investigate the effectiveness of water gazing in promoting the psychic transfer of mental images.

Thirty-four subjects (13 males and 21 females), all college students enrolled in a college course in parapsychology, participated in the study, which was organized into two phases. In Phase I, water gazing was not utilized; in Phase II, the spherical bowl of water and water gazing were introduced into the experimental situation.

The experiment was conducted in a classroom setting as an instructional exercise. The 34 participants were randomly divided into two groups of 17 subjects each, with one group designated as the sending group and the other as the receiving group. The two groups were then seated facing each other with a table situated between them. At one end of the table was a brown envelope containing a photograph with three essential elements known only to a research assistant who was not present for the exercise. Participants in the receiving group were provided note pads upon which to record their responses. The following instructions were then presented to the two groups by the instructor:

> For this phase of our exercise, the sending group will view a photograph, which will then be turned top-side down on the table. The sending group will then attempt to convey images of the photograph's three essential elements to the receiving group. The receiving group will attempt to receive the images from the sending group. Upon receiving the images, please re-

cord them on the note pads provided. Starting now, five minutes will be allowed for the sending and receiving process.

A color photograph of a snow scene was then presented to the sending group, and seen only by that group. The three essential elements were snow, a red bird, and snow-laden evergreens.

The evaluation of the exercise was based on the number of instances of essential elements recorded by the receiving group. A total of 12 instances were noted as follows: red bird—12 instances; snow—2 instances; and evergreens—3 instances. One subject identified all three of the essential elements.

In Phase II of the study, water gazing was introduced into the experimental situation. A spherical bowl of water was placed at the center of the table, and a brown envelope containing a new photograph with three essential elements was placed at the end of the table by a research assistant who alone knew the envelopes contents and who was not present for the exercise. The instructions presented to the two groups were as follows:

> For this second phase, the sending group will view a new photograph and then attempt to convey images of its three essential elements to the receiving group by focusing on the spherical bowl of water. The receiving group will attempt to receive images of the photograph's three essential elements from the sending group while also focusing on the bowl of water. Upon receiving the images, the receiving group will record them on the note pads provided. Starting now, five minutes will be allowed for the sending and receiving process.

The color photograph for this phase, again seen only by the sending group, was that of a mother holding an infant against a pink curtain. The composition of the sending and receiving groups remained unchanged.

The evaluation for Phase II, as for Phase I, was based on the total number of essential elements—the woman, baby, and pink curtain—

recorded by the receiving group. A total of 30 instances of essential elements for Phase II as compared to a total of 12 instances for Phase I was recorded by the receiving group. Included were the following: Woman—16 instances; baby—7 instances; and pink curtain—7 instances. Five subjects in Phase II as compared to one subject in Phase I identified all of the three essential elements.

Statistical analysis of the data revealed a significant difference between the results of Phase I and Phase II (x square=17.2, reject Ho; significant at p<.01).

Although the controls were weak for this study—it was designed primarily as a classroom learning exercise—the results did suggest that the introduction of water gazing could appreciably enhance the telepathic sending and receiving process. We could expect that water gazing, when introduced into training programs in ESP, could facilitate telepathy and activate the imagery process which seems to be a critical component in many telepathic sending and receiving situations.

Water Gazing and Psychic Imagery

This study (TR-20: Water Gazing and Psychic Imagery) was a four phase classroom learning exercise structured to investigate the use of water gazing in telepathy and clairvoyance. A group of 30 college students enrolled in a parapsychology seminar participated in the study. In Phase I, the students were randomly divided into two groups of 15 students each. A spherical bowl of water was situated on a table between the two groups that faced each other. The sending group was presented an envelope containing a color photograph left in the room by a research assistant who was not present for the experiment and who alone knew the characteristics of the photograph.

The photograph was that of a child playing on a beach with the sea in the background.

After briefly viewing the photograph, the sending group then focused on the bowl of water, and with the picture removed, attempted to send images of its essential elements to the receiving group over a 5-minute period. The receiving group was likewise instructed to focus on the bowl of water in an effort to receive the picture's three essential elements. Each member of the receiving group was provided with an unruled writing pad and instructed to record the print's essential elements by either writing them down or drawing them.

Analysis of the results found that 8 receivers identified the child, 6 identified the beach, and 7 identified the sea. Three receivers (2 females and one male) identified all three essential elements, and 3 identified two essential elements. The total correct elements identified in this phase were 21 out of a possible total of 45.

Phase II of the exercise was a replication of phase I with the same sending and receiving groups but with a new picture and without the bowl of water and water gazing. The picture for Phase II consisted of a child, a dog, and a house in the background. The results of that phase indicated a total of 9 correct elements received as compared with a total of 21 in Phase I. None of the subjects in Phase II received all three essential elements and only one subject identified two essential elements.

In Phase III of the exercise, the group of 30 students engaged in water gazing to determine the characteristics of a concealed picture in a large brown envelope which had been placed under a spherical bowl of water situated on a table at the center of the group seated in a circular arrangement around it. A research assistant, who alone knew the contents of the envelope and was absent for the experiment, had placed it in the experimental situation during a class break and prior to the re-assembling of the group.

The essential elements of the picture were a house, an automobile, and a tree. The group was provided an unruled writing pad and instructed to gaze at the bowl of water, then record the three essential elements of the sketch by either writing or drawing their impressions on the pad.

A total of 48 instances of essential elements were identified. The highest possible score was 90.

In Phase IV, the experimental situation was the same as for Phase III but with a new picture and without the bowl of water. The picture consisted of a lake, a sailboat, and mountains as essential elements. In this phase with the same subjects, the total number of essential elements identified was reduced to 28 as compared to 48 for Phase III.

This study, notwithstanding its limitations, indicated that the introduction of water gazing into the experimental situation could dramatically improve group performance in both telepathy and clairvoyance.

Water Gazing and Telepathy #2

The purpose of this study (TR-21: Water Gazing and Telepathy) was to investigate the use of a spherical bowl of water and water gazing to facilitate the sending-receiving process in telepathy.

A total of 34 college students (13 males, 21 females) enrolled in a parapsychology seminar participated in the study, which was organized into two phases. In Phase I, the bowl of water was not used; in Phase II all conditions remained the same except that a spherical bowl of water and water gazing were introduced into the experimental situation.

Water Gazing: Telepathy, Phase I (Without Water)

The experiment was conducted in a classroom setting as a learning exercise. The 34 participants were randomly divided into two groups of 17 subjects each. The two groups were then seated facing each other with a table situated between them. On the table was a brown envelope containing a photograph, which had been, placed there by a research assistant who was not present for the experiment and who alone knew the characteristics of the photograph. The course instructor presented the envelope to the sending group with instructions to remove the photograph and send a description of it telepathically to the receiving group. The receiving group in turn was instructed to record on a note pad a description of the photograph, to include its three essential elements. Five minutes were allowed for the sending/receiving process. The instructions presented to the groups by the instructor were as follows:

The sending group will focus on the photograph and attempt to telepathically convey its characteristics to the receiving group. The receiving group will attempt to telepathically receive information from the sending group and record a description of the photograph on the note pad provided. You will be allowed 5 minutes for the sending/receiving exercise.

The color photograph consisted of a child, red balloon, and white cat.

The evaluation of the exercise was based on the number of the photograph's three essential elements recorded by the receiving group. A total of 12 essential elements were recorded as follows: Child—5, balloon—1, and cat—1. Only one subject identified all three essential elements.

Water Gazing: Telepathy, Phase II

Phase II was a replication of Phase I with two exceptions: A new photograph was selected for use in sending and receiving, and a spherical bowl of water and water gazing were introduced into the experimental situation. The bowl of water was situated at approximately eye level on the table between the two groups. The composition and functions (sending/receiving) of the two groups remained unchanged.

The instructions for Phase II were as follows:

For this phase, your task as senders is to focus on the bowl of water in an effort to transfer to the receiving group the image of the picture you have just viewed. The receiving group will attempt to telepathically receive information from the sending group and record a description of the photograph on the note pad provided. You will be allowed 5 minutes for the sending/ receiving exercise.

The color photograph in this instance was that of a man playing a violin with a dog at his side.

As in Phase I, the evaluation for Phase II was based on the total number of the photograph's three essential elements—man, violin, and dog—that was recorded by the receiving group. A total of 31 essential elements—an increase of 19 instances over Phase I—was recorded for

Phase II. Five subjects in phase II as compared to one subject in Phase I identified all three essential elements.

Statistical analysis of the data revealed a significant difference between the results of Phase I Telepathy and Phase II Water Gazing and Telepathy (x square=17.2, reject Ho; significant at p<.01). It is noted, however that this experiment as an informal classroom exercise lacked certain controls. Aside from the bowl of water and water gazing, the practice effect provided by Phase I could have contributed to the significant increase in telepathic performance noted in Phase II.

The results of this study suggested, nevertheless, that the introduction of water gazing could appreciably enhance the telepathic sending/receiving process.

Water Gazing and Creative Writing

In addition to its demonstrated usefulness in promoting various psychic functions, water gazing is sometimes used to enhance creativity. To investigate that application, water gazing was introduced into the second half of a college-level course in creative writing with the cooperation of the course instructor. The experiment (TR-22: Water Gazing and Creative Writing) was initiated after the students in the course had submitted four creative compositions for evaluation by the course instructor.

From the class of 19 students, all volunteered for the study. Ten students were randomly selected from the group as experimental subjects who would participate in the water gazing exercises. The remaining 9 students were designated as control subjects who did not participate in the water gazing exercises. A blind technique was used in which the instructor was not informed regarding the identity of the two groups.

The water gazing activity for this experiment consisted of a group exercise in which the experimental subjects formed a circular seating arrangement around a table upon which had been positioned at its center a spherical bowl of water situated so as to facilitate a comfortable, slightly downward gaze. Prior to gazing, the group was instructed to relax physically and mentally using a technique in which the eyes were closed and the physical body was scanned from the head region downward. Areas of tension were noted and then mentally relaxed. The group's attention was then focused on the bowl of water. Following a five-minute period of focusing, the subjects were instructed to close their eyes and allow mental images and creative ideas to unfold. Following each gazing exercise, the creative products, including both images and ideas, were discussed, with the duration of the discussion period varying from session to session.

Following a period of two weeks during which the water gazing group sessions were conducted twice weekly, each of the 19 students enrolled in the course completed a creative writing composition which was then rated by the course instructor on a 5-point scale. Over the next 2 weeks during which no additional gazing sessions were scheduled, three additional creative writing compositions were completed for a total of 4 compositions altogether by each of the 19 students, and the creative quality of each composition was then rated by the instructor on a 5-point scale.

Analysis of instructor ratings revealed that all subjects in the experimental group experienced improvements in the average ratings on creative quality for their four compositions following the introduction of water gazing. Although seven of the nine control subjects experienced improvements in their average ratings for their last four compositions, the degree of improvement was less than that of the experimental group. The average improvement in ratings on the 5-point scale for the control group was .25; whereas the average improvement for the experimental groups was .98, an overall improvement of almost 4 times that of the control group and almost the equivalent of a letter grade increase on the average for the experimental subjects. These findings strongly suggest that practice in water gazing could be an effective technique for stimulating creativity and increasing the quality of creating writing.

The expectancy effect and the absence of sufficient controls could be considered a major limitation of this study.

Water Gazing and Creative Expression in Art

To investigate the effect of water gazing on the quality of artistic expression, arrangements were made with an art instructor to introduce water gazing at the mid-point in a college-level art course in painting (TR-23: Water Gazing and Creative Expression in Art). The instructor provided the researcher with ratings of students enrolled in the course before and after the four-week experimental period. The ratings were based on a 5-point scale, with 1 representing excellent and 5 signifying poor. The class of 16 students was randomly divided into two groups consisting of a control group of 8 students (3 males and 5 females) who did not participate in water gazing, and an experimental group of the remaining 8 subjects (4 males and 4 females) who practiced water gazing once weekly over a 4-week period. A blind technique was used in which the instructor was not informed regarding the identity of the two groups.

The experimental arrangement for the water gazing sessions consisted of a circular seating of subjects around a table upon which had been placed a spherical bowl of water. The sessions were conducted in a laboratory setting free from interruptions or distractions.

The weekly water gazing exercise consisted of a 30-minute session, which included gazing at the bowl of water and then closing the eyes to allow imagery to unfold. The gazing segments were flexible, usually no more than a few minutes, as were the imagery segments. Following the series of gazing and imagery exercises, the subjects engaged in a discussion of their experiences in a relaxed and informal setting.

Analysis of instructor's ratings at the end of the 4 week period indicated that the average improvement in ratings for the control group was .50 whereas the average improvement for the experimental group was 1.22, which indicated a substantially greater increase in instructor ratings of creative quality for the experimental group than for the control group. Among the 8 participants in the experimental group, 6 experienced an increase in instructor rating with the remaining 2 subjects obtaining a final rating equivalent to their earlier ratings. Among the control subjects, four subjects obtained an increase in instructor rating with the remaining four students retaining their mid-course ratings.

The results of this study suggested that water gazing could be potentially useful in increasing the quality of creative expression in art. A major weakness of the study, however, was the absence of controls. The expectancy effect could have influenced the results of this study.

Water Gazing: Effects on Memory

The purpose of this study (TR 24: The Effects of Water Gazing on Memory) was to investigate the capacity of water gazing to facilitate memory. Forty undergraduate students (24 males and 16 females) volunteered for the study. The age range of the subjects was 21 through 31 years. The 40 subjects were randomly divided into two groups of 20 subjects each. Each group was provided a note pad and instructed as follows:

> This experiment explores your ability to recall words presented to you verbally. I will now read to you a list of 20 words. At the end of the reading, your task is to record in any order as many of the 20 words as possible on the note pad provided.

The list of 20 words was then presented and the group was instructed to record their responses.

The experimental group, prior to being presented the same 20 words, engaged in group water gazing for a period of 5 minutes. For gazing, a spherical bowl of water was positioned on a round table in the center of the laboratory. The experimental subjects were arranged in a circular seating arrangement to facilitate comfortable gazing. The water gazing exercise was initiated by the researcher who presented the following instructions:

> The purpose of this exercise is to help you to clear your mind and build your memory powers by focusing on the bowl of water. Simply relax as you gaze at the bowl. Should your eyes tire, close them briefly and then continue gazing at the bowl

of water. Gazing at the bowl will help you to think clearly and remember better. You will be allowed 5 minutes to gaze at the bowl of water. Go ahead. I will tell you when your time is up.

Upon conclusion of the gazing period, the same instructions and list of words used for the control group were presented to the experimental group.

Analysis of results revealed the serial position effect for both groups, with items near the beginning and end of the list being remembered with greater frequency than those items in the middle. The experimental (water gazing) group, however, performed at a higher average percentage recall level for all words in the list, regardless of position, when compared with the control group. (t=5.00, reject Ho; significant at p<.01).

The results of this study suggested that water gazing, when introduced into the learning exercise, could appreciably increase retention. It could be argued, of course, that such an effect could be due to expectancy rather than to water gazing. Inadequate controls could be considered a deficiency of this study. Admittedly, more research is needed to determine precisely the effects of water gazing on retention involving various learning situations.

Water Gazing with The Triangle of Power

The triangle is often seen as a symbol of power with its three sides symbolizing mind, body, and spirit. The Triangle of Power in Water Gazing as developed in our labs is based on preliminary observations that simply visualizing the triangle tends to generate a relaxed state in which mental, physical, and spiritual functions become increasingly attuned and balanced. When formed by the hands and appropriately incorporated into water gazing, the triangle becomes not only a balancing and attuning force, it activates an energized state required for the achievement of personal goals, such as self-enlightenment, better health and fitness, career advancement, and even rejuvenation, to mention but a few.

*Figure 13. Triangle of Power. A triangle formed by the fingers
is used to facilitate productive water gazing.*

THE TRIANGLE OF POWER PROCEDURE

The procedure requires simply a spherical bowl of water situated for
easy viewing in a comfortable, safe setting free of distractions. Here's
the procedure:

1. While relaxing comfortably in a seated position, take in a few
   deep breaths and exhale slowly as you view the spherical bowl
   of water. State your personal goals while viewing the spherical
   bowl and think of it as your connection to the highest sources
   of enlightenment and power required for your complete success.
   Note the emerging sense of security permeating your being.

2. Following a few moments of relaxed viewing, form a triangle
   with your hands by joining the tips of your thumbs to form its
   base and the tips of your index fingers to form its peak.

3. View the spherical bowl of water through the triangle held at
   arm's length as you note your sense of connection to it.

4. While continuing to gaze at the spherical bowl through the triangle, slowly expand your peripheral vision as you note a glow
   enveloping first the bowl and then the full triangle. As the glow
   extends outward beyond the triangle, note the mental, physical,

and spiritual state of attunement and balance spreading throughout your being.

5. Close your eyes and form an image of the triangle with the
   spherical bowl of water at its center. Think of the bowl of water
   as your connection to the highest sources of energy and power.

6. Mentally re-state your goals and affirm your complete success in
   achieving them.

7. Conclude by relaxing your hands with palm sides turned upward while affirming: *I am fully empowered mentally, physically,
   and spiritually. I can activate the power of this procedure by simply
   forming a triangle with my hands and affirming "I am now fully
   empowered!"*

Following your completion of the exercise, take a few moments to reflect on the experience. Note your sense of connection to the highest
sources of power and success.

Should you prefer, you can substitute other objects as points of
focusing within the triangle. Objects or scenes of nature when framed
by the triangle and viewed from a distance are especially effective for
this procedure. Examples include a tree, lake, mountain, or even a star
or the moon. An empowering sense of becoming connected to nature
almost always accompanies the viewing of objects or scenes of nature
through the triangle of power.

Conclusion

Requiring only a spherical bowl of clear water and a willingness to
explore its applications, water gazing is a multi-functional technique
that can generate a host of psychic functions required to simulate
paranormal development. The simplicity of the technique belies the
complexity of its functions. It can activate the paranormal functions
required to generate psychic imagery, activate various forms of ESP,
promote creativity, improve artistic expression, and facilitate creative
writing, to list but a few of the possibilities. The evidence is clear:

Through practice and experience, water gazing can promote the paranormal actualization of our highest paranormal potentials.

Validated in the lab setting and successfully applied beyond the lab, water gazing is among the most effective self-empowerment techniques known. Whether to increase creativity in writing and art, activate telepathic sending and receiving, facilitating clairvoyance, improve memory, promote successful goal attainment, or generate a state of mental, physical, and spiritual attunement, the powers of water gazing appear to be without limits. Taken together, the evidence is clear: Water gazing effectively accesses the wealth of unlimited powers, both within ourselves and beyond.

Water Gazing and Crystal Gazing

While the similarity of Crystal Gazing to Water Gazing may seem obvious, the differences are important. The first distinction is that of function: the Crystal Ball is used in Divination while the bowl of Water is used in a Creative Process of growth attunement. The second is that of substance: the Crystal is a solid representing the element of Earth. Water is the element Water and retains the character of a fluid substance even when placed in a bowl and thus temporarily becoming a device.

The Crystal Ball is an object that is retained, used again and again, and becomes "charged" through usage and intent, and perhaps by ritual. It is an object that is permanent and has a memory. Water is a fluid that is disposed of, and even though the bowl may be retained and not used in any other way, its function does not include that of memory. Water alone is not a real Object and has no memory. Water, however, is vital for life. Neither Crystal by itself or shaped into an object is essential to life, but the Earth Element provides the substance we walk on, stand on, and build on.

Psychic Reading with Earth, Water, Fire, or Air

The real value of crystal or any other substance comes from its Elemental composition and the ways in which it is transformed into an object. Crystal, when shaped and polished into a semi-transparent and semi-reflective ball is a device with particular qualities that enable it to function as a psychic device. However, Crystal Gazing employs an Object born of Earth, and psychic readings with it may have a different character than Water Gazing. Likewise, as with Fire Gazing and Cloud (Air) Gazing, all are worthy topics for experiment and research.

In psychic work, the qualities and character of an object are important to its usage and function. As always, the more you know, the further you can go, and grow.

CHAPTER SIX
Objectology and Psychokinesis (PK):
Mind Over Matter

PK: Moving Objects and Influencing Events by Mind Alone

Perhaps nothing short of resurrection is as impressive as the demonstrated ability to move physical objects—even objects as small as coins, dice, or even a golf ball already in motion. Yet the exercise of that ability, whether by human intervention or that of unknown other-dimensional beings, has been observed in the avoidance of accidents, stopping falls already happening, and other seeming miracles.

Figure 14. Suspended Quartz Crystal.
A quartz crystal is suspended under a laboratory jar.

The trouble is that the bigger things—like a car sliding on an icy road or a man falling off a cliff—don't happen in labs, while the little things are too often passed off as statistical anomalies, misperceptions or outright trickery.

This chapter proves otherwise.

Psychokinesis (PK) is defined as the human ability to influence objects, events, and/or processes in the apparent absence of physical intervention or intermediary instrumentation. In both the controlled laboratory and classroom instructional situation, the psychokinetic induction of movement in material objects from a distance have repeatedly illustrated this phenomenon.

PK Potentials to influence both External and Internal Realities

Research has consistently shown that the PK potential exists in everyone. It illustrates our capacity to reach beyond physiology to influence realities at a distance. Through both individual and group practice, the capacity for PK can be dramatically improved. Implied in the research studies that follow is the capacity, not only for PK power to influence external conditions but for this remarkable power to influence internal physiology—a possibility that has *near-unlimited possibilities toward promoting health, fitness, longevity, and quality of life.*

Inducing PK Movement in the Crystal Pendulum

The purpose of this classroom exercise (TR-25: Inducing Movement in the Crystal Pendulum) was to explore the effectiveness of a group of college students to mentally induce movement in a crystal pendulum from a spatial distance.

The group of 44 students, all enrolled in a college level course in experimental parapsychology, were randomly divided into 2 subgroups of 22 students each. Each group was seated so as to face the other group on opposite sides of a laboratory table. At the center of the table was positioned, at a comfortable viewing level, an inverted laboratory bell jar, to the inside bottom of which had been affixed a crystal pendulum on a copper chain so that the pendulum swung freely inside the inverted jar. The crystal had been cleared but non-inscribed. The task of the two sub-groups was to bring about motion in the pendulum. A metronome was placed at one end of the table to pace their efforts. As the metronome's needle at its slowest setting moved away from a sub-group, that sub-group mentally pushed against the pendulum while the members of the other sub-group mentally pulled the pendulum toward them, thus establishing a rhythmic "push/pull" pattern. These push/pull efforts, which were paced by the sound of the metronome, continued for a series of 5 minute practice sessions with a one minute rest period between sessions.

At three minutes into the second practice session, the pendulum began a slight turning motion and then began to swing slowly to and fro. The metronome was stopped at that point and the pendulum's movement paced the group's push-pull efforts. These efforts continued for a period of 5 minutes, 20 seconds, during which the pendulum's movement steadily accelerated until it struck the sides of the bell jar. At that point, members of both sub-groups were instructed to bring the pendulum to a stop by reversing their push/pull efforts. As the pendulum moved toward a sub-group, that group was instructed to push against it; as it moved away from a sub-group, members of that group were instructed to pull the pendulum toward them. The pendulum's movements rapidly slowed over a period of 2 minutes, 30 seconds whereupon it came to a complete rest.

This exercise did suggest that this "push-pull strategy" could be effective in bringing forth PK movement in a crystal pendulum.

PK, Crystal Gazing, and the Human Aura

The aura is an energy phenomenon thought to envelop the human body and other living things. One view of the aura holds that it is an external manifestation of an inner life force energy core with the capacity to influence both inner and outer realities. It would follow that PK as a manifestation of energy could conceivably utilize the aura system to directly influence matter, a phenomenon we call *Aura PK*.

This study (TR-26. Psychokinesis, the Human Aura, and Crystal Gazing) was designed to investigate the effectiveness of a PK procedure that utilized the aura in which 6 volunteer subjects (3 males and 3 females) attempted to induce movement in a quartz crystal pendulum suspended by a copper chain under an inverted bell jar in the controlled laboratory setting. The crystal had been cleared but non-inscribed. The subjects had all been trained in aura PK procedures that utilized physical relaxation, aura imagery, and certain energy releasing techniques.

The experiment was conducted in a quiet, controlled laboratory situation. The inverted bell jar with the pendulum suspended under it was centered on a laboratory table at a comfortable viewing level with the 6 subjects, 3 on opposite sides of the table, facing the pendulum. To pace the PK efforts, a metronome was placed facing the two groups at one end of the table.

VISUALIZING THE AURA

The subjects were instructed by the experimenter who was present throughout the session to engage in physical relaxation using a technique in which the physical body was mentally scanned from the head region downward in an effort to release any build-up of physical tension and replace it with relaxation.

The experimenter instructed the subjects to engage in sensory focusing by noting such specific physical sensations as pressure, tingling, coolness, and warmth anywhere in the body. With their eyes closed, the subjects then engaged in aura imagery by first forming a mental image of a glowing nucleus of power centered in the solar plexus region of the body. They then visualized a brilliant, expanding energy field enveloping the physical body.

AURA ENERGY and THE PUSH-PULL TECHNIQUE
TO MOVE THE PENDULUM

At that point, the experimenter put the metronome into a slow, rhythmic motion, and the subjects were instructed to open their eyes and view the pendulum and target their aura energies by individually forming an imaginary beam of light from themselves to the pendulum. As the metronome needle began to swing away from either of the groups, that group was instructed to push against the pendulum using "antimagnetic" powers. As the metronome needle swung toward either group, that group was instructed to pull the pendulum by using positive magnetic powers. Thus, a rhythmic, alternating push-pull procedure was established between the two groups.

With the sound of the metronome pacing their push-pull efforts, the two groups were instructed to induce a swinging movement in the pendulum, whereupon the metronome would be stopped and the pendulum itself would pace the push-pull efforts. Until movement of the pendulum occurred, a distributed practice schedule was implemented with the two groups engaging in a 4-minute push-pull session followed by a 2-minute rest session.

On the fourth push-pull session, a distinct turning motion was noted in the pendulum followed by to-and-fro movements in the pendulum. The metronome was then stopped and the session continued for 6 minutes during which the pendulum's movements steadily increased until the pendulum struck the sides of the bell jar. The participants were then instructed to arrest the pendulum's movements by reversing their push-pull efforts. By pushing against the pendulum when it moved toward them and pulling toward it when it swung away from them, the two groups were successful in bringing the pendulum to a complete stop within a one-minute period.

This study suggested that concentrated aura energy could be used as a force capable of influencing matter, in this case a crystal pendulum.

The Effects of PK Experience on Crystal Pendulum Performance

The quartz crystal pendulum suspended by a copper chain is valued as a psychic instrument because of its apparent capacity to gain objective data not readily available through other strategies. When suspended from the hand and held over objects being studied, it has been used to answer a wide range of questions and convey highly meaningful information by the nature of its movements.

Among the many potential applications of the pendulum are its usefulness in locating lost objects, assessing career interests, and solving personal problems, to list only a few.

The purpose of this study (TR-27: The Effects of Experience on Crystal Pendulum Performance.) was to determine the effects of experience on the use of the crystal pendulum as a psychic instrument by comparing the performance of an experienced group with the performance of an inexperienced group. All participants of the study were drawn from a student population and given the task of identifying the location of a silver coin placed in one of three boxes on a table in front of the seated subject. Each subject was given up to 5 minutes to determine the location of the coin.

For the experiment, three groups were formed as follows:

Group 1. The Inexperienced Group with no formal training in parapsychology, including the use of the crystal pendulum as a psychic instrument.

Group 2. The Pendulum Group with formal training in a college level course in parapsychology, which included training in the use of the crystal pendulum as a psychic instrument.

Group 3. The Experienced Group with formal training in a college-level course in parapsychology, but which did not include training in the use of the crystal pendulum as a psychic instrument.

Each group consisted of 12 volunteer subjects drawn from a college student population.

Each subject entered the laboratory and was seated at a table on which had been placed three boxes, one of which had a coin concealed inside. The placement position of the coin was known only to a laboratory technician who was absent for the experiment. In front of each box was a letter—an A, B, or C. One-by-one, each research subject upon entering the laboratory was provided a cleared but non-inscribed crystal pendulum suspended on a small copper chain and instructed by a second laboratory technician (who observed the exercise but did not know the location of the coin) to locate the coin within a 5-minute period by simply suspending the pendulum over each box and observing its movements.

The performance of Group 1 which had no formal training in areas of psychic phenomena including the use of the crystal pendulum was around that expected by chance (4 correct responses out of 12). Similarly, the performance of Group 3 which had formal training in parapsychology but no training in the use of the crystal pendulum was also around that expected by chance (3 correct responses). In contrast, the performance of Group 2 which had formal training in parapsychology to include the use of the crystal pendulum as a psychic instrument performed at a level considerably above that expected by chance alone. For that group, 9 of the 12 subjects identified the location of the coin. These results indicated that Group 2 fell one percent short of statistical significance. Groups 1 and 3 had very low success and, statistically, only guessed.

This study, though limited, suggested that specialized training in crystal pendulum techniques could appreciably enhance the accuracy of the crystal pendulum as a psychic instrument.

The Crystal Pendulum: Detecting Gender Influences

One of the most highly refined psychic skills is the ability to detect the residual gender effects of physical contact with tangible objects, a skill with particular relevance to criminal investigations.

As energy beings, we could conceivably energize at least temporarily the objects we touch. It would follow that the residual energy resulting from touch could be influenced by gender. To investigate that possibility, this study (TR-28: The Pendulum and Gender Influences) was designed to determine the effectiveness of the crystal pendulum in detecting the residual effects of gender on a physical object.

In this experiment, 6 pendulum subjects (3 males and 3 females) who had completed a course in parapsychology that included the use of the crystal pendulum as a psychic instrument applied the technique in an effort to detect the gender of the person who had last held a playing card. Prior to the pendulum exercise, 12 volunteer subjects (6 males and 6 females) drawn from the student population were seated randomly at a long laboratory table and instructed by a laboratory technician to draw a playing card from a new deck which had been provided each student. After holding the card for one minute, the subject placed the card face down on the table and then left the laboratory. Upon completion of the drawing procedure, the remaining decks of cards were removed from the laboratory by a technician.

The 6 trained pendulum subjects who had been waiting in a room on another floor of the building entered the laboratory, one at a time, and with a pendulum (a cleared but non-inscribed crystal weight at the end of a copper chain) provided them at the beginning of the experiment, attempted to detect the gender of the person who had last held each card by suspending the pendulum over the card. They were cautioned not to touch the cards, which remained on the table undisturbed and in the order as originally placed there by the 12 subjects. A circular motion of the pendulum was designated by the researcher to indicated female, and a to-and-fro motion was designated to indicate male. The male/female ratio of the 12 subjects who had drawn the cards was not divulged to the 6 pendulum subjects.

Each of the 6 pendulum subjects was allowed 5 minutes alone in the laboratory to detect gender. Before leaving the laboratory, they each recorded their responses on score cards, which had been provided them.

Analysis of the 72 trials (12 cards x 6 subjects) showed only 17 trials to be incorrect. This study suggested the crystal pendulum could be effectively applied following appropriate training to detect the residual influences of gender on objects.

The ability to detect the residual gender effects of physical contact with tangible objects is a highly refined skilled that is receptive to practice. Once developed, it holds special relevance as an investigative technique in such settings as espionage and the criminal justice system.

The Crystal Pendulum: Detecting Gender of the Unborn

Given the potential usefulness of the crystal pendulum as a psychic instrument for identifying the residual influence of gender on tangible objects, it would seem reasonable that the pendulum would hold even greater usefulness in detecting gender of the unborn. To investigate that possibility, an experimental study (TR-29: The Crystal Pendulum and Detecting Gender of the Unborn) was devised in which 6 crystal pendulum technicians (3 males and 3 females) attempted to detect the gender of the unborn for women who were at various stages of pregnancy. Each technician had completed a college level course in parapsychology, which included the use of the crystal pendulum as a psychic instrument.

Six women in various stages of pregnancy volunteered for the study, which was conducted in a quiet campus office setting. At the time of the study, the gender of her unborn was unknown to each expectant mother. The women, individually and by appointment, reported to the office for the experiment and were seated comfortably in a recliner. Each of the 6 technicians entered the office and, one by one, attempted to identify the gender of the unborn by suspending a cleared but non-inscribed crystal pendulum on a copper chain a few inches over the subject's abdomen. A circular motion of the pendulum was designated to indicate female, and a to-and-fro motion was designated to indicate male. The results of each trial were recorded by the technician but not divulged to either the subject or other technicians until the end of the study.

The women were instructed to notify the researcher upon later becoming informed of the gender of their offspring.

The results of this experiment strongly suggested the usefulness of the crystal pendulum in detecting gender of the unborn. For the 6 women, the gender of each offspring was correctly identified when the highest frequencies were considered, including subject 6 whose unborn children were fraternal twins (a male and a female). For that subject, four of the six technicians obtained results indicating both male and female.

The findings of this study revealed a statistical significance between the pendulum results and actual gender (r=.59, reject Ho, significant at p<.01). Reliability check revealed that, overall, the pendulum technician's combined reliability was 77.78%.

Conclusion

Given verification through research of PK as a human trait, the possibilities of this interesting phenomenon has far reaching implications. As a goal oriented phenomenon, the PK process typically targets external realities to influence or produce desired results. In emergency situations demanding high level of physical energy, PK appears capable of generating and mobilizing energy that interacts with physiology to result in apparent superhuman feats of strength. On the other hand, PK can include the capacity to influence objects in motion, such as slowing a skidding automobile to prevent or lessen the impact of a collision and slowing a fall to prevent physical injury. In an un-related group situation, spontaneous PK in which spectators "pull" for an individual or team, can influence the mental state of athletes and thus improve physical performance. The potential of PK to influence physiology remains among its most highly promising applications.

CHAPTER SEVEN
Objectology and Dowsing: The Earth Speaks

THE DOWSING ROD

Dowsing, as conventionally defined, is a technique in which a single Y-shaped instrument or a pair of L-shaped rods is used to gather information not otherwise available to conscious awareness. When held lightly in a perpendicular position in the hands, the rods are typically seen functioning as "antennae" or sensitive extensions to the physical body, enabling a capacity of interacting with external conditions.

The rods, properly held, and in association with a receptive state of consciousness, respond to a variety of information sources and conditions, including but not limited to the existence of subterranean conditions and Earth resources such as water, oil, gas, and metal as well as buried artifacts.

The Dowser's State of Awareness

It is important in all aspects of Objectology to realize that the "Power" is not in the Object itself but works in connection with the user' state of awareness, and understanding of the "science" involved. Combined with that is the necessity to use the object—*like any other tool*—correctly. At the same time, tools made of certain materials, shaped in particular ways, and sized appropriately, are going to function better than those that are not.

Dowsing as a Science

Yes, even though Dowsing and most forms of divination are rejected by materialist science as—at best—a "pseudo-science," there is a "science" to all such practices. In other words, there is a constantly developing system of organized knowledge based on theory and experimentation, improved through practice and observation, with results verified objectively and comparatively.

Dowsing's Origins and History

Dowsing, as practiced today, probably originated in 15th century Germany, but likely was practiced in other forms long before. Like so much else not officially approved by medieval Christian religion, dowsing was condemned as a breaking of the first commandment by Martin Luther in 1518. Nevertheless, German expertise in both dowsing and mining technology was in demand all over Europe and later, in America.

The traditional dowsing rod is a forked branch freshly cut from the American Witch-hazel or the European hazel also known as the Filbert. Also popular are branches cut from the Willow.

How the Dowsing Rod Works

Among the typical responses of the single Y-shaped rods are vibrations and forceful downward pulls, while for pairs of L-shaped rods, it is a crossing movement or a widening of distance between the rods. A downward pull typically indicates the location of a subterranean resource while a rhythmic up-and-down movement is believed to gauge distance. A side-to-side movement is thought to signify an energy field while vibrator movements are thought to signify motion, such as a flowing stream. When pairs of rods are used, a crossing of the rods is usually associated with incompatible or repelling energies such as pollution and radioactivity. A separation of the rods suggests the existence of non-repelling energies.

The movements of rods are likewise seen as receptive to a variety of subterranean resources and conditions. Aside from the discovery of subterranean resources, dowsing with metal or wood rods has shown remarkable success in locating subterranean faults and the imminence of volcanic eruptions. Copper rods, particularly when the ends are equipped with quartz crystal, have shown remarkable sensitivity in gaining information available from no other source.

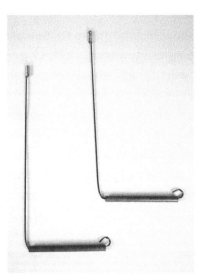

*Figure 15. Dowsing Rods. An L-shaped pair of copper dowsing rods
with a quartz crystal affixed at the end of each rod.*

*Figure 16. Dowsing with Metal Rods. The L-shaped rods are balanced
perpendicularly to permit easy, unobstructed movement.*

Interviews with Dowsers

Numerous studies have investigated the nature of dowsing and its effectiveness, including its industrial applications. Of special interest to non-dowsers are the perceptions of dowsers themselves concerning the nature of dowsing and their own dowsing skills. To explore those perceptions, this study (TR-30: Interviews with Dowsers) conducted personal interviews with 27 practicing dowsers (22 males and 5 females) whose ages ranged from 17 to 74 years. The period during which participants of this study had practiced dowsing ranged from 2 to 54 years, with an average of 29 years. Here's a summary of the interview results:

- The frequency of dowsing among interviewees ranged from "almost daily" to "once or twice a year".
- Eighteen of the 27 dowsers reported having been taught the techniques by a relative or friend.
- Eight of the dowsers reported having acquired the technique by observing other dowsers.
- One dowser reported having independently learned how to dowse.
- Eighteen of the 27 dowsers considered the dowsing ability to be a genetic trait.
- Twenty-six dowsers conceded that even when genetics are involved, learning remains critical to mastering dowsing skills.
- Twenty-two dowsers in our sample reported having relatives who also dowsed.
- All the subjects of this study considered dowsing to be a valuable skill with many useful applications.

Among the items recovered by the dowsers in our study were coins, Native American relics, articles of jewelry, water lines, buried cables, Civil War relics, and subterranean resources such as mineral deposits, water, and oil, to list but a few.

The Effects of Practice in Dowsing

Locating subterranean water sources is one of the most common applications of dowsing technology. This study (TR-31: The Effects of Practice in Dowsing to Detect Water) was designed to investigate the effects of specialized training in dowsing using quartz crystal-tipped dowsing rods to locate water in a controlled laboratory setting.

Eight subjects (5 males and 3 females), all college students with no experience in dowsing, volunteered for the study which was conducted over a period of 4 weeks with two sessions weekly.

Each of the eight sessions over the 4-week period included instruction, demonstrations, and practice in locating water using L-shaped copper dowsing rods with a clear quartz crystal affixed by copper wire at each rod's elongated end. Each crystal was carefully affixed to the rod so that the crystal's six-sided pyramid's terminated end is pointed forward. The crystal had been cleared but non-inscribed before being attached to the end of the rod. The experimental set-up for each session included 5 black plastic gallon containers, all identical in appearance, situated in a row on a laboratory table with a space of 36" between the containers. All the containers were empty except the one that contained water.

Each practice session consisted of 4 trials for each subject in an effort to determine through dowsing which black plastic container among the 4 other empty containers contained water. The subjects were provided two dowsing rods and instructed to hold them perpendicularly by the short end, one in each hand. Rather than holding them firmly, the rods were held lightly in the hands, with the elongated prongs balanced on the index finger to permit easy, unobstructed movement. The subjects were instructed that a crossing of the rods over a container indicated the presence of water.

At the beginning of each session, dowsing techniques were demonstrated and discussed in a relaxed, permissive atmosphere. Each subject was then given 4 practice trials in locating through dowsing the container filled with water. Feedback was provided immediately at the end of each of the 4 trials.

A research assistant recorded the performance of each subject on each of the 4 trials, which was always conducted in the presence of the full research group. Upon completion of a trial, a second research assistant entered the laboratory and while screened from the group, repositioned the containers randomly for the next trial, whereupon the assistant left the laboratory.

The results of the study indicated continuous group progress in identifying the container of water. All participants improved their performance record over the experimental period, though considerable variations in rates of improvement were noted.

Over the eight sessions, the total correct responses more than doubled. Statistical analysis of the data revealed a significant difference between the first session and the final session (t=4.53, reject Ho; significant at p<.01), a finding which suggests that dowsing skills can be significantly improved through specialized training and practice.

Detecting Contaminated Substances through Crystal Dowsing

The detection of contaminated substances is often cited as one of the many practical applications of dowsing. Examples include noxious subterranean streams and contaminated landfills. To investigate that application, a laboratory exercise (TR-32: Detecting Contaminated Substances through Crystal Dowsing) was designed in which experienced and non-experienced dowsers were given the task of detecting a contaminated substance placed among other non-contaminated substances in a controlled laboratory setting.

Twenty subjects consisting of 10 experimental subjects (ages 19 through 27 years) and 10 control subjects (ages 20 through 25 years) participated in the study. The experimental subjects were students who had taken an introductory course in parapsychology which included supervised practice in dowsing using L-shaped copper rods with a clear quartz crystal affixed by copper wire at the elongated end of each rod with the terminated end of the crystal pointing forward. The crystals had been cleared but not inscribed prior to the experiment. The 10 control subjects, who were selected randomly from a college student group of 14 volunteers, had no experience in dowsing.

Prior to the laboratory exercise, the control and experimental subjects were briefly oriented by the project director concerning the nature of dowsing, followed by demonstrations in the use of the crystal rods as dowsing instruments.

For this study, nine black plastic gallon containers of water, all sealed and identical in appearance, were placed on a laboratory table, with a space of 36" between containers. The placement of the containers was done randomly by a laboratory technician after each container had been assigned a number. Container number 7 contained water contaminated with a pesticide; the remaining containers contained non-contaminated water. Only the laboratory technician, who was not present for the dowsing segment of the experiment, knew the identity of the contaminated container.

The experimenter and control subjects, one at a time, entered the laboratory, and with dowsing rods in hand, were instructed to locate the container of contaminated water. The results of each trial were not divulged to other subjects until all trials were completed.

The results of this experiment showed a remarkable performance record for the 10 experimental subjects with no errors in their responses. Only two control subjects correctly identified the contaminated substance. In a post-test discussion session, which included both the control and experimental groups, the successful experimental subjects typically described the contaminated water's influence upon the rods as negative or repelling. The two successful control subjects explained their success as due to chance.

Statistical treatment of the data revealed a significant difference between the experimental group and the control group (x square=13.34, reject Ho; significant at p<.01).

The results of this study suggested that past experience in dowsing significantly increased dowsing skills, specifically in detecting contaminated substances.

Crystal Dowsing in the Industrial Setting

Many dowsers and industrial organizations alike recognize the potential application of dowsing in the industrial setting. To explore the possible benefits of dowsing to industry, this study (TR-33: Crystal Dowsing in the Industrial Setting) consisted of a two-phase investigation focusing on the use of crystal dowsing as a non-destructive testing strategy to identify the presence of flaws not detected visually in specimens of plastic and steel.

The subjects of the study were 14 college students (4 males and 10 females) with an age range of 20 through 27 years. All had completed a college course in parapsychology that included the use of L-shaped copper dowsing rods with a cleared but non-inscribed quartz crystal affixed by copper wire at the elongated end of each rod to identify subterranean resources and to locate concealed objects. The course included limited practice in the application of the technique. The same 14 subjects participated in both phases of the study.

The materials used for the study were (a) a pair of L-shaped copper dowsing rods with crystals affixed; (b) three specimens of steel, size 2" x 5" x ¼", all identical in appearance but one of which had an internal flaw—a small fissure that had been previously detected through a non-destructive testing procedure; and (c) three specimens of plastic, also 2" x 5" x ¼", that were also identical in appearance but one of which contained an air bubble previously detected through a non-destructive testing procedure.

For both phases, the samples were spaced at 36" apart on a laboratory table by a technician who alone knew the position of the flawed sample and who was not present during dowsing. The 14 subjects, equipped with dowsing rods, entered the laboratory, one at a time, and attempted to identify the defective samples. They reported their choices to another technician stationed in the laboratory to ensure that the position of the samples remained fixed.

In Phase I, 8 of 14 subjects correctly identified the defective steel sample: in Phase II, 9 subjects correctly identified the defective plastic sample. Six of the subjects identified the defective sample in both phases. Only 2 subjects identified neither of the defective samples. No significant difference was found between Phases I and II (x square=.16, accept Ho; not significant).

The results of this study suggested that crystal dowsing holds interesting promise as a non-destructive testing or quality control technique. It is not a perfect technique—it may lack the reliability of modern non-destructive testing technology—but in situations where advanced technology is not available, crystal dowsing could have important applications.

Conclusion

Taken together, the available research findings suggest that dowsing, if developed to its fullest, could have significant applications not only in such familiar applications as finding lost objects, discovering cultural artifacts, or locating subterranean resources but also in science and technology, business and industry, and the military. The major challenge facing dowsing as both an art and science is fourfold:

- To discover and differentiate the multiple dowsing abilities.
- To determine more fully the psychodynamics of dowsing.
- To develop optimal educational approaches to maximize development of dowsing skills.
- To identify and validate the many potential applications of dowsing.

With additional research into the nature of this old phenomenon, a new dowsing technology could emerge that would significantly advance our search for better ways of probing the unknown and directly acquiring new and useful information.

CHAPTER EIGHT
Objectology and the Crumpled Paper Technique:
Air Talks

Elemental Air is Wrapped in the Folds and Creases

Air is that primary element that represents Communication, and yet is ephemeral like a moving cloud. Hence, we commonly record information on paper and return to paper to find and recover information. Today, paper as a final resource is challenged by another form of Air, Cloud Technology. Crumpled Paper contains a lot of Air in its folds and creases, and like a moving cloud in the sky above can serve as a <u>medium </u>for our paranormal needs.

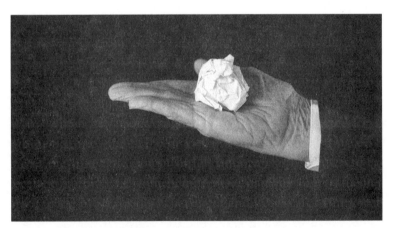

Figure 17. The Crumpled Paper Technique. A sheet of paper crumpled into a mass is ready for opening.

Figure 18. The Open Crumpled Paper. The crumpled mass,
once opened, becomes a unique source of
potential enlightenment and power.

The Object and the User's State of Consciousness

The Crumpled Paper Technique as developed in our labs at Athens State University is a procedure in which a standard sheet of copy paper, size 8.5" x 11", is crumpled by the subject into a mass and then used as a psychic instrument with two major functions: First, to gain relevant information not readily available from other sources, and second, to initiate a self-empowered state that is conducive to the achievement of a wide range of personal goals.

The self-administered technique is based on the concept that all growth is continuous and interrelated. As the crumpled mass rests loosely in your hands, it can become a source of personal empowerment through its energizing, attuning, and balancing effects. Once the crumpled sheet is unfolded or opened, its empowering potential can be magnified by focusing attention on its unique patterns and their past, present, and future relevance.

The Crumpled Paper is like Cloud Technology

As a goal-oriented exercise, the Crumpled Paper Technique was designed to generate a positive state of self-empowerment with strong expectations of success. It is effective for such diverse goals as break-ing unwanted habits, extinguishing phobias, managing stress, over-coming depression, accelerating learning, increasing creativity, and improving memory. Aside from these, the procedure often generates increased awareness of higher dimensions of power and in some in-stances, the comforting presence of ministering teachers and guides.

Like the Cloud, the Crumpled Paper has near Infinite Capacity

The research participants who assisted in our development of this technique often reported rapid progress in achieving their personal goals. During practice of the procedure, they often experienced clair-voyance as well as precognition. Not infrequently, they experienced increased awareness of relevant past-life experiences. Examples in-cluded the discovery of the past-life sources of phobias, obsessions, and compulsions.

Recovery of the Past as a Psychic Resource

The results reported by our research participants often included a complete liberation from the disempowering effects of unresolved past-life experiences. In their views, the unfolding of the crumpled paper was almost always accompanied by the unfolding of the psy-chic mind. According to them, the technique helped to identify their hidden potential and activate their full development. Through this program, students often discovered new and more effective ways of accelerating learning, improving retention, overcoming blockages, in-creasing creativity, and clarifying their career goals.

Facilitating Clairvoyance

Outside the academic world, the Crumpled Paper Technique has been used as a valued information source in a variety of settings. It has been used in the criminal justice setting to gather important evidence and effectively locate missing persons, including prison escapees. As an espionage technique, it has reportedly been used to clairvoyantly view classified documents, monitor certain weapons' development programs, and observe secret military operations. It has been used to locate misplaced documents and on a broader scale, to identify sources of environmental contamination while uncovering workable corrective measures. It has recently gained popularity as a highly effective clairvoyant technique for locating lost or wayfaring animal companions.

Here's the technique as developed in our labs, which requires a quiet, comfortable setting free of distractions.

THE CRUMPLED PAPER TECHNIQUE, STEP BY STEP

Step 1. With a writing pen and blank sheet of 8.5 x 11 inch paper at hand, formulate your goals in positive terms and affirm in your own words your commitment to achieve them. Having stated your goals, write your name across the top of the blank sheet of paper, and then crumple it into a mass just as you would if you intended to throw it away.

Step 2. While the crumpled sheet of paper is resting loosely in your hands, view the crumpled mass and note its unique characteristics, to include its size, shape, and other features.

Step 3. Having viewed the crumpled sheet with its distinctive features, settle back and with your eyes closed, visualize the crumpled mass resting loosely in your hands. Take plenty of time for a clear, detailed image to emerge. Remind yourself that the crumpled mass of paper resting in your hands is a unique creation. It is unlike any other crumpled mass, whether past, present, or future. Remind yourself further that the crumpled mass is a unique repository of energy. It is your energy that created it, and it is your energy that sustains and retains its form. Sense your connection and interaction with the crumpled mass.

Step 4. As the crumpled sheet of paper continues to rest loosely in your hands, clear your mind of active thought and visualize a distant orb of radiant energy of any color you choose. As the distant sphere of energy increases in brightness, let the energized sphere of paper in your hands become your link to it as a higher source of enlightenment and power.

Step 5. Visualize rays of energy from the distant sphere interacting with the crumpled sphere in your hands and from there, infusing your total being with energy and power. Sense especially the attuning and balancing effects of that interaction. Notice the images and impressions that accompany the interaction. Take plenty of time for the infusion of energy to reach its peak.

Step 6. With the infusion of energy now complete, carefully unfold the crumpled sheet, place it between your hands, and allow additional images and impressions to spontaneously emerge. For clairvoyant viewing of distant situations and conditions, including detailed records or documents, allow the unfolded sheet of paper to become a visual manifestation of the situation or condition. For viewing present happenings, think of the unfolded sheet as a screen upon which the unfolding events appear. For precognitive viewing, think of the unfolded sheet as a projection screen upon which future events of important relevance become clearly visible

Step 7. View the unfolded sheet of paper with the name side up and notice its wide ranging characteristics, including straight lines, clusters of wrinkles, triangles, and stars, to name but a few. Triangles and stars appearing in the wrinkled sheet are particularly significant in that they typically signify psychic enlightenment; whereas crossed lines typically suggest a present or future challenge. A cluster pattern resulting from the intermeshing of small wrinkles typically suggests a complex life situation with multiple interactive factors. Straight lines, on the other hand, suggest a significant force or influence, the longer the line, the more significant its meaning. These are but a few of the possibilities. It remains up to the receptive clairvoyant mind to determine the full significance of the unfolded sheet's array of patterns. Take plenty of time to view the sheet's specific features while allowing relevant images and impressions to spontaneously emerge.

Step 8. Place the unfolded sheet aside and reflect on the experience. Review your specific goals and the relevance of the wrinkled sheet to them. Clearly specify each of your goals and in your own words, affirm your complete success in achieving them. As you visualize each of your goals as realities in progress, affirm: I am now empowered to achieve each of my goals.

THE FINGERTIP ENGAGEMENT PROCEDURE

Upon completion of the Crumpled Paper Technique, you can maximize the empowering effects of the exercise through the so-called Fingertip Engagement Procedure. Also developed in our labs, it is one of the simplest and yet most effective approaches known for generating a state of mental and physical harmony conducive to full self-empowerment. It is especially effective as a rejuvenation technique that slows aging and in some instances, literally reverses the visible effects of aging (Slate, Joe H.: *Rejuvenation: Living Younger, Longer, and Better*, Llewellyn, 2001). Here's the technique:

Step A. To begin the procedure, settle back, take in a few deep breaths, and develop a slow, rhythmic breathing pattern. Close your eyes and mentally scan your body from your head downward, pausing at tight, tense areas and releasing the tension. Let your total body become increasingly loose and limp.

Step B. Once your body is fully relaxed, turn the palms of your hands upward and sense positive energy slowly gathering in the center of your palms. Let the accumulation of energy in your palms slowly radiate to energize both hands. You may note a warm, tingling sensation as the energy builds in your hands.

Step C. Slowly bring your fingertips together, one pair at a time beginning with the thumbs and progressing to the little fingers. Let each progressive engagement of the fingers represent a word in the five-word affirmation: I am now fully empowered. At this point, you can introduce specific affirmations related to your life goals.

Step D. Conclude the procedure with the self-empowerment cue that by simply bringing your fingertips together, you can unleash all the power you need to meet the demands of any life situation.

Upon completing the fingertip exercise, take a few moments to reflect on the self-empowering effects of the experience. With repeated practice of the Crumpled Paper Technique and the supplemental Fingertip Engagement Procedure, you can increase your power to initiate an empowering state with seemingly unlimited possibilities. Once equipped with these skills, you can unleash a wealth of new possibilities in your life. From everyday decision-making to innovative planning, you can access all the resources you need for your complete success.

Figure 19. Hand Dynamometer.
The device is designed to measure strength of hand grip.

*Figure 20. Hand Dynamometer Applied. The device as applied
here specifically measures strength of right hand grip.*

Gender Differences and Pattern Stability

In an effort to determine gender difference and pattern stability in the
crumpled sheet of paper, a two-phase study was designed and conducted in our labs (TR-34: The Crumpled Paper Technique, Gender
Difference, and Pattern Stability). Phase I of the study investigated the
similarities and differences in the crumpled sheets produced by males
and females. The variables studied included the time required to
crumple the sheets, circumference of the crumpled mass, strength of
hand grip, and the presence of geometric patterns in the wrinkled paper patterns when the crumpled sheet is opened. Phase II of the study
investigated the stability characteristics of the technique to again include the time required to crumple the sheet and circumference of the
wrinkled mass along with frequency, intensity, and intricacy of crease
lines in repeated trials.

Twenty males and 20 females, all college students with an age
range from 19 to 24 years volunteered for the study. Each participant
in the study was individually administered the crumpled sheet ex-

ercise in a quiet laboratory setting. The subject was seated at a table across from the laboratory technician and instructed as follows:

Here is a blank sheet of paper. Please write your name across the top, and then crumple it into a mass, just as you would if you were going to throw it away, and then place it on the table. A stop watch was used to time the exercise, starting when the subject received the sheet of paper, and ending when the crumpled mass was placed on the table. Immediately following the exercise, a measure of strength of hand grip was obtained for each subject using a hand dynamometer (Lafayette Instrument Co.), which yielded strength in kilograms.

The circumference of the crumpled mass was then obtained using a tape measure. For elongated masses, two measures were obtained and averaged. The wrinkled mass was then carefully opened and the frequencies of geometric patterns found in the sheet's lines were noted. Among the patterns recorded were triangles, squares, circles, stars, wavy lines, and pyramids consisting of a cluster of triangles occurring together to create a slightly raised pattern.

Analysis of results revealed several gender differences in the circumference of the wrinkled masses, with female circumferences considerably greater than those of males. Males, on average, required less time to crumple the sheet, and their crumpled masses were smaller in circumference than those of females. For males and females, a statistically significant correlation was found between the circumference of the crumpled masses and the strength of grip with the smaller the masses the greater the strength of grip (for males, $r=-.97$, reject Ho; significant at $p<.01$; for females, $r=-.79$, reject Ho; significant at $p<.01$). No significant correlation was found for either males or females for circumference and time to crumple (for males, $r=.32$, accept Ho; p not significant; for females, $r=.275$, accept Ho; p not significant). A greater frequency of geometric designs was found in the crumpled sheets for males than for females, possibly a result of the more tightly crumple masses typically produced by males.

In Phase II of the project, the 20 subjects participating in Phase I volunteered to participate in an effort to determine the degree of pattern stability in the wrinkled sheet. Each subject was administered four additional crumpled paper exercises. Time and circumference measures were again obtained for each exercise as in Phase I in an effort to measure the stability of repeated trials.

Analysis of results for Phase II indicated strong stability among repeated trials for the same subjects, both in time to crumple the sheets an in circumference of the crumpled product. Subjective inspection of the repeated products for each subject likewise indicated strong stability of line patterns when the masses were opened. The masses with a smaller circumference characteristically showed more lines, more geometric patterns, and fewer voids or areas without wrinkles.

The Crumpled Paper Technique in the Industrial Setting

Casual observations of the crumpled paper technique suggested that persons who had achieved a high level of success in their careers tended to produce unusually small crumpled masses. This study (TR-35: The Crumpled Paper Technique in the Industrial Setting) was designed to compare the crumpled paper mass size of men and women at different position ranks in a major industrial organization.

With the approval of the organization's management to conduct the study on site, the crumpled paper technique was administered to 20 employees (10 men and 10 women) of various position ranks who had been selected for the study by the company's personnel director. The crumpled masses were obtained at the work site of the employee, typically the employee's work station. The following instructions were verbally presented to the employee for the crumpling procedure:

> We are conducting a study to see if there are differences in the way people crumple sheets of paper when they are about to throw them away. Would you volunteer to be one of our subjects?

None of the employees approached declined the request. Some expressed amusement at the study, but no additional information was provided.

The subject was then presented a blank sheet of letter size unruled white paper and instructed as follows:

> Thank you for volunteering for this study. Would you please write your name across the top of this sheet of paper and then crumple it into a mass—just as you would if you were going to throw it away?

A stop watch was used to carefully record the time required to crumple the sheet, beginning at the time the subject received the sheet and ending at the point when it was returned to the examiner.

Upon completion of the crumpled sheet procedures, the circumferences of the 20 collected masses were measured using a flexible plastic tape measure. Unusual characteristics such as "ears" or protruding corners and asymmetry of the masses were noted. Protruding corners, however, were not included in the circumference measurements. Elongated masses were measured in both directions and then average. The unfolded crumpled sheets were not analyzed.

The study found that employees in lower ranks of the organization typically produced larger masses than the employees in higher management or supervisory positions.

Statistical analysis of the data showed a significant correlation between the circumference of the crumpled mass and the time required to crumple it ($r=.48$, reject Ho; significant at $p<.05$). A statistically significant correlation was also noted between the overall circumference and the rank position in the organization for both men and women ($r=.94$, reject Ho; significant at $p<.01$). Other significant correlations were noted between rank order and the circumference for men ($r=.66$, reject Ho; significant at $p< .01$) and for women ($r=.83$, reject Ho; significant at $p< .01$). However no statistical significance was found between rank order of position and the time to crumple the mass for either males ($r= .47$, accept Ho, not significant) or females ($r=.26$, accept Ho; not significant).

This study suggested at least two interesting possibilities: First, employees who produce smaller crumpled masses could be more likely to rise to higher ranks in the organization, and second, it is possible that as employees rise to higher ranks in the organization, their crumpled masses change to become more similar to those of other employees at those ranks.

THE CRUMPLED LEAF TECHNIQUE

The crumpled paper technique has been modified to include the crumpling of a tree leaf as a substitute for paper. Arguably, insight related to the crumpled paper technique could have relevance to the crumpled leaf technique.

The crumpled leaf technique is similar to the crumpled paper technique but different in that it uses a tree leaf instead of a sheet of paper. Casual inspection of the crumpled sheet of paper as well as the crumpled leaf produced by individuals who were practicing psychics revealed when opened (or uncrumpled) the presence of numerous geometric designs, particularly a design known as the "psychic star"— a four or five pointed star design appearing in the central region of the crumpled sheet. Other designs found frequently in the crumpled sheets of psychics included the pyramid, cross, heart, octagon, wavy line, and circle.

In an effort to objectively assess the crumpled leaf features associated with psychic ability, the crumpled leaf procedure was administered to 10 well-known practicing psychics (4 males and 6 females) and 10 volunteer subjects (5 males and 5 females) drawn from the general population (TR-36. Psychic Signals in the Crumpled leaf). Each of the 20 subjects of the study was presented a fresh maple leaf and instructed as follows:

> Thank you for your participation in this study. Would you please take this leaf, and with the top side up and the stem pointing toward you, crumple it into a mass.

The leaf was then opened and the geometric designs were counted by viewing either the top or underside of the leaf.

The frequency of geometric designs found in the crumpled leaves of the 10 general population subjects averaged 2.0 for males and 3.3 for females; whereas the average frequency of geometric designs found in the crumpled leaves of the 10 gifted psychics averaged 10.5 for males and 8.5 for females. Among the crumpled leaf patterns of gifted psychics, a total of 4 star designs were noted. No star designs were found in the crumpled leaf patterns for the general population.

While the population for this study was small, the Crumpled Leaf Technique does show promise as a strategy for assessing psychic ability.

Conclusion

In the vast ocean of illimitable knowledge, each new discovery can generate a small but exciting ripple of power that is a reminder of our destiny for endless growth and greatness. The Crumpled Paper Technique along with the Finger Tip Engagement Procedure as developed in our labs is among the most powerful self-administered approaches known for activating dormant potentials and focusing them on desired goals.

CHAPTER NINE
The Next Step:
Activating Dormant Potentials

From the Unknown to the Known, from the Lab to Real Life, and from the "Other" to YOUR OWN Personal Empowerment.

While observations of paranormal phenomena and the direct exercise of paranormal powers are as old as human history (and even older than historical accounts when we consider those of myth and lore), it is only in the last two centuries that the paranormal has been subjected to consistent scientific research, verification, and to the development of structured psychic and psychological technologies for their personal and practical application in everyday life.

The research programs described in the previous chapters not only verified the reality of paranormal phenomena but those of various traditional methods for their perception and purposeful usage. Through such research we've taken away "mystery" from the seeming "miraculous"—the *Mysteries* and the *Miracles* that are often exploited by charlatans and religionists for their personal or organizational agendas.

Moving further ahead, we explored the metaphysical foundations for certain methodologies in the relationship between <u>Objects</u> used for psychic perception and their composition in terms of the <u>Primary Cosmological Elements</u> of Earth, Water, Fire, and Air—demonstrating the interrelationships between *Astral* and *Physical* dimensions and of domination of Mind over Matter. It is through our understanding of these interrelationships that human *Will* and *Desire* are imposed on external realities to bring about change and development in accord with our inner programming.

Awakening "Dormant" Powers

These are not *new* powers: they are innate but lack development in most humans. This concept relates to the esoteric belief that "In the Beginning was the Word," and that *Word* was and is a **"Program"**—in the modern sense of the word—that essentially outlined what was to come at all levels of the Cosmos without regard as to the Who or What or How of Creation itself. In other words, that Program set in motion everything that has since happened in the visible Universe from the "Big Bang" to the formation of our Solar System, our Planet Earth, the eventual appearance of Life and the evolution of life, to the evolution of Humanity, and to the continuing evolution and Development of today's Individual Humans. The Program builds on itself, spinning out mini-programs to augment the originals, and Onward and Upward we go. What was Yesterday, what is Today, and what will be Tomorrow is all there as programmed from the Beginning.

Paranormal vs. Supernatural

Before going further, we want to distinguish the "paranormal" from the "supernatural" as for many people they are the same. While we have established that paranormal phenomena are beyond or aside from what is comparatively experienced as *normal,* we do mean beyond or above "Natural." We believe the paranormal phenomenon and psychic powers are all natural and follow the "Laws of Nature"—*as programmed.* As mentioned previously, the "Cosmos" is inclusive of many levels of reality beyond that of the physical universe—levels that are named Astral, Mental, Causal, and Spiritual. Not only do we believe them not to be *supernatural* we believe that nothing in the Cosmos is. And, in that sense, there is nothing supernatural or "religious" in the paranormal—*Spiritual, yes, but not Religious.* Another term, among many, for this Belief System, is **"Deism."***

Deists accept that there is a Creator God, but affirm also that this Creator is not an interventionalist, and that the on-going creative process follows established "Laws of Nature" which can be intelligently observed and rationally interpreted to guide Human action. Deism is a Natural Belief System rather than a Revealed Religion defined by prophets and messengers, codified into theology and sacred books interpreted and managed by priests and religious "authorities" supposedly above natural and human law.

Deism does not reject apparent "miracles," but only that they are of Supernatural origin; Deism does not reject the apparent power of prayer, but only that it results in Divine intervention; nor does Deism reject *natural* powers that may be called *spirits, angels, gods, guides, entities,* etc.—only when they are claimed to be beyond natural law.

A few well-known Deists include Descartes, Voltaire, Bacon, Isaac Newton, Adam Smith, John Locke, Carl Friedrich Gauss, Benjamin Franklin, James Madison, Thomas Paine, Ethan Allen, Thomas Jefferson, James Watt, Max Planck, Charles Sanders Peirce, Leonardo da Vinci, Jules Verne, Neil Armstrong, Thomas Edison, and—obviously—many other intellectuals and scientists.

Contrary to recent fundamentalist claims, the United States was not founded as a "Christian nation." The American Declaration of Independence mentions God once, in Deist terms, with no reference to Moses, Jesus, the Bible, or other Religious authority. Both Presidents George Washington and John Adams officially affirmed that **"the government of the United States of America is not in any sense founded on the Christian religion."**

Today, other than in name and preference for organization and the social functions of "church" there is little difference between Deism, Naturalism, and Unitarianism. (See our *Communicating with Spirit*, 2015, for greater detail on many old religions and modern belief systems.)

Paranormal phenomena and powers are in no way "supernatural," but do often have that appearance as *not seen*, for example, in the collective or so-called "instinctive" behavior of many animals, aquatics, birds, and even insects. Yet, while mostly demonstrated in the collective or group (crowd, herd, flock, school) forms of consciousness, we do also observe and *experience* it in our direct relationship with *individual* pet and work animals such as dogs, horses, elephants, dolphins, and some birds where some form of telepathy or some non-physical sense is at work.

And, even with plants, as famously demonstrated by Cleve Backster whose plants—when hooked up to a lie detector—not only *measurably* reacted to the threat of a burning match (see The International Journal of Parapsychology, Volume X) but physically *recoiled* by moving away from Backster's hand holding the match *before it was ignited,* possibly indicating some degree of precognition.

Just as our *normal* five senses of seeing, hearing, smelling, tasting, and touching can be further developed and strengthened through training and exercise (like any other physical attribute), so can our "sixth" or psychic sense in our *Next Step in Personal Empowerment.*

This **"Sixth Sense"** or power is part of the personal evolution that we all, collectively and individually are undertaking at this time. The more we *intentionally* do in this respect, the faster and further we will *step ahead,* awakening dormant powers and no longer be <u>asleep at the switch</u> when circumstances call that extra empowerment.

Conscious and Unconscious, Two-Way Communication

We acknowledge that much of this *instinctive* communication is unconscious, but we also need to point out that All Communication, conscious and unconscious, happens in both directions between all the parties involved and sometimes even beyond those directly involved to broadly manifest in the whole immediate environment.

Our environment is full of vibrations*

*Please refer to Tables at the end of this chapter for supplemental and comparative information.

Everything *vibrates,* including every part of our bodies, and everything in the *world* around us whether perceived by our normal senses or not. Everything manifest is either Matter or Energy, or a mixture of both, and that mixture is characterized by vibrating particles that we perceive to the degree that our sensory perception responds and adjusts to the particular *apparent reality* of the object of our interest. **Anything other than normal is <u>paranormal</u>.**

To otherwise perceive the Paranormal, we can enlist the various objects and methodologies described in the previous eight chapters of Lab research and technology development. To **<u>directly</u> experience or perceive the paranormal, we must alter our own normal sensory vi-**

bratory capacity, activating our own dormant potentials (innate psychic powers), altering and raising our consciousness in a controlled manner.

Nothing in the Cosmos is permanent and unchanging. Just as a plant grows from a tiny sprout into a mighty oak tree, and eventually dies, falls to the ground, and rots into nutriment for new life, a new tree or other plant likely takes its place in a continuing round of existence. Or, something else altogether takes its _space_ in an ever-changing environment. Life, as we know it, goes on—but its form often changes.

Death and its Alternatives

Humans, too, like trees, still die*, and their space** is most often taken by a person of a new generation. For many people in the Western world, biological death is felt to be the final curtain and the grave the "final resting place." In contrast, many of the new _millennial_ generation and students of self-improvement practices and of the Paranormal are increasingly open-minded and ready to explore alternatives.

> *Others of us do believe that the Person's Spirit moves on to grow in alternate realities to eventually incarnate into a new physical body, and the soul advances a step or two in its new life. (See our book, _Communicating with Spirit_, 2015.)
>
> _Or, is death any longer a biological necessity?_ New "Longevity and Age Reversal" Research predicts otherwise and that age limitations are falling away. Whether through reincarnation or longer lives, humans grow and evolve, faster and faster. Yes, within our own lifetime, no matter how long or short, we _can_ individually grow, develop, and take the _Next Step_ in personal evolution that we identify as Personal (and Psychic) Empowerment.

Evolution is commonly believed to be a slow and species-wide _Response_ to new environmental _Challenges_ in terms of biological development. Historian Arnold Toynbee coined this phrase—"Challenge and Response"—in relation to the decline and birth of civilizations. It is only over the past two or three centuries that personal growth is recognized as contributing to the evolution of the entire human species.

> **"Space"** We use that word as an occasional alternative to "place" in recognition of what is, ultimately, a *fourth* dimension for Humanity entering the New Age. Whereas "place" is still *earthbound*, "Space" is more than an *extreme upward direction*. Rather, it is indeed Humanity's New Frontier. To move *into* Space requires not only new technologies but also new morality, new laws, and the founding of a New Civilization. Unfortunately, Space will also add a new dimension to warfare.

New Age Challenges

Today, more and more people worldwide are challenged by accelerating population growth threatening the capacity of natural, social and health resources, economic development, energy and transportation networks, home and national security, quality education and good government. We are all challenged by the new agriculture (antibiotics in meat and poultry, massive feedlots, long-distance transportation, factory farms, etc.); by radical and transformative new technologies (the personal computer in all its forms; the Internet in all its permeations; the continuous flow of news, information, opinion, and propaganda); the replacement of widely accepted systems of communication by new variations (newspapers, radio, television, cameras everywhere, cell phones); the advent of new energy and material resources (coal to oil to gas, drilling to fracking, mining to capture of wind and solar energies, the lithium battery and graphene); fast and vast changes in cultural relations between men and women (contraception, hormone supplements, fetish in fashion, women CEOs and generals); vast new opportunities in education and knowledge resources, from pre-school to post-graduate and independent study; from religious empires to no religion, from Church over State to State over Church to Church and State to No Church and Free Spirit; and more challenges in health and wealth, stealth bombers and drones, extreme weather and threats of war, terrorism and guns, street drugs and mental health, and a future that is both bright and promising and scary and threatening.

Yes, a long list, but it is part of the new reality. At the same time—challenge and response mean growth, evolutionary development, self-empowerment, and new psychic skills.

Species and Individual Evolution and Personal Empowerment

Evolution happens in response to challenge. It happens both to the human species and to the individual person who in turn reflects back to the species in never completed cycles of change and growth. Some of it is precipitated by long term Cosmic and Solar cycles, others by shorter Zodiacal and Planetary cycles. These are beyond our control, although knowledge and understanding allows us to consciously "swim with the tide" rather than struggle against it. Doing so has both universal and individual benefits that are beyond the purpose of this book.

Personal Empowerment, however, results from the study, practice, and growth of the individual taking the *next step* in sensory development: that of the Sixth Sense of paranormal perception and psychic powers that will be discussed in the next chapters. Please review the Tables of Three Levels of Self-Consciousness and the Seven Planes and Seven Bodies in the Introduction, the Tables of the Seven Planes of the Solar System and Seven Levels of the Human Structure in Chapter Three, and the Tables of Vibrations here in Chapter Nine in preparation.

VIBRATIONS
MACROCOSM and MICROCOSM
Vibration Ranges of different phenomena

Infrasonic to Very Low Frequency (VLF) Waves, Magnetism and Gravity: (measured in **G** Gauss (not a prefix) 10^{-2} or minus 2 zeros to 100 Hz)

Certain Paranormal senses and phenomena, including levitation.

.00000	.0000	.000	.00	0 gauss
ESP	Dowsing	Black	Gravity	Magnetic
	Field	Streams*	Field	Field

*Described as "harmful earth rays" studied by members of the Institute of Electrical and Electronics Engineers in John Keel's *The Eighth Tower*.

Physical Senses—Frequency (approximate Vibrations, Beats, Waves, Cycles or Hertz (Hz) per Second)

Touch	2 to 16			
Hearing	(from 16 in infants) 20 to 28,000			
	Infrasonic	*Base*	*Treble*	*Ultrasonic*
Taste				
Smell				
Sight	370 THz to 750 THz			
	Infrared Red	*Violet*	*Ultraviolet*	

BrainWaves in vibrations per second (Hertz):

Delta	1 to 3			
Theta	4 to 7			
Alpha	8 to 13			
Beta	14 to 28			

Earth's Schumann Resonant Frequency: 7.8 Hertz

Electromagnetic Spectrum, longer waves: in Hertz:				
Electric Power and AC Motors		60 to 100		
Very Low Frequency Radio		3 KHz to 300 KHz		
Radio, AM		540 KHz to 1630 KHz		
Radio, Shortwave Broadcast		5.95 MHz to 26.1 MHz		
Very High Frequency (VHF)		30 MHz to 300 MHz		
Television, Band I		54 MHz to 88 MHz		
FM Radio, Band II		88 MHz to 174 MHz		
Television, Band III		174 MHz to 216 MHz		
Ultra High Frequency (UHF)		300 MHz to 3000 MHz		
Television, Bands IV and V, Channels 14-70		470 MHz to 806 MHz		
Super high frequencies (SHF)— Microwaves:		**3 GHzto 30 GHz**		
Infrared, Heat		**300 GHz to 430 GHz**		
Visible Light (visible to human, *physical*, sight):		**430 THz to 750 THz**		
Red	400 to 484 THz			
Orange	484 to 508 THz			
Yellow	508 to 526 THz			
Green	526 to 606 THz			
Cyan	606 to 630 THz			
Blue	631 to 668 THz			
Violet	668 to 789 THz			
Ultraviolet		**1.62 PHz to 30 PHz**		
Spirit Light (visible to human, *psychic*, sight)		**300 GHz to 40 PHz**		
X-Ray		**30 PHz to 30 EHz**		

Gamma Rays			30 EHz to 3000 EHz		
and					
Cosmic Rays			10^{20} to 10^{21}		

Includes levels of Psychic Projections, and of Soul Essence
(Source: page 27–28, Slate and Weschcke, *Llewellyn Complete Book of Psychic Empowerment*)

Mathematical Measurement Prefixes and their Meanings

nano-means	**n** 10^{-9} or 0.000000001 (minus 8 zeros = milliardth)
micro-	**u** 10^{-6} or 0.000001 (minus 5 zeros = millionth)
milli-	***m*** 10^{-3} or 0.001 (minus 2 zeros = thousandth
centi-	**c** 10^{-2} or 0.01 (minus 1 zero = hundredth)
deci-	**d** 10^{-1} or 0.1 (no zeros—tenth)
	10^{0} or 1
Deca-	**D** 10^{1} or 1 zero = ten
Hector-	**H** 10^{2} or 100 (2 zeros = hundred)
Kilo-	**K** 10^{3} or 1,000 (3 zeros = thousand)
Mega-	**M** 10^{6} or 1,000,000 (6 zeros = million)
Giga-	**G** 10^{9} or 1,000,000,000 (9 zeros = billion)
Tera-	**T** 10^{12} or 1,000,000,000,000 (12 zeros = trillion)
Peta-	**P** 10^{15} or 1,000,000,000,000,000 (15 zeros)
Exa-	**E** 10^{18} or 1,000,000,000,000,000,000 (18 zeros)
Zeta-	**Z** 10^{21} (21 zeros)
Yotta-	**B** 10^{24} (24 zeros)
yocto-	**y** 10^{24} (minus 14 zeros = quadrillionth)
zepta-	**z** 10^{21} (minus 21 zeros = trillardth)
atto-	**a** 10^{18} (minus 18 zeros = trillionth)
femto-	**f** 10^{15} (minus 15 zeros = billiardth)
pico-	**p** 10^{12} (minus 12 zeros = trillionth)

(Source: page 27–28, Slate and Weschcke, *Llewellyn Complete Book of Psychic Empowerment*)

CHAPTER TEN
Psychic Development:
Challenge and Response

History is the story of Challenge and Response; Evolution is the reality of Response to Challenge.

Both History and Evolution are *developmental responses* to the Challenge set forth by Creation itself "**in the Beginning**." The first Response was-and-is the self-regulating *system of programs* we call "the Laws of Nature," and the first Law of Nature was-and-is "**the Word,**" that always will-be the *progressing* program we call "Evolution."

As time progressed, the *continuing* Evolutionary Process generated the first existential units and endowed them with *innate* consciousness. Challenge becomes more and more specific in form and structure, and the systemized responses generate the World we know, a World varied by its surface features, climate and geography, history, and diverse in human "culture."

Ever Onward, Always Progressing

As "populations" of all types—from sub-atomic particles to complex life forms, from botanical and biological to animal and human co-existent with "spiritual" and perhaps other forms—have increased in numbers and complexity, their "cultures" have become more competitive and intrusive. *We are not "Alone!" Our World, and the Whole Cosmos, is rich in Life, Consciousness, and Spirit with much, still mostly unknown and unrecognized, in form and interaction.*

At the same time, both Challenge and Response has become more singular and focused, the one generating the other, building upon what went before, and progressing in what comes next through recognizable stages. Each progressively selecting and modifying the other so that Nature (and its "laws") also evolves along with its "progeny"—both Collective and individual. Evolution continues with no foreseeable ending

157

but with meaning and purpose we begin to understand. With Understanding comes Awareness and increasing acceptance of Responsibility for human Action.

Personal Empowerment: Command and Control
Individual Response progresses from *involuntary, and sometimes* compulsive, reaction to *voluntary* and *increasingly rational* action, and Challenge is met with a Personal Response that <u>can</u> become a Developmental Opportunity to *Become More than You Are,* and the Potential to *Become All You Can Be.*

Individuals today are cumulatively rich in attributes and innate potentials, and each person has the opportunity to raise consciousness, expand awareness, and "initiate" the Next Evolutionary Step by developing their innate paranormal potential into advanced Psychic Powers and dependable Skills.

Psychic Development and Empowerment:
The Next Step in Human Evolution
We see this Next Step of Psychic Development as one of Personal Empowerment, raising your innate paranormal "sensitivity" to a true psychic skill under your Command and Control. Unlike much of our evolutionary past, this is a step that should be taken with intention and full understanding—just as any other advancement like that of higher education and professional training. Yet, unlike traditional group-oriented classroom learning or classical apprenticeship, it is an *act of self-development.* History and Evolution have brought us to this stage, but the next step must be an act of personal culmination.

"Ye are Gods in the Making"
This is both a Biblical saying and an esoteric principle recognizing that we have the *potential* of evolving physically and mentally through *acts of will* and *acceptance of responsibility* for the consequences of our actions. The Next Step is the *Causal Act of True Will* to deliberately develop the "Sixth Sense" and transform further Psychic abilities as *NORMAL* to everyday life.

We can't emphasize this enough—just as we must accept responsibility for our actions,—individually and collectively—as they affect the physical environment, as they contribute to our national and global security and well-being, to our personal, local and world health, to financial and economic growth and success, and much more, and that we understand the dynamic interrelationship between Past, Present and Future and how our future depends on what we do now to increase education at all levels, to invest in science and technology, and move beyond ideological limitations. *Knowledge is Power, and the Power must be correctly and responsibly employed.*

The Challenge to old, Materialist Science

This esoteric promise is also a statement of belief in spiritual reality that goes "above and beyond" the perceptions of *materialist* science. This is not to say that all scientists are *Materialists,* but *Physical* Science is—by definition—limited to *measurable* Material Reality. In other words, materialist science says if you cannot perceive it via the *normal* five physical senses, and measure it by *normal* physical means, *it does not exist!*—Except, *perhaps*—for something beyond *paranormal* called "god."

However, while not generally recognized, <u>modern</u> physical science actually does measure both matter and energy not directly perceivable, and recognizes astronomical and quantum factors known only indirectly as reactions to other factors also not directly perceived. That's part of the New Physical Science.

The Great Leap Forward

History, Evolution, and Circumstances will keep on challenging individuals for an evolutionary response to the present critical situations just as consequential as was humanity's Great Leap Forward some 60,000 years ago when climate change led to mass migrations out of the African homeland and that challenge led to the beginning of *technology* with tools purposefully invented for the specific job at hand. A stone hammer became more than a blunt instrument, a piece of cracked flint could ignite a fire, clay molded into a pot, fire used to boil a pot full of water that widened and improved choice and quality of food, and so on.

Here, too, was the beginning of general education, for tool-making had to be taught by one person to another, and group action increased value and opportunity, stimulating discovery and invention. Knowledge leads to more knowledge, and to social progress, and tools used to make goods traded for other goods, and Trade could lead to what today we call "Economic Development."

While scholars don't classify this "Great Leap" in relation to human capacity, we perceive it as the vital evolutionary step when Mind was directly used to resolve human problems, and *Civilization was born.*

There's more to Reality than the Physical Dimension

We can further say, as esotericists have long taught, that there are levels of sense and reality *beyond* the physical. The most immediate *paranormal* level is generally called the "Astral Plane" (as encountered earlier in Chapter Three), and the concurrent level of consciousness is inclusive of that perception experienced as Clairvoyance and often called the **"Sixth Sense."**

The Astral Plane and Astral Consciousness are not anything "new" to the world. What we refer to as the "Astral Plane" and the "Astral Body" have been integral parts of the greater Cosmos and human Person since the Beginning. (Please refer back to the *Table of Seven Planes and Seven Bodies* at the end of the Introduction for more detail.)

Beyond the Astral, there are levels generally called the "Mental" and the "Causal," and more beyond these that for practical purposes at this stage we simply call "Spiritual." Traditional terminology can be confusing because so many words and related concepts were simply "borrowed" from Sanskrit, Hebrew, Greek, and other languages, and even more diverse sources via a multitude of channels. "Astral," for example, means *Starry,* but from a practical understanding, it is the world of Emotion, and another way of understanding emotion is "E-Motion," or *Energy in Motion.* Yes, of course, we also define emotion as "feelings," and feelings are often a manner of *sensing:* hence, our Sixth Sense of Clairvoyance.

How we develop Clairvoyance

While we are not, in this book, providing systematic training for the development of clairvoyance and other psychic skills (for that, see our *Clairvoyance for Psychic Empowerment*), one simple self-administered procedure is: **Pay Attention to Your "Feelings."** By that, we don't mean to *get all emotional* when "feeling" an idea, concept, event, situation, person, etc., but rather to analyze: *what your feelings are telling you, what is it you are sensing, what is the basis for your emotional reaction, etc.* And then *let yourself Explore the "answers"* to those questions.

An alternate word for "explore" is to "*meditate*" on those answers. Too often people think of *meditation* mainly in connection with yogic practices or for meditation upon such broad ideals as Peace, Harmony, Impersonal Love, etc. rather than to focus on current questions and personal needs.

And this raises another important and often overlooked point: The "Esoteric," the "Spiritual," even the "Psychic" and the "Paranormal" do not mean *above and beyond the practical, the personal, and matters of self-concern like health, wealth, love, and sex.* (Or as one once well-known travelling spiritual teacher would have it: "Nothing below the belt!")

The New Science of the Paranormal

The Paranormal is no longer beyond science. Quantum Theory brings us toward a new scientific understanding of Clairvoyance and other paranormal actions. At the sub-atomic level we encounter the phenomena known as "entanglement" where two particles once related one to another remain in *instantaneous* communication no matter how distant they become separated one from the other. Another quantum phenomena is called "superposition" which allows a particle to have a value of one or zero at the same time and to appear in two places at once and hence to "tunnel" through a wall as if were not there. Albert Einstein called Quantum Mechanics "spooky" science, it was quantum physics that led to nuclear bombs and power, and opened the computer generation and Information Age.

Quantum Theory, the "Bridge" between Physical and Esoteric Science

Without getting into more complex discussion, the fact is that quantum science is at the founding of a new generation of computers able to solve the most complex problems millions times faster than existing machines and technology, and opening "doors" to knowledge once thought of as purely esoteric. In an alternate view, quantum theory says that *Intention becomes Reality.* In other words, a disciplined mind can produce "miracles."

It also means that tomorrow's technology will fulfill all the dreams of science fiction and the marvels seen on *Star Trek*, and that, indeed, we will be *going "where no man has gone before."* Science and Technology, and the New Science of the Paranormal, is taking us into domains once thought of as spiritual and beyond human, but they are really just the Next Step in the development of our innate potential.

Vision to Solve Tomorrow's Problems Now!

An Old Lesson, but one still challenging to learn, is to Think and Plan Ahead to meet tomorrow's needs before they are needed! And, for that we need the Vision to develop the technology to replace our planet's dwindling resources, for space travel to open new frontiers, but beyond all, to see and understand that we ourselves are all that we envision. Spiritually and physically, along with the astral, the mental, the causal, and more, we are all that there can be.

Becoming More than You Are

Becoming more: If there is an object associated with what you want to explore, you may actually be able to *feel it with your hands.* Even though clairvoyance is not a physical sense, it is a *sense* and can function as an *extension,* or expansion, of the physical senses of Touch, Sight, Taste, Smell, and Hearing. And, this is a major point in our thesis: the *expansion* and *extension* of awareness is the Growth and Development of innate psychic faculties that we describe as the Evolutionary Next Step in this New Age.

There are many permutations and broad applications to this as well as new Challenges and Responses that we will discuss in Chapters Eleven and Twelve, but this is the *transitional time* of our "Initiation" into both the Zodiacal Age of Aquarius and the culminating 26,000 year cycle called the Galactic Alignment when the Sun passes the galactic equator at the furthest point from our galactic center and now we leave the darkness called "Kali Yuga" and begin the 13,000 year journey of increasing *Light*—both in the physical and the spiritual sense.

Learning to "Think" long

It is a true Challenge to everyone to really think in such long spans of time—not merely of lifetimes and centuries but millennia and even millions of years—as the Past and Future for us as "units of human consciousness." We transitioned *down* into physical incarnation sequentially through the Causal, Mental, Astral, and Etheric planes. According to esoteric teachings and Hindu Sacred History, we descended *down* from "Heavenly Beginnings" and will eventually ascend back to our "Heavenly origins." From the "Beginning" back to the "Beginning," *but with this difference:* We will have grown in Knowledge and Power to "Become All we can Be," thus fulfilling the potentials set forth in the First Program of our Cosmic Beginning.

We need the perspective of History to give meaning to our present being. The age of the physical universe is believed to be nearly 14 *billion* years, and that of our Solar System nearly 5 billion years, while that of Planet Earth is just over 4 billion years. Life on Earth began about 3 billion years ago. *It takes a long time to grow up, and we have a long time to go.*

The Importance of Personal Vision

Ultimately, all action is individual and personal for no matter the structure and purpose of any "collective" it is a group of individuals, and each person is responsible for their own chosen actions. Even if that group or the individual person is being *led* by a religionist priest or minister, or being *trained* by a professional instructor or teacher, or is simply "following the leader" or "going with the crowd, "the responsibility is personal. Likewise, if emotionally responding to a charismatic evangelist or populist politician using all the tools of "mass hypnosis" (stirring music, powerful rituals, or trance-inducing chants), the response is personal. The same is true of the consumer's emotional response to sophisticated advertising or the mass response to the "emotional frenzy" associated with major sports events, religious revivals, or music concerts: The responsibility for individual action is personal.

Life is a constant series of challenges to which there are always responses—for even no action is a form of action in response to challenge. You can and should study and consider all aspects of the challenges of your awareness, and your development of Clairvoyance and Pre-cognition will increasingly enhance your Personal Vision to see all aspects of your potential actions and thus make better decisions.

Our Potential is Infinite: Our Consciousness and Spirit extends far beyond physical limitations. What we commonly call Astral and other subtle bodies are better understood as "Vehicles" of particular levels of Consciousness by which we can experience and explore those other worlds of matter and energy called "Planes."

As you use your vehicles to explore these greater domains while at the same time extending and expanding the depth of your physical as well as the higher levels, you grow, your vision extends, your power expands, and you become aware of your role as "Co-Creator."

CHAPTER ELEVEN
Psychic Empowerment:
An Evolutionary "Movement"

MOVEMENT IS LIFE—LIFE IS MOVEMENT
There is Power in Movement,
and there are many Kinds of Movement

There are many things meant by the word, "movement," and a "movement" can mean many things—including other and related movements. *Movement makes things happen and gives meaning to their Happenings.*

The Power of Combined Movements

In Music, for example, there are many related "movements," variations among instruments and counter-movements, but also the related physical movements as in dance, drama, and opera, in marching and gymnastics. In addition, the combination of music and physical movement is used to create powerful television commercials.

Music with movement, and movement with music is a powerful combination stirring emotions, communicating ideas, and stimulating particular actions. Such music combinations are intentionally used for their power in connection with other actions to augment their emotional impact. Examples of such usage include politics, religion, marketing, sports, motion picture and television dramas. But music is only one example of combined two or more kinds of movement.

"Natural" and "Cultural" Movements

"*Natural*" movements include all forms of non-personal physical movement such as particle movement, atomic and molecular movement, internal and external physiological movements, seasonal and migratory movements, geo-physical movements, planetary movements, and more. Everything moves, just as everything changes. But other than such natural movements we can see two basic human

"*Cultural*" movements: those that are reflective of coincidental activity and those that appear as planned by an individual or small group including the forced movement of entire population groups.

Revolutionary and Developmental Movements

From a historic perspective, there have been many kinds of cultural movements with their various related emotional, mental, and physical actions and resultant reaction. There have been powerful Literary, Artistic, Political, Religious, Philosophical, and Scientific movements that often are associated with particular people; and then there are other movements that go beyond individual or small group efforts that have marked entire generations. Citizen Democracy, Digital Technology, Mass Education, and Quantum Theory are examples of "Evolutionary Movements" that are both *Revolutionary* and *Developmental*—changing the very foundations of world culture and setting forth new patterns of Life for coming generations.

Human <u>Response</u> to the <u>Challenge</u> of Cosmic Vibrations

How do we explain the existence of these movements? We like to think of these as entirely "human" in origin—but: *Are they?* Rather than suggesting any kind of "Divine" Guidance or Inspiration we suggest that these dynamic Evolutionary Movements are "powered" by broad astronomical/astrological cycles. Of course it takes human agents to *respond* to the *challenge* of the "Cosmic Vibrations." But, the bigger the movement the fewer are the individual names distinctly identified as founders and leaders. In other words, these movements are not "human" in origin but seemingly planetary in dimension and causal in action.

The Extension of Physical Power and Personal Empowerment

Human potential has been constantly enriched through such Evolutionary Movements reaching far beyond their initial "subject content." Citizen Democracy led to the American Revolution, to freedom from imposed religion, to free public education, to the rejection of slavery, to the spread of individual entrepreneurship, the Industrial Revolution, the spread of higher education, the rise of the Middle Class overcoming the elitist class system, and more and more, *ever onward to the empowered individual.*

Yes, we see that "Knowledge is Power," but even more important is "Personal Empowerment." We don't just *use* Knowledge as a means to power, wealth, and security, but to personal growth, freedom, independence, and *Self*-Development.

The Next Step: Reaching Beyond Physical Limitations

The "Next Step" of Psychic Development described in Chapter Ten is actually a "Movement" as important in the 21st Century as was the birth of Citizen Democracy in the 18th Century, of Public Education in the early 19th, of Quantum Theory at the turn of the 20th, and of Digital Technology in the mid-20th.

Think of how each movement has led to vast enhancement and *extension* of our individual personal capabilities. Our personal computers and the Internet place history, information, and knowledge at our fingertips, and enable us to conduct business, undertake advanced studies right from home; computer power and memory (and the "cloud") **Extend Personal "Work-Power"** equal to that of hundreds of people in the previous century; our cell phones communicate across the world and even translate languages for us; smart watches transmit current medical history directly to doctors; we can shop, pay bills, invest our money, check our home security from a distance while riding safely in driverless cars, etc., while benefiting from the same enhancements empowering our co-workers, service people, suppliers, consultants, advisors, contractors, etc.

The Digital Revolution and Its Evolution

The Digital Revolution forms the foundation of global communication, culture, finance, and information sharing in the fields of health, medical emergencies, and world weather forecasting, which in its inclusiveness becomes the first best chance for World Peace.

Everything we can "dream of" becomes a new technology program, more and more magickal, issuing from a combination of emotional energy and mental conception guided by will. That, practically speaking, is what "software" is. Software is what manages the Hardware, just like "Mind over Matter" and for Thought to guide Emotion and control the Physical.

The Extension of Psychological and Psychic Powers for Self-Empowerment

Unlike the growing, easily-seen *Exterior* extension of Personal Physical Empowerment of the recent decades and centuries, the Psychic Empowerment of the 21st Century reaches beyond the Physical Plane to the Astral, Mental, and Causal Planes via the related "vehicles" comparable to the physical plane and physical body. Unseen and not being physical, their senses and powers are generally considered to be an extension of *Interior* Psychological or Spiritual Powers inherent to the vehicles of the Inner Planes.

In earlier chapters we explored some of these psychic (or paranormal) powers with the help of physical methodology to demonstrate the enhancement of personal power through practices of Divination, Dowsing, Extra-Sensory Perception, Mental Telepathy, Astral Projection, Clairvoyance, Past Life Memories, and more. So long as we are incarnate,

Even the most "spiritual" power builds upon the physical. We are a "whole" being, not a collection of separate parts (other than in conditions of complete unconsciousness, coma, schizophrenia, etc.)

The Spiritual Movement and "Religion" in the New Age

In some ways—or maybe totally so—Psychic Empowerment as a *Spiritual Movement* is the "religion" of the New Age. Science has replaced religion as a source for the "story" of our origins, and rationality has replaced outdated theology as a source of ethical and "moral guidance," while spirituality is embodied in the personal need to Grow and become one with the Source of "All Creation."

The Difference from Religions of the Past

But we have to recognize *this New Age movement is different from* religions of the past with their appearance of being "channeled" to select humans by some *external* Divine Power, Agent, or Messenger. Such focus further involved designated humans to interpret what the Source gave, and then to train and guide ordinary (normal) *dependent* human beings in the ways proclaimed as coming from the exterior Source.

Western Religions Dominated by the Old Judaic Bible

The Old Religions of India and China are very old, as were those of Egypt and Greece, but much of the Western World is still dominated by the Judaic Bible centered on the Book of Genesis believed to have been written by Moses around 1400 BC. In it we are told that "God created man in his *own* image, in the image of God created he him; male and female created he them."

What is Overlooked and Long Forgotten

Moses doesn't give a date for when his God created the World and the men and women entrusted with its care, but that need not concern us. What does concern us is the prevailing concept that we are created by God in his own image. Overlooked here is the logical conclusion that humans, being of God's substance in God's image are all "God's children" and, hence, "Gods in the making" for children grow up to carry on from the parent.

Also overlooked and forgotten is the statement that God's image is both male and female. So not only is God both male and female, but so are each of us of Divine Substance and both male and female in the matrix of our *inner* being that guides us developmentally. Within each of us is the Source of our being and the Resource for our Knowledge, Understanding, and Guidance. Our Source is internal and always contemporary, and not some externally channeled antiquarian teaching that must be interpreted for us by out-of-touch "organization men."

A Viable Creation Myth

Is this "creation story" history? No. Is this science? No, but, presumably, it is "divinely" inspired myth and hence the story of who we are at the core of our being. And while this is a Western myth, it is little different from other Creation Myths—East and West, North and South. And as simply a myth, it is, a logical guess that happens to be pretty universal and that is essentially reflected in modern psychological and physical science. It's a sufficient foundation for us to project certain conclusions.

The Role of Religion

In much of past history, religion was a "given" to a particular group of people serving at least in part to unify the people under a common leader or belief system. The word *religion* itself derives from the Latin *relig* (to tie, fasten) and *ligare* (to bind), hence "to bind together." While the source might be a creation myth as interpreted by the leader, the ground purpose was political: to lead and control a tribe or nation. No matter the elements of the belief system, religions have been either the main cause or the method behind most wars.

Exploring the Inner Nature of Physical Reality

First we must examine a creation myth. We are long accustomed to think that the non-scientists of the past had no means of perceiving and understanding the reality of the physical world. Not true, for the seers and shamans of old had the means to explore the *inner dimensions* of both man and his world. While clairvoyance and other paranormal powers were rare and mostly dependent on physical methods of consciousness alteration, these men and women did explore and catalog the inner worlds.

Mostly working as teams, men and women travel the astral world, cataloging the inner substance of healing herbs and the corresponding attributes of crystals and minerals, learning the role of posture and sound in healing mind and body, seeing the correspondences between aura colors and shapes to emotional and physical health, and much more. Notice the use of the *present tense* in the above description: these procedures have not been lost and forgotten—they are practiced today as ever and no longer are dependent on psychoactive substances and other traditional methods. Both clairvoyance and astral projection can be learned and applied to such exploration.

Modern Religions and the Role of Churches and Ministers

There are more than 4,000 active religions in the world, and while the three Abraham religions of Judaism, Christianity, and Islam not only dominate the Western religious scene, they represent half the world's population with Christianity and Islam, each having around two billion adherents while Judaism has only 14 million. Hinduism has just over a billion followers and Buddhism just under a half billion.

Some religions totally control the lives and practices of their adherents—even to the point of life or death—while others are primarily supportive in relation to their members spiritual studies and practices, including discussion and classes on world religions and philosophies, the technologies of prayer and meditation, even the evocation and invocation of various deific forms and forces. A few, like the non-theological Unitarian-Universalist, primarily provide social services and counseling in their churches, celebrating life events from birth to death including naming, coming of age, marriage, funeral and burial (or cremation), and even celebrating the culmination of menopause.

"Religion," as relayed by the traditional tax-exempt big-moneyed organizations, is increasingly of little purpose in the modern world other than as a resource for spiritual studies and community services but those functions are important and fulfill deep social and psychological needs. And, while an external place and environment is far from necessary for your own program of Psychic Development and Empowerment, such a service can be very helpful under the conditions of busy, crowded, and often noisy urban life, that is better provided by the non-theological churches.

Will, Mind, and Self-Discipline in the New Age Movement

You don't have to wait until tomorrow or any special time or place to start a program of psychic development and empowerment. All that is really required is your determination and a plan of action. Yes, your plan can and should include reading a few books and might benefit from classes and lectures, but it is your own mind that makes sense of everything. It is your Mind that organizes your observations into your own Belief System. It is your mind that creates your plan of action employing the whole of your being:

CREATING YOUR PLAN OF ACTION

Will motivates and disciplines;

Mind plans and organizes;

Emotion energizes, evaluates, and rewards;

Body is the vehicle of action.

You study to learn technologies of Mind and Spirit—the "software" to manage the "hardware" of your Body and Emotion. You employ those technologies of Astral Projection, Communication with Spirit, Divination and Precognition, Meditation and Self-Hypnosis, and Personal Alchemy (Self-Transformation) to Grow and *Become More than You Are.* They are all there for you to use, but the most fundamental method is to:

QUIET THE MIND, ASK THE BIG QUESTIONS, AND LISTEN TO THE ANSWERS

You can call it "Personal Meditation" because you are the source of the Big Question and it is your creative core that is the source of the answers. Of course, you must write both in a personal journal. And you must study your journal and let it suggest the next Big Question to ask. And so on.

What are "Big Questions?" This is important! They are <u>not</u>, at this stage, those typical questions asked of an astrologer or of a psychic "reader" of any kind—*Will Gloria and Henry make it together? Is Gwen pregnant? Will Robert get that job? Who will be the next president?*

Which team will win? Will it rain on the picnic? Don't belittle your true power in this manner for which other technologies can be used. Later you will have no limitations.

The Ultimate Secret

Having asked the Big Question and recorded the Big Answer, you can further explore its permutations using any of the other technologies as they are part of your personal clairvoyance that is central to your innate psychic empowerment that increases as you use it. That—*using it*—is the ultimate secret to your psychic development.

Everything you do in this program is "Personal." Personal Magick, Personal Alchemy, Personal Divination, Personal Development—or call it all self-development, self-empowerment, etc. The point is that your psychic development and empowerment are all self-centered at this stage. *You are becoming all you can be, and there is no limit to what you can become!*

CHAPTER TWELVE
A Lifelong Plan for Success

Not in the clamor of the crowded street,
Not in the shouts and plaudits of the throng,
But in ourselves are triumph and defeat.
Henry Wadsworth Longfellow, "The Poets" (1876)

Overcome All Barriers

The potential for greatness exists in everyone. Through the *Lifelong Plan for Success* as presented in this chapter, you can access that potential and activate a dynamic, endless growth process. You can overcome barriers to your success and create totally new growth possibilities. By dissolving growth blockages, you can activate inner sources of power, including dormant sub-conscious functions. You can accelerate the growth process and improve cognitive abilities such as memory, problem-solving, and reasoning. You can build a more positive self-concept and become more fully attuned both inwardly and outwardly. You can promote better health and fitness, slow the aging process, and even reverse the effects of aging. You can uncover past life experiences and add totally new meaning to your existence. When you add to these the abundant resources available from other dimensions, including higher astral realms of power, the possibilities become unlimited.

Varying levels of Personal Consciousness

As an optimistic concept that focuses on the multifunctional dynamics of self-empowerment and success, the lifelong plan as presented here recognizes the relevance of varying levels of personal consciousness, not as opposing inner forces but as co-existing processes with the capacity to interact. Their contents include experiences and potentials with critical empowering possibilities at varying levels of development. Even undeveloped potentials existing at the deepest levels of consciousness are critical to success because they are energized with empowering possibilities. A major goal of the Lifelong Plan for

Success is to facilitate a continuous growth process that activates the full unfoldment of personal growth potentials.

Becoming Connected

Self-empowerment through the Lifelong Plan for Success is an optimistic concept. Neither heredity nor environment is seen as the major determinant of growth, but rather the emerging self. The limitations of heredity and the adverse effect of environmental influences yield to the empowered self and its capacity to overcome growth barriers.

The Self-Empowerment Potential

By recognizing the empowerment potential existing in everyone, the self-empowerment potential rejects all alibis for disempowerment and failure. Mastery of specific empowerment techniques not only increases enlightenment, it initiates a growth interaction with unbounded possibilities. Included is not only the activation of empowering potentials within the self, but also the reversing of those disempowering processes that impede our growth. Through becoming connected to the powers within and beyond, success becomes your destiny.

The Plan for Self-Empowerment and Lifelong Success

The Lifelong Plan for Success recognizes the self-empowering potential existing in everyone. It can be used to accelerate personal growth and achieve an endless range of person goals while contributing to the common good. The plan begins with a Preliminary Exercise that builds self-esteem and establishes a positive mind-set, both of which are essential to the lifelong plan. These essentials, however, must emerge from within: they cannot be externally assigned. Once generated through regular practice of appropriate mental or verbal dialogue, they become a dynamic force that sustains a driving life-style of success. The self-dialogue is engaged either in whole or in part as the first step of the plan. It can also be engaged independently of the full plan, including upon awaking and at intervals throughout the day.

THE ELEVEN-STEP PLAN

1. Self-dialogue. A daily component of the Plan.

- I am a person of worth
- I believe in myself and my power to succeed.
- I am capable and secure within myself.
- I have the power to achieve any goal.
- I can overcome any barrier, meet any challenge, and overcome any resistance.
- Nothing can deter me from succeeding.
- I am destined for success.

2. Specify your goals. Decide what you want to achieve and write it down. Identify the outcomes as clearly as possible. If your goal is to lose weight, specify the amount. If you want to be successful in business, describe success in concrete, quantifiable terms. If you want to improve your memory, identify the nature and degree of improvement. If your goal is to complete a college degree, set a projected completion date.

3. Think Visually. Use imagery to envision yourself in both the process (goal achieving) and product (goal attainment).Surround yourself with the positive energies of success as you work toward your goals. Imagine yourself in the future success environment.

4. Develop a Plan. Formulate a step-by-step plan. List your existing resources and explore the relationship of each resource to your objective. Explore ways that your present resources can be applied toward gaining other relevant assets. Identify any additional resources required to achieve your goal. For each deficiency in resources, identify as many potential remediations as possible. List each of them. Be sure the deficiency is related to your stated goal; and remember, many unexplored and underdeveloped resources exist within yourself.

5. Generate Commitment. The commitment process will usually consider such questions as: *Why is this goal important to me? What are the immediate and long range effects of achieving the goal? What empowerment techniques related to this goal are at my command and how can I apply them? Can I equip myself to overcome obstacles?* Through commitment, you invest yourself and your energies in the goal.

6. Maintain Motivation. A strong motivational state is the result of first, identifying and visualizing your goal and second, committing your energies to achieve it. The motivational state, however, is not fixed. You can maintain a high level of motivation by recognizing the intrinsic value of personal progress and growth associated with your goal-oriented strivings as well as through self-reinforcement in which you reward yourself for progress.

7. Use Positive Self-Affirmations. Recognize your progress with affirmations of success. If your progress is interrupted, look for ways to overcome resistance and re-affirm your commitment to achieve your goal. Remember that dwelling on failure is disempowering. If one strategy fails, try another. The most powerful self-affirmation known is simply: "I CAN DO IT!" When presented three times—the first time with emphasis on **I**, the second time with emphasis on **CAN**, and the third time with emphasis on both **I** and **Can**—the simple affirmation becomes a fountainhead of power!

8. Sustain Balance. Balance (along with variety) is the spice of life. Active striving is typically more effective when balanced with effortless flowing. Aggressive, overt strategies are often enriched when accompanied by creative visualization. Keep your balance. You will find such balancing techniques as meditation, relaxation, and self-hypnosis not only facilitate your problem-solving efforts and progress in achieving your goals, they contribute to your well-being and general self-empowerment as well.

9. Exercise Variety. By using a variety of self-empowerment strategies, you will build your self-confidence and expand your empowerment skills. Seek new and different self-empowering techniques.

10. Develop an internal locus of control. The most important sources of power rest within yourself. Develop awareness of those sources, and open the inner power channels.

11. Start Now. Procrastination is disempowering. Claim ownership of your goals, and activate your *Lifelong Plan for Success*.

ASCENDING THE PYRAMID

Ascending the Pyramid is among the most effective techniques known for promoting personal empowerment and lifelong success. Developed in the laboratory setting at Athens State University, the procedure is based on the finding that simply visualizing a pyramid can be effective in generating a positive mental state conducive to success. Adding an appropriate inscription to each level of the pyramid was found to generate an even greater empowering effect.

The procedure is initiated by slowed breathing and a peaceful, passive mental state. A pyramid with 12 levels leading to its apex is then visualized with each level inscribed with a word that evokes certain empowering affirmations. At each level, the inscription is visualized as related affirmations are presented either verbally or non-verbally. Aside from the affirmations presented in the procedure as follows, additional affirmations, whether general or specific, can be included. Here is the procedure:

The Twelve Levels

Level 1: LOVE. Love is basic to my life. It is the energizing foundation of my existence and the center of my being. In my capacity to love, I discover myself and the meaning of my existence

Level 2: FORGIVENESS. By forgiving myself and others, I unblock the flow of growth in my live. Forgiveness is the transforming inner force that soars always upward toward harmony and peace.

Level 3: PEACE. Peace is the river that flows throughout my being. It is deep; abiding, and secure. Infused with inner peace, I can weather any storm. Disappointments, misfortunes, uncertainties—all yield to the quieting force of inner peace.

Level 4: FAITH. Faith is the elevating, motivating power in my life. It is my belief in my own being and the essence of my existence in the multiverse. In adversity it sustains and upholds me. It reveals the possibility of unlimited power in the present and a larger dimension of meaning in the future. Faith is the eternal energy of my being.

Level 5: CHOICE. In each moment of my life, I am choosing. I choose to act or not to act. I choose to think or not to think, I choose to feel or not to feel. Because I choose, I am responsible for my actions, thoughts, and feelings. They are all mine, and I choose to own them. I am what I choose to be at any moment. The present state of my being is the product of my choice.

Level 6. CHANGE. Change is the energizing current of growth and progress in my life. Positive change carries me always forward to experience something new and vital about my existence each day.

Level 7: AWARENESS. Through expanded awareness, my life is enriched and the meaning of my existence clarified. As I become more aware, I become more completely attuned to my being. I know myself best when I come face-to-face with the totality of my being in the here-and-now.

Level 8: KNOWLEDGE. Knowledge is power. Through knowledge of my inner being, I gain power to direct my life and control my destiny. Through knowledge of outer reality, I gain power to function more productively in the present and engage more effectively in the future.

Given knowledge, whatever its source, I become empowered to achieve my objectives and to help bring about needed change in the world.

Level 9: BALANCE. Balance in my life enables me to be spontaneous and free. My thoughts, feelings, and actions are integrated into a harmonious system of interacting functions. My mental, physical, and spiritual functions are integrated into a harmonious system that liberates my highest potentials and facilitates my total growth.

Level 10: ENLIGHTENMENT. Through knowing myself and the deeper meaning of my existence, I become empowered to take command of my life, expand my potential, and determine the consequences of my strivings. I thus become the master of my own destiny.

Level 11: ENDLESS EMPOWERMENT. My existence is bi-directional and endless. It spans the endless past and future alike. Because I am without beginning and end, my potential for growth and success is forever unlimited.

Level 12: ALTRUISM. At its peak, self-empowerment transcends the self and centers on world needs and global concerns. The result is an empowered state sufficient to deal effectively with global concerns and find solutions to such issues as hunger, poverty, injustice, abuse of human and animal rights, environmental pollution, and reckless depletion of our natural resources. Through altruistic acts that promote the common good, my personal existence is authenticated as relevant to the advancement of the world today.

Global Advancement
The world today is in the middle of global change. In our transition from an era that emphasized individualism somewhat free of world concerns, we are increasingly becoming participants in an interdependent global process. Because personal existence is no longer self-contained but rather globally related, the self-empowerment perspective becomes even more relevant. We become engaged in the complex

challenge of achieving personal empowerment while promoting global advancement The global advancement implications are profound and the possibilities are far reaching. These include:

THE IMPLICATIONS OF OUR GLOBAL ADVANCEMENT

1. A growth-fostering world that moves us toward a more worthwhile life for all.

2. Global harmony that flows from a new understanding of the rights, dignity, and worth of each human being.

3. An end to the indignities of suffering and hunger because of a new wave of caring and trust.

4. A solution to global strife and unrest through a humanistic fusion of the dichotomies that alienate people and cultures.

5. A new caring and nurturing of our physical and biological environment.

6. A genuine concern for the generations of people that are to follow us.

Conclusion

The Lifelong Plan for Success is an onward and upward plan that suggests new and advanced approaches in our search for knowledge and understanding of our existence—mentally, physically, and spiritually. Its major focus throughout is on the indestructible nature of our personal being and the potential for continuous growth and success existing within everyone. It challenges us to find ways of discovering that potential and developing it to its fullest.

GLOSSARY

The role of a glossary is not to "dictionary define" a word or phrase but to *functionally* relate to its usage in the book. If the word involved is specifically pertinent to the *context* in a singular place, then an immediate footnote may better serve the need of the reader at that point. In contrast, the glossary gives expanded and alternative meanings to the words as they relate to the multiple *concepts* being developed in the book.

This is especially the case when the subject matter is new or is a new approach to an old subject as in the transformation of the old 19th century Psychic Science and 20th century Parapsychology into the 21st century *New Science of the Paranormal.* Ideally, it opens "new doors" for the reader to explore and new dimensions to pursue. Thus, as in any research project, the potentials are greater than imagined.

Afterlife: After life, comes death, and after death comes the **Afterlife** in which the "surviving personality" moves on to begin a new chapter in the Ultimate Journey. In leaving the dying and then dead physical body, that Personality begins losing bits of memory that have no importance while retaining others that do in the continuity of being. After leaving the physical body, consciousness continues in the astral vehicle much as it did in the physical vehicle. *It has a "job" to do*—of continuing growth and development until such time as it discards the astral to continue on in the mental vehicle, and finally in the causal vehicle from which the lessons of that life are abstracted by the permanent Soul in the sense of a "Spirit Vehicle." After a time of preparation, the Soul initiates a process of descent forming a series of new vehicles that culminate in a new physical incarnation. And, so on, Life after Life, learning and growing until the job is done.

Age Reversal Research: One of the great challenges and opportunities in the New Age is to improve and lengthen physical life. As longevity research continues, it brings new knowledge of the causes of physical aging, some of which can be mitigated and even "reversed." While some of this involves improvements in nutrition and particular therapies such as cell regeneration, other aspects include meditation, visualization and forms of *self-conditioning* through self-hypnosis programs. The point is that physical life is the initial foundation in each series of incarnations, and the further we can extend it in time and quality the more we grow and develop in our multi-life journey.

Agritherapy: A psychotherapy approach based on the therapeutic value of working in soil and nurturing plants. Physical and emotional contact with growing plants nurtures and feeds living energy to their "care providers." Earth and Nature are a unity in which humans participate even when we think of ourselves apart and "above" Nature. Our environmental abuse has reached a critical point that only we can reverse to restore health to all.

Air as Object: In his pioneering research programs at Athens State University, Dr. Slate has developed an approach to the "tools" of divination under the name of *Objectology,* and has further innovated such new forms of divination as Sand Reading and the Crumpled Paper Techniques. The "Objects" used provide an *objective* (measurable) *resource* for paranormal information and further taps into the five primary "alchemical" elements of Spirit, Air, Fire, Water, and Earth giving added empowerment to the particular tool. See individual entries for Objectology, Crumpled Paper, Dowsing, Sand Reading, and Water Gazing. Also *think for yourself* how each of these primary elements relate to such traditional divinatory practices as Astrology, Tarot, Rune Casting, Dream Interpretation, Aura Reading, Palmistry, etc.

Altered States of Consciousness (ASCs): There is a fair amount of nonsense floating around (I am using these words deliberately) about ASCs, yet we all experience them daily: Waking and sleeping are each altered states of our personal consciousness. Any specific *function:* Dreaming, imagination, creative thinking, sexual fantasy, and even more "ecstatic" alterations are familiar. Likewise sexual orgasm, sports mania, various trance and trance-like states associated with Evangelical religious services, Driver Fatigue, Hypnosis, Meditation, and so on.

In other words, an alteration of consciousness does not depend on the use of drugs or other *chemical* alterations of the physical body. Any *focused* state leading to a specialized *function* of mind or emotion is an ASC such as those producing paranormal experiences of astral projection, clairvoyance, divination, healing, etc. involves an intentional or spontaneous alteration of consciousness that can be easily learned.

Our goal is knowing what we want, focus mind and emotion on its accomplishment, follow a program or step-by-step procedure to do it, and then proceed to your goal. *Always have a goal.*

Altering Sensory Vibratory Capacity: Each of our Senses is a reaction to particular vibratory input. In the physical body we have developed organs specific to the five physical senses. But for the "higher" senses we don't have sense organs but rather alterations in consciousness and the "awakening" in particular of the *chakras.* Also see Vibrations.

Ancient Wisdom: "The Ancient Wisdom" remains a mystery, perhaps a myth, perhaps lost history of a time when "Men were Gods." Or, was it when "The Gods walked on Earth?" or when "Space Visitors seeded the Earth?"

However we treat it, the Ancient Wisdom purportedly included knowledge of great powers and energies, of technologies still surpassing those of the modern world, and of wisdom that would transform our present world into one of peace, prosperity, and progress. It's the real concept underlying the belief in the "New Age," and in *Novus Ordo Seclorum*—a "New Order of the Ages."

Real or not, we are pushing back the edge of known history and finding that the artifacts we see—the Great Pyramid, the Great Sphinx, the mountain monuments in Peru, and more—are far older than previously believed and indicative of technologies still to be "rediscovered" today.

Was that Ancient Wisdom hidden away in the Tarot? Are whispers of it contained in the symbols and signs of Freemasonry? Is it waiting for us in the practices of Magick, Yoga, and the Martial Arts? Can it be glimpsed in the ecstasies of Sex Magick?

The mystery remains. All our esoteric practices are founded in the belief that we can each solve the mystery and move beyond the still luminescence of the Ancients. Is any such discussion appropriate to a *science* book? Of course—it's a series of mysteries to be solved, each promising benefit to modern man in this New Age.

Animal Communication: While some still speak of "dumb animals" in contrast to (hopefully) more intelligent humans, we are increasingly recognizing the special intelligence of many animals and have learned to partner with them in practical applications. Perhaps none more so than "Man's best friend," the dog. Dogs happily learn to work as hunting companions, as "seeing eye" guides to the blind, as bomb and drug sniffers, watch dogs, as scent trackers in search and rescue and criminal apprehension, as child and home protectors, and more.

Other familiar animal companions include the horse, the elephant, the chimpanzee, and some will claim the household cat. But all such companion relationships depend on *Communication*—the exchange of intelligence (special information) between animal and human supported by *emotion*. Well, animals "talk," but in their own languages, just as humans do. Yes, animals learn human words, inflections, and gestures, and humans increasingly learn what their animals mean with different dog barks, horse nickers, cat meows, etc.—but we increasingly realize that ALL communication is more than sound and gesture and includes degrees of paranormal exchange. The relationship between animal and trainer, and owner and companion is ultimately more dependent on the paranormal communication of "feelings" than anything else.

Apparent Reality: In most situations, *Reality* is what we see and otherwise perceive. In general, what we don't see is presumed not to exist. "Spirits," for example, are rarely seen other than through the appearance of physical manifestations and hence their reality is largely defined by that appearance and/or your Belief System.

However, "Reality can be deceiving" as when mountain ranges are reflected on clouds in the sky. Nevertheless, we tend to act upon appearances and it is through experience that we learn to look beyond normal physical appearances and sense the paranormal as well.

Application Programs: Many of the paranormal developmental procedures and the aptitudes and capabilities you develop working with them can be reduced to step-by-step programs suited for "home use" via your personal computer, tablet or smart phone for ready and practical applications. *Ascending the Pyramid* is one such strategy.

Ascending the Pyramid: A 12-Level developmental technology combining imagery of a step pyramid and self-affirmations to promote psychic empowerment.

Suggested Reading:

Slate, Joe H., and Carl Llewellyn Weschcke: *Llewellyn Complete Book of Psychic Empowerment—Tools and Techniques*, Llewellyn, 2011.

Astral Body (aka Astral Vehicle): The extra-biological part of our being, which exists as a conscious, intelligent, and indestructible entity, is the third *Vehicle* ("upward" in the general scheme) or level of consciousness, also called the Desire or Emotional Body, or Emotional "Envelope." In the process of incarnation, the astral vehicle is composed of the planetary energies in their aspects to one another to form a matrix for the physical body. This matrix is, in a sense, the true *horoscope* guiding the structure of the body and defining karmic factors.

The Astral Vehicle is the Lower Self of Emotion, Imagination, Thinking, Memory and Will—all the functions of the mind in response to sensory perception and emotional reaction. It is the field of dreams and the subconscious mind. It is the vehicle for most psychic activities including the "spirit" or *Surviving Personality* following death of the physical body.

Yet, a distinction must be made: The Physical Body is the field of ordinary conscious mind and the Astral is that of the sub-conscious mind, and a doorway to the super-conscious mind and the collective unconscious. It is the vehicle of astral projection and the Shamanic Journey, the means of exploration of the Inner Worlds.

Astral Projection and Astral Travel: (Also see out-of-body experience [OBE])It is desirable to treat these two subjects together because of the confusion in terminology over the years. Astral projection is a particular state of consciousness in which the astral body is perceived as separating from the physical and is able to travel on the astral plane, obtain information, communicate with other beings, consciously experience distant realities, and return to the physical with full memory. In most situations, we are interested in using the astral plane to explore the non-physical universe and to influence physical actions. Still anchored in the physical body, we make use of various OBE procedures to do these things. In most cases, it is vital to set specific goals, and it is through such work that we do gain skills, train our astral "muscles," and grow in consciousness. Among Spiritualists, it is referred to as "spirit leaving the body."

It is commonly thought that the astral body separates from the physical during sleep, but does not travel. Non-physical movement in the familiar physical world is more likely to involve the Etheric body than the astral. But, the astral plane is not the physical world, and it lacks the "solidity" of the physical plane even though there is replication of physical structures as astral images. However, things may appear on the astral that are not in the physical. The etheric is the energy double of the physical body, able to function separately from the physical body while connected to it with the "silver cord" that transfers energy and consciousness between the two. The etheric body can travel anywhere in the physical world, moving with the speed of thought, and can interact with the physical in a limited manner.

In recent metaphysical thinking, it is more often believed that the Astral Body does not *spatially* leave the physical body because it is not really an independent "body" but is the sub-conscious mind and "moves" within the field of consciousness without moving at all. Consciousness is everywhere, and in consciousness you can be anywhere. To the extent you want a body, you need to create a "Body of Light" in your imagination and then just imagine it doing what you want, going where you want.

Suggested Reading:

Bruce, Robert, and Brian Mercer: *Mastering Astral Projection* book and CD companion, Llewellyn, 2004.

Phillips, Osborne: *Astral Projection Plain and Simple—the Out-of-Body Experience,* Llewellyn, 2003.

Denning, Melita, and Osborne Phillips: *Practical Guide to Astral Projection, the Out-of-Body Experience,* Llewellyn, 2001.

Goldberg, Bruce: *Astral Voyages, Mastering the Art of Interdimensional Travel,* Llewellyn, 2002.

McCoy, Edain: *Astral Projection for Beginners—Six Techniques for Traveling to Other Realms,* Llewellyn, 1999.

Slate, Joe H., and Carl Llewellyn Weschcke: *Astral Projection for Psychic Empowerment,* Llewellyn, 2012.

Webster, Richard: *Astral Travel for Beginners, Transcend Time and Space with Out-of-Body Experiences,* Llewellyn, 2002.

Aura: An egg-shaped sphere of energy extending two to three feet beyond the physical body and viewed by clairvoyants in colorful layers that may be "read" and interpreted.

It includes layers outward from the physical: the Etheric, Astral, Mental, and Spiritual bodies. The aura is also known as the "magical mirror of the universe" in which our inner activities of thought and feeling are perceived in colors. It is also the matrix of planetary forces that shapes and sustains the physical body and the lower personality.

Clairvoyants may analyze the aura in relation to health, ethics and spiritual development, and the aura can be shaped and its surface made to reflect psychic attacks back to their origin.

Suggested Reading:

Andrews, Ted: *How to See and Read the Aura,* Llewellyn, 2006.

Slate, Joe H.: *Aura Energy for Health, Healing and Balance,* Llewellyn, 1999.

Webster, Richard: *Aura Reading for Beginners, Develop Your Psychic Awareness for Health and Success,* Llewellyn, 2002.

Aura Massage: An energy interaction in which the energies enveloping the physical body are massaged in the absence of physical touch.

Aura PK: A procedure in which aura energy is used to induce psychokinesis (PK).

Aura Seeing: The perception of the aura is a major step in psychic sensory development. Its value in health analysis and healing is immense. Mark Smith in his book, *Auras: See Them in Only 60 Seconds!,* he breaks this instruction down into a few easy steps:

- Stand the subject eighteen inches to two feet in front of a bare white wall. Avoid walls with colors or patterns. (Joe Slate in his *Aura Energy for Health, Healing and Balance* suggests that you place a small shiny object such as a thumb tack or adhesive dot on the wall a few inches to the upper left or right of the subject.)
- Use indirect lighting—natural ambient daylight, if possible. Avoid fluorescent light or direct sunlight.
- View the subject from at least ten feet away.
- Ask the subject to relax, breathe deeply, and rock gently from side to side with hands unclasped at his or her side.
- Look past the subject's head and shoulders and focus on the wall behind.
- Avoid looking at the subject, concentrating instead on the texture of the wall or the shiny object behind him or her, *using your peripheral rather than direct vision.*

- As you look past the outline of the body, you will see a band of fuzzy light around the subject, about one-quarter inch to one-half inch in depth. This is the *etheric* aura.
- Continue to look past the outline of the body, and you should see the subject as if he or she is illuminated from behind, sometimes with a bright yellow or silver color. One side might glow more strongly or slowly pulsate. Auras rarely are uniform.
- As you progress you will soon see a second, larger band of light three inches to two feet around the body. This is the astral aura. It is usually darker and more diffuse than the etheric.
- Joe Slate says that once you see the aura you should shift your attention from the shiny object to the aura and observe its various characteristics. Should the aura begin to fade away, shift your focus back to the shiny object, and repeat the procedure.

Suggested Reading:

Andrews, Ted: *How to See and Read the Aura,* Llewellyn, 2006.

Slate, Joe H.: *Aura Energy for Health, Healing and Balance,* Llewellyn, 1999.

Slate, Joe H., and Carl Llewellyn Weschcke: *Astral Projection for Psychic Empowerment,* Llewellyn, 2012.

Smith, Mark: *Auras: See Them in Only 60 Seconds!,* Llewellyn, 2002.

Automatic Writing: A procedure designed to access subconscious sources of information through effortless, spontaneous writing. It is generally considered a form of Channeling in which a person, sometimes in trance, writes or even keyboards messages generally believed to originate with spiritual beings, or with aspects of the subconscious mind. Typically the hand holding a writing pen rests lightly upon a sheet of blank paper and is *allowed* to write spontaneously. Not infrequently, meaningless scribble will precede meaningful writing that becomes the channel between consciousness and the information source.

Also, studied as a procedure to access subconscious sources through spontaneous and relaxed writing.

Suggested Reading:

Wiseman, Sara: *Writing the Divine—How to Use Channeling for Soul Growth and Healing,* Llewellyn, 2009.

Awakening Dormant Powers: The importance of this is the realization that we do have innate power, potential strengths and capabilities that can and should be developed to fulfill the wholeness of our being. No matter what we may name it, we are programmed for greatness but like any other potential it is up to us individually to activate each and all of that is potential to become all that we can be.

Backster, Cleve: 1924–2013, was an interrogator for the CIA who connected a polygraph (lie-detector) to live plants and claimed that his experiments proved both that plants "feel pain" when burned and have ESP to sense in advance the good and the bad of forthcoming experiments. Backster's work was inspired by that of physicist Jagadish Chandra Bose who demonstrated that plants grew better when harmonious music was part of their environment.

Becoming Connected: Humans are complex beings—physically and emotionally, socially, and mentally, psychologically and spiritually—rich in our potential but most are too **disconnected** to bring that potential into realization. By recognizing, and accepting, the self-empowering potential existing in everyone, that potential itself rejects failure. Mastery of specific empowerment techniques initiates a growth interaction with unbounded possibilities, activating empowerment processes within while rejecting and reversing disempowering processes that impede our growth.

Self-realization depends on becoming connected to the powers within and beyond. Belief in Self ignites the process of internal growth and connection. Self-unification and self-empowerment leads to growth and self-realization. Self-understanding, self-discipline, and the rejection of distortion and division from outside influences—mostly those with strong emotional impact distorting the self-empowering process.

Self-empowerment through the Lifelong Plan for Success overcomes such self-division. Neither the limitations of heredity nor the adverse effect of environmental influences can deny the empowered self and its capacity to overcome growth barriers.

The Lifelong Plan for Success recognizes the self-empowering potential existing in everyone. It can be used to accelerate personal growth and achieve an endless range of personal goals while contributing to the common good. The plan begins with a Preliminary Exercise that builds self-esteem and establishes a positive mind-set, both of which are essential to the lifelong plan. These essentials, however, must emerge from within: they cannot be externally assigned. Once generated through regular practice of appropriate mental or verbal dialogue, they become a dynamic force that sustains a driving life-style of success. Self-dialogue is engaged either in whole or in part as the first step of the plan that can then be continued at intervals throughout the day.

Beginning, The: It is important to understand evolution as a continuous process of Challenge and Response in relation to Self-empowerment. "In God's image" does not mean in any external appearance. Or that humans, angels, other beings, or even physical matter and the physical world were "created" as they appear today, or as they were in some past glory,

While evolution moves within a multi-level scheme in which a series of matrices function as "next steps" building upon the past, those steps work as experimental "trial and error" from which the "better" survived and went on while others met a *dead end*. There is a spiritual impulse, a kind of spiritual guidance that is relentless and continuous, but becomes increasingly *participatory* as humans evolve into "co-creators." For all we know, that may lead to an eventual merger of human with the robots and drones of their creation. Along with replacement parts that are improvements on their processors, physical immortality may be achieved. On the other hand, self-empowerment may lead to some form of self-regeneration. Be open to all possibilities.

Believing Enables Seeing: Belief in possibilities opens the "Doors of Perception." Denial of possibilities is self-blinding to the opportunities of growth and development. All is possible to the Open Mind.

Big Bang: The name of the present concept of the creation for the physical universe believed to have occurred 13.8 billion years ago. Since that moment, the universe continues to expand. Note: In this theory the physical universe is the final step in the sequential process following the creation of the greater Cosmos, inclusive of the non-physical planes and dimensions (astral, mental, etc.) Different theories posit different numbers for these "higher" planes—seven, ten, twelve, or more.

Big Questions: The suggestion that psychic powers should not be wasted answering "little" personal questions about lotteries, romance, etc., but should instead focus on Bigger questions dealing with the Meaning of Life, the Nature of the Creative Process, the Quest for World Peace, etc.

Born Again, to be: While this expression applies primarily to Christian Evangelical practices involving adult baptism in water (often total immersion), the intent is to induce an ecstatic, even an out-of-body experience of union with deific power. In the esoteric sense, being born again is to unite the Lower and Middle Selves with the Higher Self. In Magickal terms, it is the union with one's Holy Guardian Angel while in Jungian terms is the Integrated Psyche.

Bottomless Pool Ritual: A practice of tossing a ring or other object representing a relationship into a certain pool believed by some to be bottomless as a gesture to fully disengage a no longer viable relationship and extinguish its residual effects. See Disengagement Toss Procedure.

Causal Self: Basic to esoteric (occult) science is the recognition that each person has not just one but many "bodies" (vehicles or envelopes) or levels of consciousness, substance, and energy variously working together as a composite. As physically incarnate beings, we are primarily focused in the physical/etheric body but we are also simultaneously functioning in the astral (emotional), mental, and causal bodies. Of far less concern for us at this stage of our being is a second composite of still higher bodies functioning independently of the first composite.

As the alternate name indicates, the astral is the *vehicle* for our emotionality. And just as the name suggests, the mental is the vehicle for our mentality, while the causal is the vehicle for what we commonly think of as our spirituality. It can be said that the basic lessons of esoteric science and magickal practice are how to focus, experience, and operate in and with these bodies, thus turning them into vehicles of purposeful activity at (not <u>on</u>) each level or *plane* of our whole being as contained in this first composite.

We can't explore all the details of this in a single entry in this glossary. Most readers are somewhat familiar with the "out-of-body" experience otherwise known as *Astral Projection* in which the focus of consciousness is centered within the astral vehicle which can then "travel" (but not in the same manner as the physical body moves about) to experience and act in this non-physical dimension. But, remember, in our emotionality, we already experience, act, and react through our astral "self." Likewise, through our mentality, we do function in and through our mental self.

But "feeling" and "thinking" are not the whole story for these bodies any more than "walking about" is the whole story for the physical body, and—by now—it should be clear all function together but in different degrees of awareness and <u>willful</u> intention. Will is the primary function of the Causal Self, and integration of the physical/energy, emotional and mental bodies are spiritual will is the goal of incarnation and hence of all esoteric, magickal, and "spiritual" practice.

I placed that word, spiritual in quotes because it is one of the most misunderstood and misused terms. We are Spirit—<u>not</u> a spirit—but SPIRIT. Spirit, like Consciousness, extends everywhere even as we function as individual conscious and spiritual entities. Spirit and Consciousness function in all our bodies and through Spirit and Consciousness we can potentially function at all levels and depths of the Cosmos.

But our concern is with Spirit expressed through WILL in the Causal Self. Will means purpose, and to function as the Causal Self means we should have a Vision of our purpose in each and all the lives we live. To gain that vision requires the integration, *under Will,* of all the lower selves, and with that consciousness becomes centered in the Causal Self. The Causal Self carries the essence of all previous lives and thus is the summation of all we've been and are.

The Causal Self is NOT the Soul. The Ultimate Individuality that we mean by the word *Soul* is part of a yet higher composite— but we can refer to the Causal Self as the "Son" of the Soul.

One great difficulty arises because spirituality is thought to be the province of religion, and the institutions of religion limit themselves and their adherents to rigid theological interpretations of scriptures written down long ago within specific cultural environments vastly different than today. Spirituality is not religion but involves study of the higher levels of the psyche and an understanding of their role in the growth of the Whole Person and their beneficial applications to personal life and cosmic relationship.

See also the Consciousness Model in the Conscious Entry.

Chakras: These are etheric/astral energy centers located in the aura on the surface of the etheric double and functioning through etheric/astral connections to exchange particular energies between the physical and non-physical bodies, the psyche, and the higher sources of energy associated with the planets, the solar system, and the cosmos. They are interfaces between Mind and Body.

There are seven traditional "master" chakras located along the spine from its base to above the head, and dozens of minor ones located in such places as the palms of the hands, soles of the feet, joints of arms and legs, and just about any place traditionally adorned with jewelry.

Chakras are whirling centers of energy associated with particular areas of the body. In Yogic/Tantric practice, *Muladhara* is located at the base of the spine and is the source of *Kundalini* and the power used in sex magic to raise consciousness and create thought forms to carry pre-determined objectives. *Svadhisthna* is located at the sacrum. *Muladhara* and *Svadhisthna* are linked to the physical body. *Manipura* is located at the solar plexus. *Muladhara*, *Svadhisthna*, and *Manipura* are together associated as the Personality, and their energies can be projected through the solar plexus in such psychic phenomena as rapping, ectoplasm, and the creation of familiars. *Manipura* is linked to the lower astral body. *Anahata* is located at the heart level and is associated with group consciousness. *Vishuddha* is located at the throat and is associated with clairvoyance. *Anahata* and *Ajna are linked to the higher astral body. Ajna* is located at the brow and is associated with clairvoyance. *Sahasrara* is located at the crown and is associated with spiritual consciousness. *Anahata, Vishuddha, and Sahasrara* are together associated as the spiritual self.

These master, or major, chakras are as follows. While we are listing some correspondences to planets, colors and the Kabbalistic sephiroth, there is considerable debate about these and the correlations cannot be specific because the chakras and the sephiroth involve two different systems. Likewise, although not listed, there are differences between both these systems and those of Oriental martial arts and healing systems.

Base Chakra—*Muladhara*, base of spine, color red, associated planet Saturn, Sephirah Malkuth, associated Tattwa *Prithivi*, symbol of the element of Earth. Sense of Smell.

Sacral Chakra—*Svadhisthana*, genital area, color orange, associated planet Jupiter or Moon, Sephirah Yesod, associated Tattva *Apas*, symbol of the element of Water. Sense of Taste.

Solar Plexus Chakra—*Manipura*, solar plexus just above the navel, color yellow, associated planet Mars, Sephiroth: none suggested, associated Tattva *Tejas*, symbol of the element of Fire. Sense of Sight

Heart Chakra—*Anahata*, heart, color green, associated planet Sun or Venus, sephirah Tiphareth, associated Tattva *Vayu*, symbol of the element of air. Sense of Touch.

Throat Chakra—*Vishuddha,* throat, color blue, associated planet Mercury, Sephirah Daath, associated Tattva *Akasha,* symbol of the element of Spirit. Sense of Hearing.

Brow Chakra—*Ajna* (the Third Eye), brow (just above and between the eyes), color indigo, associated planet Moon, Sephiroth Chokmah and Binah. Sense of Intuition.

Crown Chakra—*Sahasrara,* color violet, associated planet none, Sephirah Kether. Sense of Empathy.

The following chart is a simplification of the primary chakra system.

No.	Common Name	Sanskrit Name	Location[2]	Color[1] or Petals
1	Base	Muladhara	Base of Spine[5]	Red
2	Sacral	Svadhist-hana	Over Spleen	Orange
3	Solar Plexus	Manipura	Over Navel	Yellow
4	Heart	Anahata	Over Heart	Green
5	Throat	Vishuddha	Throat	Blue
6	Brow	Ajna	Brow	Indigo
7	Crown	Sahasrara	Top of Head	Violet

1. These are the most commonly assigned colors, but authorities differ.
2. These are the most commonly assigned locations, but authorities differ. Instead of the Solar Plexus, Theosophists identify it with the Spleen, others with the Navel.
3. Commonly, this is given as two, but it is really two "wings" of 48 each.
4. Most commonly, it is identified as a thousand petaled lotus. The crown chakra has 960 spokes plus another 12 in its center which is gleaming white with gold at its core.
5. Between anus and perineum.
6. Again, there are disagreements among authorities. Remember that there is no direct physical connection between the etheric chakras and the physical body.

Source: Slate, Joe H., and Carl Llewellyn Weschcke: *Llewellyn Complete Book of Psychic Empowerment—Tools and Techniques,* Llewellyn, 2011.

For specific detail, see each of the individual listings alphabetically by their Sanskrit Name.

Suggested Reading:

Judith, Anodea: *Wheels of Life, A User's Guide to the Chakra System,* Lewellyn 1999.

Mumford, Jonn: *Chakra and Kundalini Workbook, Psycho-spiritual Techniques for Health, Rejuvenation, Psychic Powers and Spiritual Rejuvenation,* Llewellyn, 2002.

Challenge and Response: The concept of Response in relation to Challenge was developed by historian Arnold Toynbee to theorize about the rise and fall of civilizations, but we also apply it to the story of Evolution. Evolution happens in response to challenge. It happens both to the human species and to the individual person who in turn reflects back to the species in spirals of change, development, and growth. Some changes are precipitated by long term Cosmic and Solar cycles, others by shorter Zodiacal and Planetary cycles. These are beyond our control, although knowledge and understanding allows us to prepare for the future and consciously "swim with the tide" rather than struggle against it. Doing so has both universal and individual benefits that are beyond the purpose of this book.

Nevertheless, Challenge and Response is the story of life as well as of evolution. Understanding and anticipating inevitable challenges in the journey of life allows you to prepare response in advance of need and thus succeed against all obstacles. Knowing the future is the key to success.

Channels of Power: A distinguishing characteristic of any application of "Power" is *FOCUS.* Without focus, power is wasted. Think of a waterfall—it may be beautiful to see, and even to hear, but unless the power of falling water is focused and applied, that natural resource for electric power is wasted.

The same is true of any application whether it be Mind power (concentration), Physical power (labor, machinery), Emotional power (drama, ritual), of Psychic power (psychokinesis, clairvoyance, divination, etc.). "Power" is everywhere, but is perceived through *Movement,* increased through Concentration, and applied through *Focus.*

Citizen Democracy: Democracy is a system of government in which ALL the qualified people within a "polity" (a defined unit such as a state or city, or other grouping) are directly involved or represented in the development and administration of policies. Essentially, "Citizen Democracy" by-passes political parties, churches, corporations, labor unions, and other organized "special interests" and proclaimed authorities to vote directly for its representative without interference or "guidance" other than debate among themselves. It was the founding ideal of America.

Clairvoyance: Clairvoyance simply means "clear seeing," the implication being that the particular *psychic vision* involved reveals the hidden nature of an object, event, or person.

When we look at any object with our physical eyes we are limited to its three ordinary physical dimensions. We are not only unaware of the sub-atomic aspects functioning in the object, but many of us are not truly observant of the finer details of color, shape, odor, taste and feel and of **the *resident consciousness* fundamental to the object itself.** There is consciousness even in a brick, and more so in a blade of grass, a swimming fish, etc. And, where there is consciousness, there is *life. The universe is alive at all levels and in every dimension.*

We have to learn the art and practice of clairvoyance just as we do any other human skill, and there's a science to that. We believe its development should be encouraged as a matter of growth and movement into wholeness. We believe psychic empowerment should be your goal because you should be an empowered person. There will be many practical benefits to your developed clairvoyance as well—extending your inter-dimensional perceptions of reality means that you see more and are better able to judge the meaning and value of your inter-actions with the complex world in which you live. It gives you a greater foundation for the decisions you must make in life. You will gain deeper insights into your own physical and emotional reactions to both external events and internal issues.

On the physical level, we perceive with our physical senses. As we focus consciousness at higher levels, we don't perceive with "sense organs" but through awareness of the substance and changing vibrations emitted from the object of our attention. The higher we ascend in awareness, the greater our vision. At the astral level, we are aware of a fourth dimension, and at the mental level we perceive five dimensions.

Both clairaudience and clairvoyance, and other psychic skills, have been induced through hypnosis and self-hypnosis showing them to be innate to the human psyche.

Clairvoyance can dramatically expand our world of awareness and perception of spatially distant realities, uncover critical sources of new knowledge and power. Precognition can provide advanced awareness allowing us to prepare for future events and, sometimes, to influence or prevent them altogether. While some future events seem to be unalterable destinies, others may be probabilities subject to our intervention. Through precognition we are empowered to eliminate negative probabilities while accentuating the positive. Given precognitive knowledge, we can generate a powerful expectancy of success that literally transforms probabilities into realities. We *can* literally create the future of our choice.

Dr. Joe H. Slate, working at Athens (Alabama) State University, shows an emerging body of evidence that ESP, rather than an unexplained extension of sensory perception, is a fine-tuned manifestation of the non-biological or spiritual nature of our being, and includes interactions with spirit realm.

"As part of the unfoldment of the human intellect into omniscience, the development occurs at a certain stage of human evolution of fully-conscious, positive clairvoyance. This implies an extension, which can be hastened by means of self-training, of the normal range of visual response to include both physical rays beyond the violet and, beyond them again, the light of the super physical worlds . . . It is important to differentiate between the passive psychism of the medium, and even the extra-sensory perception (ESP of parapsychology), and the positive clairvoyance of the student of occultism. This later, completely under the control of the will and used in full waking consciousness, is the instrument of research . . . to enter and explore the Kingdom of the Gods."(Hodson, Geoffrey: *The Kingdom of the Gods*, 1953, Theosophical Pub. House, Madras, India)

Suggested Reading:

Slate, Joe H., and Carl Llewellyn Weschcke: *Clairvoyance for Psychic Empowerment—the Art and Science of "Clear Seeing" Past the Illusions of Space and Time and Self-Deception*, Llewellyn, 2013.

Slate, Joe H., and Carl Llewellyn Weschcke: *Psychic Empowerment for Everyone—You Have the Power, Learn How to Use it*, Llewellyn, 2009.

Co-Creators: (Self-Empowerment) We are coming to realize that all along we have been unconscious co-creators, and now we have the growing realization that we must become <u>conscious</u> co-creators, broadly aware of our own transgressions of natural law, or else the human experiment will end in failure. In this New Age, we come to know that we are evolving toward becoming gods and co-creators, with the powers to create and destroy, but our "salvation" can only come through the exercise of personal responsibility and of participation for the good of the community rather than following corrupt and ideologically motivated politicians and self-serving elitist "leaders."

The Deity Within each human is the unconscious Life Force and the Conscious Presence of the Creative Force. The Deity Within is the source of our free will and conscious creativity. It is the Deity Within that makes us a "Co-Creator"—even though presently and still mostly unconscious and unaware and hence "blind" and thus the source of many of our own destructive actions that bring harm and terror to other humans and harm and terror to the environment that is the global home we share with all beings on this planet.

Only by becoming conscious do we become constructive rather than destructive. Only by *becoming more than we are* do we fulfill our obligation to the Creative Force that programmed the evolutionary drama from the Beginning. It is by making conscious the many blind forces within our body and psyche through the practices of Invocation and Evocation of associated deities that we become wholly "all that we can be" to fulfill the role assigned to us as co-creators.

All esoteric teachings have been dedicated to advancing humans as "Gods in the Making." This is the Dawning of the Age of Aquarius, when East and West come together in the New Age of Awakening Humanity. The call is to everybody, not the elite few. Everyone must be responsible both to himself and his neighbor as brother and sister, not as leader and follower. We begin now.

Suggested Reading:

Culling, Louis T., and Weschcke, Carl Llewellyn: *The Complete Magick Curriculum of the Secret Order G.B.G.*, Llewellyn, 2010.

Collective Unconscious: A kind of group mind inherited from all our ancestors and including all the memories and knowledge acquired by humans. It is believed to exist on the higher astral and lower mental planes and to be accessible by the super consciousness through the personal subconscious mind in deep trance states induced through hypnosis, self-hypnosis, meditation and guided meditation. The ability to call up infinite information and integrate it into your present life needs is of enormous benefit—similar to but beyond the capacity of any present-day Internet Search Engine.

It is the function of the Personal Consciousness to bridge to the collective tribal, racial, cultural, national, mythic, even planetary memories and the world of archetypes of the Universal Consciousness, making them available to the Psyche mainly through the Sub-Conscious Mind.

The memories of all of humanity, perhaps of more than human, and inclusive of the archetypes. The contents of the collective unconscious seem to progress from individual memories to universal memories as the person grows in his or her spiritual development and integration of the whole being. There is some suggestion that this progression also moves from individual memories through various groups or small collectives—family, tribe, race, and nation—so the character of each level is reflected in consciousness until the individual progresses to join in group consciousness with all humanity. This would seem to account for some of the variations of the universal archetypes each person encounters in life. Also see Akashic Records

Suggested Reading:

Dale: *The Subtle Body—An Encyclopedia of Your Energetic Anatomy*

Conscious Awareness: The "objective" consciousness, i.e. the "aware" consciousness with which we exercise control and direction over our "awake" lives.

With your Conscious Mind you can take charge of the great resource of the Sub-Conscious Mind. Information is constantly coming in, more than you can take full cognizance of, and so much of it is automatically diverted to the Sub-Conscious Mind. The Sub-Conscious Mind is more than a passive collection of memories, it is also your personal connection to the Universal Consciousness containing all that is from the very Beginning. Within this are all the potentials for all that you may become. This includes what we call "powers"—generally thought of as *psychic* powers. But before these powers are fully meaningful, they must be developed to become consciously directed <u>skills</u>.

But wait, as they say in television commercials, *there's more!* All that is the Conscious-Mind—with its magnificent potentials for rational thinking, for creative development, for abstract analysis, for organization, for the use of imagination, for planning, and all those skills that make it possible for the human being to manage the resources of the natural world—rose out of the Sub-Conscious Mind. Outwardly, that's what we do; inwardly, we manage Consciousness, because that is what we are. In particular, the job of the Conscious Mind is to manage the Sub-Consciousness and develop its innate powers into skills that we can then deploy consciously with awareness and intention to work with the Great Plan of evolving life. In another sense, it is to make Conscious the Unconscious through careful management of its resources.

When you take deliberate charge of the subconscious, your life takes on a new dimension of both meaning and power. Rather than a risky existential leap into a dark cavern of the unknown, your probe of the subconscious is an "inward leap of power" that clarifies the nature of your existence and reaffirms your destiny for greatness and meaning. It's a leap of progress that not only accelerates your growth, but guides you toward greater happiness and fulfillment as well.

As we became more aware of ourselves as individuals and operated more in the Conscious Mind, developing personal memory, rationality and new ways of thinking, we perceived ourselves in relationship to the natural world rather than as part of it. We learned to store knowledge in our memory rather than having immediate "feeling" access to it. Rather than relating internally to the rhythms of Sun, Moon and Planets, we saw them externally and developed sciences of astronomy, astrology and agriculture. And we became aware of linear time.

Nature can show the ways to knowledge and understanding of her secret powers when you learn to listen. The Sun, the Moon, and the Planets, too, have powers to share with Man in his wholeness.

As Manager, it is the job of the Conscious Mind to know, understand, and direct all these resources. It's the most exciting, most gratifying, most rewarding and grandest job you will ever have, and it's one that is yours forever! You can't be fired, nor can you abdicate.

Consciousness: Everything that is, out of which Energy and Matter manifest and Life evolves. Consciousness is the beginning of all things and part of the trinity of Consciousness, Energy and Matter. "Consciousness just IS!" We can't really define consciousness because we are nothing but consciousness and consciousness cannot really define itself. "I AM THAT I AM."

Our personal consciousness includes all states of awareness and our experiences of fear, love, hope, desire, happiness, sadness, depression, ecstasy, mystical union, etc. We experience connectedness through consciousness

Consciousness is not a "thing" nor is it a function of a "thing" called the brain. Killing the brain doesn't kill consciousness but it limits its expression in the familiar physical world. Consciousness is expressed through the brain, but it exists outside the brain. Consciousness acts upon the physical world, like a "force," as in telekinesis.

There are three levels of consciousness:

1. I for Instinct, a function of the lower subconscious

2. I for Intelligence, a function of the ordinary consciousness

3. I for Intuition, a function of the super-consciousness

The ancients were far more sophisticated in their understanding of "consciousness" than we give them credit. Moderns tend to judge everything from the background of technology and material sciences, believing that the lack of advanced scientific instrumentation means a lack of understanding about "how things really work."

In more than one sense, today's science is still catching up with the "Ancient Wisdom" which expressed understanding of the universe through myth and symbol. The single greatest difference is that the "old" wisdom was the *property* of the few and today we extend our knowledge to nearly any and every one. Modern education seeks to give everyone a basic knowledge of physical science, although there is a serious gap when it comes to "spiritual science."

One great difficulty arises because spirituality is thought to be the province of religion, and the institutions of religion limit themselves and their adherents to rigid theological interpretations of scriptures written down long ago within specific cultural environments vastly different than today. The truth is that spirituality is not religion but involves study of the higher levels of the psyche and an understanding of their role in the growth of the Whole Person and their beneficial applications to personal life and cosmic relationship.

CONSCIOUSNESS MODEL (the general esoteric concept)

Logos   Adi   Father, Son and Holy Ghost
Anupadaka   Son and Holy Ghost
Atma   Holy Ghost
Monad—   Lower Adi
        Anupadaka
        Higher Atma
Spirit   -   Atma
Ego, Incarnating Individuality, the Higher Self—Atma, the Spirit, or the Will
        Buddhi, the Intuition, or Wisdom
        Manas, the Abstract Mind, or Activity

Soul's Vehicles :

Causal Body (Higher Mental)—To evolve with— Ideals and Abstract Thought.
Mental Body (Lower Mental)—To think with— Ideas and Concrete Thoughts
Astral Body (Upper and Lower)—To feel with— Emotions and Desires
Physical Body (incl. Etheric Body)—To act with—Sensorial Reactions and Actions
Personality, the Lower Self—   Lower Manas, Concrete Mind
Mental Body
Astral, Desire Nature   Astral Body
Physical, Functioning Body
Physical/Etheric Body
Body Consciousness-Autonomic nervous system
(Source: Jinarajadasa: *First Principles of Theosophy*, 1861)

Controlled Laboratory Research: In the Preface to this book, Dr. Slate has shown that consistent research programs have validated the existence of paranormal phenomena and powers and makes the case for further research to help us understand these greater dimensions of the universe and of the human psyche. The scientific method consists of these stages:

    1. The Development of a Comprehensive Theory that seems to account for the observed elements.

2. The Design of Laboratory Experiments to test the validity of the Theory.

3. Observation and Isolation of those elements shown by Experiment, or additional Observations, to violate the Theory.

4. Repeat until the Theory consistently accounts for all the Elements.

5. Test the Theory outside Laboratory Conditions in the Real World.

6. Repeat as necessary. Until proven in the Real World, a Theory is only reasonable speculation.

Cosmic Multi-Dimensional Reality: Both the Cosmos and our Selves are multi-dimensional, and we are connected one to the other, and to each other across many layers and levels of consciousness. Mind provides the direction and means to creating and exploring these connections, i.e. "Thoughts create Reality," but you must expand your awareness to penetrate the deeper meanings and determine the course of your own personal and collective life. This New Age itself brings opportunities for self-empowerment, expanded awareness, and unlimited spiritual growth. Indeed, it is a time for a global spiritual revolution.

Cosmos: The Cosmos is not to be confused with the physical universe, which is limited to the single physical plane, while the Cosmos is inclusive of the physical and all other planes, and is far more complex and infinitely larger than what we ordinarily see and think.

Many esoteric writers chart a Cosmos of eight dimensions within seven planes of manifestation, plus three more planes beyond manifestation that guide the process, and three more above and outside of manifestation from which it is sourced. This corresponds with the structure of the Kabbalistic Tree of Life with the seven plus three Sephiroth and the three levels outside manifestation.

Creation Myth: Creation myths reflect the natural environment in particular geographic areas. Is the local climate predominantly hot, cold, wet, or dry? Is it characterized by mountains or deserts; forests or savannahs? Are there active volcanoes, frequent earth movement, devastating storms? What of the natural resources—is water plentiful or scarce, are there rivers across broad areas; Is the area seriously dependent on monsoons to supply needed water? is the area rich in food and is that food vegetative, animal, or fish? Are there dangerous animals? And, what of human marauders—are they painfully recurrent?

The answers to these questions form the background of the creation myths. Myths are the stories that fill in the gaps between what we know and what don't yet know. Myths make sense of the world of experience and provide structure upon which culture grows. Myths are created by the seekers of cosmological understanding about the origins of the universe and of man.

Whether through dreams and visions, or intuition or the voices of spirit, the seekers formulated stories about creation and mankind's relation to the forces and intelligence behind creation. These creation myths were peopled with supernatural beings fulfilling for the tribe and the culture those roles already familiar to the people: Father, Mother, Child, Friend, Foe, Predator, Defender, Healer, Leader, Arbiter. And those who communicated with spirits, interpreted dreams, understood signs and omens, were the shamans as the cultures expanded and continued to evolve.

These supernatural beings became gods and goddesses "ruling" the various natural, biological and social functions, and then the gods themselves sought additional specific knowledge and powers to help their "children," the people of the culture. And, nearly always, there was the person set apart from others that could travel the inner dimensions of time and space—the shaman who spoke with the deities and answered the people's questions about why things were as they were and how they could be changed.

All creation myths have certain similarities, but each culture's mythology reflects the nature of reality as it is perceived by the people and, in particular, those "seekers" attempting to explain the nature of the world and the relation of humanity to the forces of the universe and life.

Crumpled Leaf Technique: A strategy based on the capacity of a leaf to function as an instrument of power when removed from the tree.

Crumpled Paper Technique: A procedure in which a crumpled sheet of paper provides the external stimulus for activating psychic faculties.

Crystal Ball: A round ball of quartz crystal or glass used as a focal point in scrying. Gazing at the ball, one enters into a trance-like state where dream like scenes and symbols are seen and interpreted. Similar aids are the Magic Mirror, a pool of black ink, a piece of obsidian.

> Suggested Reading:
> Andrews, Ted: *Crystal Balls and Crystal Bowls, Tools for Ancient Scryingand Modern Seership*, Llewellyn, 2002.
> Cunningham, Scott: *Divination for Beginners, Reading the Past, Present and Future*, Llewellyn, 2003.
> Slate, Joe H., and Carl Llewellyn Weschcke: *Psychic Empowerment— Tools and Techniques*, Llewellyn, 2011.

Crystal Clearing: A procedure designed to clear the quartz crystal of all previous inscriptions or residual effects.

Crystal Dowsing: Dowsing with rods of metal (typically copper) with quartz crystals affixed at each of the rod's elongate end.

Crystal Inscription Procedure: A procedure designed to establish an empowering interaction with a quartz crystal in an effort to focus the crystal's energies or influences on designated goals.

Crystal Pendulum: A quartz crystal affixed as a weight at the end of a chain (typically copper) or string.

Cultural Movements: When we speak of **"Movement,"** we are referencing to a unique social phenomenon involving a wide span of people focused on a single activity centered about a mostly intellectual concept. Even an artistic or literary movement is intellectually defined. A "cultural" movement contrasts with physical movement of an army, or of the mass immigration of people, or a religious movement in that movement being directed or led from "above," whereas a cultural movement is a matter of mostly individuals joining together for discussion, development, and action upon a particular idea (or ideal).

A cultural movement can turn into a political or other movement led or sponsored from "above," but then it is no longer a "democratic" inspired movement.

Death, and its Alternatives: "Death is 'a touch of the Soul which is too strong for the body'; it is a call from divinity that brooks no denial; it is the voice of the inner Spiritual Identity saying: Return to your centre, or source, for awhile and reflect upon the experiences undergone and the lessons learnt until the time comes when you return to earth for another cycle of learning, or progress and enrichment."

(Source: Pg. 78, *The Unfinished Autobiography,* by Alice Bailey, 1951, Lucis, New York.)

The imminence of death always raises questions about what—aside from the physical body—dies. Is there a soul or spirit passing into an "afterlife" and what happens next after that? Reincarnation is the major alternative to the two alternative concepts of "death as the end" and of "death releasing a soul who then resides in Heaven or Hell."

However, increasingly, we are looking for the extension of our mortality by new understanding of the health and healing processes, and the replacement of worn-out parts—joints, lungs, heart, valves, etc. As one scientist writes "Live long enough and you'll live forever."

Deism: While Deist accept that there must have been a Creator God, a fundamental difference between the Deist belief system of Washington, Franklin, and other of America's "founding fathers" and the Abrahamic religion of Christianity is that the Deist Creator has left humanity to run the show for themselves and not depend upon prayer and worship to influence or appease God. In other words, the Deist God does not intervene in human or cosmic affairs. The on-going creative process follows established "Laws of Nature" which can be intelligently observed and rationally interpreted to guide Human action. Deism is a Natural Belief System rather than a Revealed Religion defined by prophets and messengers, codified into theology and sacred books interpreted and managed by priests and religious "authorities" supposedly above natural and human law.

Deism does not reject apparent "miracles," but only that they are of Supernatural origin; Deism does not reject the apparent power of prayer, but only that it results in Divine intervention; nor does Deism reject *natural* powers that may be called *spirits, angels, gods, guides, entities,* etc.—only when they are claimed to be beyond natural law.

A few well-known Deists include Descartes, Voltaire, Bacon, Isaac Newton, Adam Smith, John Locke, Carl Friedrich Gauss, Benjamin Franklin, James Madison, Thomas Paine, Ethan Allen, Thomas Jefferson, James Watt, Max Planck, Charles Sanders Peirce, Leonardo da Vinci, Jules Verne, Neil Armstrong, Thomas Edison, and—obviously—many other intellectuals and scientists.

Contrary to recent fundamentalist claims, the United States was not founded as a "Christian nation." The American Declaration of Independence mentions God once, in Deist terms, with no reference to Moses, Jesus, the Bible, or other Religious authority. Both Presidents George Washington and John Adams officially affirmed that **"the government of the United States of America is not in any sense founded on the Christian religion."**

Devolution: *Before time began,* when the devolution of Spirit into incarnation was incomplete, there was much interaction between spiritual entities and forces and "proto"- humans. Here we had the appearance of Gods and Goddesses, elementals, angels and other forces in fundamental relationships. Here, too, were the beginnings of Magick, the foundations of spirituality and of religions with the development of symbols with their attributes and qualities and their associations of deific accessories. Thus began the long history of "correspondences" for magical control and verification of deities, entities, forces and powers. Here there are the functions of Worship as Invocation, Meditation as Evocation, Communication as the *conscious interaction between Inner and Outer, Lower and Higher, and of Humans with Deities.*

In order to bring Spirit Power down into the Mental and Astral realms to initiate effects on the Etheric/Physical level, we now have to reach up to the Spiritual. *As spiritual beings, we have to access not only the powers within but the limitless powers beyond. Magick is what Humans do.*

Before time began, the devolution of spirit into matter led towards the ultimate structure of the Universe we know today, with "layers" of Substance, Energy and Consciousness. Within this structure certain conscious entities began to function in ways that brought about an increasingly complex structure within which the evolutionary process began, and continues.

As the Evolutionary process continued those conscious entities took on specific creative functions guiding the development of Energy into Matter and Energy and Matter into Conscious forms evolving into greater and greater complexity and *Self-manifestation.* Each "higher" level of form takes on higher levels of consciousness leading toward *Self-consciousness* and *Self-realization.*

Higher levels of conscious beings assume interactive roles in the continuing evolutionary process in fulfillment of some mythic "Great Plan" of which we can have only glimmerings at this point in our own level of *Self-awareness.* Nevertheless, we "know" that there is meaning and purpose to life and being as we more consciously experience the evolutionary process becoming more specific and individualized. We are becoming *Self-knowing.*

With the advent of self-conscious humans there comes levels of awareness of the existing higher creative entities, later called "Powers," and interaction with these Powers and the natural energies resulted in the burgeoning human imagination (often aided by natural clairvoyance) forming elemental beings around natural "power" places and even historic events. Some of the higher entities became identified as *local* or *native* Gods and Goddesses, and so did lesser beings recognized as processing manifest energies and functions in the on-going creation become identified as Gnomes, Sylphs, Undines, and Salamanders, and still other names and other beings.

These were Mythic Times, and as human consciousness became more complex so did the world of human perception. Mythology "explained" creation and the phenomena of life and the world around. Legends described the nature of the Gods and Goddesses and lesser beings. Mythology was the "science" of the day.

If worldly phenomenon could be conceptualized, then the natural powers and forces could be explained in story-form, and either deified or demonized to explain their relationships to humans. If things were beneficial, the credit went to God; if they were harmful, the blame went to the Devil.

As human consciousness grew in complexity and increased awareness of the world around, and within, these Gods and Goddesses became totally human in form and ever more detailed in their functions and their appearances. Some became very specific in their representation of human function like love, attraction, reproduction; activities like fishing, hunting, farming, fighting; concepts like beauty, leadership, intelligence; natural phenomena such as thunder, lightning, rain, plant growth and other very specific functions and happenings. All could be represented by images (mostly humanoid), gender, names, colors, costume and ornaments, even postures.

And here was the beginnings of Magick, the foundation of religion, the development of symbols and their connections, and the long history of "correspondences" for magical control and verification, and the beginning of Science.

Digital Technology: Digital Technology involves the reduction of information into "bits" which are simply units of the primary digits 1 and 0 used to represent words and images. As bits, immense amounts of information can be compressed and recorded on small storage devices that can be transported electronically. The effect has enabled humans to "think small" and to "process big." The result has been the Information Age. But "Information" becomes "controlling intelligence" and as storage devices have become smaller and smaller, operational units—all essentially miniature computers—are more and more powerful and omnipresent in all the functional elements of civilization.

This is the Digital Age. Everyone knows that even though some people wish to "hold back the tide" for various reasons, good and bad, nothing short of some sort of "Armageddon" can. More and more things, gadgets, machines, processes, etc. are managed by smaller and smaller internal computers that are often connected to one another or to "central command centers" via the Internet and wireless communication. Increasingly this is a movement of individual empowerment as the units of power and resources are "brought home" under individual control.

Thus, the Digital Age is facilitating the key element of the New Age, i.e. *individual control enables self-empowerment*. Each person can have needed information, intelligence, and power to facilitate personal management of the physical elements of a Good Life. Physical empowerment slides into Psychic empowerment.

Dimensions: Each Plane or level of Reality has certain distinctive characteristics of Space, Substance, Energy, Consciousness, Nature, and "Rules of Engagement" that must be recognized as determinate for phenomena at that particular level and for efficient and effective functioning of consciousness at the chosen level. Dimensions are the distinct functional limits of each Plane. According to the esoteric teachings of Henry Laurency the increase from three dimensions at the physical plane to four at the astral, five at the mental, etc.

Disengagement Toss Procedure: A procedure designed to facilitate disengagement in a non-viable relationship and promote resolution of its residual effects by tossing a ring or other article of jewelry representing the relationship into a body of water. See Bottomless Pool Ritual.

Distance Healing: The psychic transfer of healing influences or energies from a spatial distance.

Distance Intervention: The intervention of nature's instruments of power from a spatial distance.

Distributed Practice: It has been shown that any "practice" is better undertaken in short developmental segments than in long efforts.

Divination: Prophesy and information by "paranormal" methodologies, such as:

By reading naturally produced signs ranging from the shape of clouds to the positions of planets (astrology).

By reading artificially produced signs ranging from tea leaves to the throwing of dice or dominoes.

By reading system-developed symbols such as in Numerology, the Tarot and Rune cards or the I Ching hexagrams.

By reading visions as seen in Dreams or in Trance, in Crystal and Water Gazing, Ink Wells, etc.

By reading the movement of special objects such as Divining Rods, Swinging Pendulums, Table-tipping, Hands-on Indicators (Talking Boards, Ouija™).

By the Direct Transfer of Information as in Automatic Writing, by Mediums and Channelers.

By the Direct Receipt of Information from internal levels of consciousness via Question and Answer as in Clairvoyance.

By reading and interpreting signs and impressions as in Geomancy, Graphology, Sand Reading, Crumpled Paper, etc.

By reading and interpreting life-produced indicators as in Palmistry, Facial Features, Phrenology, etc.

In each situation, something experienced is interpreted usually by means of long-established rules justified by many years of observation across many cultures. In most cases, these interpretations are supplemented by psychic factors of impressions or intuition naturally arising in either conscious or sub-conscious (trance) states.

Divination is not a game undertaken for amusement. You should only undertake any form of divination because of true need for an answer. We ask the question when it becomes *imperative* to the questioner, so imperative that it will reverberate in your mind and cause an equal reverberation in the cosmos leading to the answer given in the form of a traditional set of rules or "code" yet to be interpreted.

It is likewise important to make the question concise and clearly worded. There should be no ambiguity, and the question should confine itself to earthy, practical matters, unconcerned with issues of morality or judgment. The best question is one that can be simply answered with either a "yes" or a "no." The simpler the question, the more precise the answer. The more serious the question, the more accurate the answer.

How Divination Works. In some sense, avoiding technical details, the future already exists; but it is also important to know that your future is *not* fixed. Changes in your current situation can make changes in your future situation. At the same time, in terms of the bigger universe of which each of us is a minute part, small changes rarely have much impact on the wider future.

Nevertheless, it is *your* future we are talking about without a lot of concern about the world around us. Always there are points of leverage that, if discovered and manipulated with willed intention, can make a difference. *But, that's magic, another subject altogether.*

However, most readings are not concerned with changing the future but with answering questions about the present and near future. Please read the following few paragraphs carefully with your full attention.

Each person is surrounded by a field of energy called the "aura." Your own aura permeates your entire body and represents your feelings, your mind, and your spirit. It's all about you.

Every cell in your body contains all of the information about you—not only the present but the past and the probable future.

Not only that, but every cell also contains a hologram of the universe; that is, all knowledge is resident within each one of us, and it is ours to retrieve if we know how.

Your aura further permeates your immediate surroundings—out to about three feet—and especially things you touch. Some substances more easily absorb the auric influence than others, and wet tea leaves are especially sensitive to this influence, serving as an ideal medium for our reading. The minute particles, actually right down to the sub-atomic level, of the tea leaves or other materials being used are responsive to your energy field—including the questions and concerns you have at the moment of the reading. The more often you practice this psychic talent, the more able will your aura project the image-forming energy to the sensitive media.

It is important to realize that all divinatory systems have to connect the Conscious Mind to the Sub-Conscious and thence to the Universal Consciousness. Successful divination and, hence, our personal "psychic empowerment" depends on our abilities to consciously *channel* our questions to these *lower* realms and to take the answers into our *awakened consciousness* for their analysis and application.

Divination, in contrast to "fortune telling" is not a *passive* mere acceptance of answers from the "cards" or the "stones" or the "stars" or other objects that are converted into "mediums," but uses those them in *inter-active* communication between the Unconscious and the Conscious Mind. The "language" of that communication—ultimately—is symbolism but the symbols themselves are not static but instead constantly evolve in response to "the times."

The challenge for the diviner is to use signs and symbols as a frame or vehicle in asking questions, and then to newly interpret those signs and symbols conveying the answers.

Suggested Reading:

Cunningham, Scott: *Divination for Beginners—Reading the Past, Present and Future*, Lleweelyn, 2003.

Slate, Joe H., and Carl Llewellyn Weschcke: *Psychic Empowerment— Tools and Technologies*, Llewellyn, 2011.

Divine Spark: Within each person there is a connection to Source of all Creation. In between the Spark and the Source, humans have introduced intermediaries, both positive and negative but all to some extent reflecting their human creators (Moses, Mahomet) or the general influence of myth and shamanic vision. As powerful "thought forms" the images have made "history." The direct impression of the human creator's (the "messengers" and "prophets") emotions of Anger, Hate, Ambition, Love, childlike Dependence, etc. upon *their* Gods created the core of religious beliefs.

The Roman Emperor, Constantine, purposely influenced Christianity to serve his imperial ambitions, laying the foundations of militant nationalism and Western Civilization.

Dormant Potentials: Every person, through various levels of consciousness, reflects all human history in varying degrees of potential. Those potentials are variously influenced by gender, genetic and cultural heredity, previous life memories, local geo-physical factors, parental and social language, educational and other formative factors in "growing up" including today's environment the mass media. Most of the potential are reflected in character and personality but some include "native" abilities and tendencies such as artistic and musical talents, educational and career interests, and paranormal powers.

Dormant Powers: We all have "natural" powers, each subject to and capable of development into strengths and capabilities. Each "power" can be modified by intent and training. Here, we are concerned with *Psychic Powers* as the next step in expanding personal awareness and the evolving Higher Self.

Dowser's State of Awareness: It should be obvious that a "non-believing" or doubtful state of mind is unfavorable to indirect perception including those employing an intermediary object as a "medium." An *Open Mind* facilitates all forms of Perception, Discovery, Development, and Invention.

Dowsing: Psychic empathy with the natural world enabling the prac-
titioner to locate water, ores, petroleum, ley lines, etc., usually aided
by a device such as a forked stick, pendulum or a modified set of
coat hangers or L-shaped rods which will strongly respond in the
dowser's hands when walking over the physical location. Some
dowers work with a pendulum and a large-scale map and obtain
equally valid results. The practice of dowsing provides valuable development of psychic sensitivities and subconscious awareness and
communication.

Many operators using pendulums and dowsing rods use "spec-
imen samples" held in one hand or incorporated into compartments on the pendulum bob or some area on a dowsing rod. The
sample is of the material objective to the outer physical dowsing
work—water, oil, gold, nickel, etc.—and functions as a *focus* for
the inner psychic, part of the operation. Other operators simply
keep the objective in mind during the mechanical process with either pendulum or dowsing rod.

Dowsing, combined with pendulum working, has become a
useful technique in forensic work and in health diagnosis. See also
"Pendulum."

Suggested Reading:

Slate, Joe H., and Carl Llewellyn Weschcke: *Psychic Empowerment:
Tools and Techniques,* Llewellyn, 2011.

Webster, Richard: *Dowsing for Beginners, How to Find Water, Wealth
and Lost Objects,* Llewellyn, 1996.

Ecstatic States of Consciousness: While numerous sensory activities
producing mild pain or pleasure, repeated movements and sounds,
forms of bondage and sensory denial, etc. can alter the "vibratory"
levels of consciousness to create those states of excitement and
pleasure called "ecstatic," our primary interest is in those that can
then be directed to psychic perception, including the Out-of- Body
Experience, Clairvoyance, Pre-cognition, etc. One of the increasing
common methods involves extended sex beyond normal orgasm.

The value comes in *directing* the ecstatic perception to a specified target.

E-MOTION (Energy-in-Motion): Emotion is always energizing, and when directed in consciousness can produce paranormal phenomena including forms of psycho-kinesis, psychic perception, magickal actions, ghostly and poltergeist events, absent and present healing, and personal transformation.

Emotional Body, Vehicle: More commonly known as the Astral Body. The reason to discuss it as the "Emotional Body" is because its *energy* is our emotional energy. As such, it is the Power of Magick, the Power of Ambition, the Power of Love, the Source of Ecstasy in Sex, the Source of Inspiration, the Source for Healing ability, and the Energy that leads or misleads the followers in politics, religion, and mass action and reaction that are the major factors in conflicts. We need to better understand and control emotional energy.

Emotional World: Otherwise known as the "Astral World" or plane. While it is somewhat challenging to perceive a cosmological reality as an emotional "resource," that is the lesson to be learned. As previously noted, "Energy-in-Motion" is the source of Magickal Power, i.e. the power to transform physical reality. Its management is the secret behind every success story, the dynamic of personal charisma, the essential factor in successful advertising and promotion, and the bridge to personal empowerment. Emotion is difficult to understand, a challenge to manage, and a hazard to peace and harmony. Yet, it is also the "engine" of human happiness. Indeed, a challenging lesson to learn.

Empathic Telepathy: "Tune in, and drop in." Empathy is a "feeling-based" connection between people that provides a channel of communication.

Empowerment Nature Walk: A procedure designed to promote a positive interaction with Nature, typically by walking in a forest and focusing the forest's energies on designated goals.

Entanglement: A physical phenomenon that occurs at the Quantum level when pairs or groups of **particles** are generated or interact in ways such that the particles remain connected and what happens to one happens to another. In other words, they share in a single quantum state. It's the physical basis for sympathetic magick, for continuous interactive communication, and—as some claim—for a long-lasting Love Relationship resulting from the shared experience of simultaneous and multiple sexual orgasms.

Esoteric Knowledge, Esotericism: In many ways, Esotericism and Occultism are just alternative words for the same teachings, yet Esotericism is commonly perceived as more Spiritual and Eastern, and Occultism as more Magickal and Western. Both teach that the human person is more than what we believe we perceive as only the physical body, and that the physical universe is the smallest aspect of the entire Cosmos.

Neither are "religions," yet they both share common themes with religion of Spirituality, Ethical Guidance, belief in a Creator Source and many Spiritual Intermediaries and Guides, some of which can be variously evoked in service to the person, to humanity as a whole, and to all life.

What's the difference between them and religion? Esotericism and Occultism perceive the human as an evolving being intrinsic to the purpose of the Cosmos, while religions perceive the human as serving God under the dictates of priests proclaiming for themselves spiritual authority.

ESP: See extra-sensory perception

Etheric Double: The "energy twin" to the physical body that bridges from the physical to the astral. The Etheric Double is the location of the Chakras and the subtle channels connecting them and conducting Prana, Kundalini and other "supra-physical" energies deployed in Yoga for Self-Development, in the Martial Arts for extraordinary *impact* effects, and in Healing Applications.

The Etheric and Astral bodies are where most paranormal activities draw their energy and are the locations of the psychic senses.

Evolution and Development: Each person is an "agent" of Evolution, and the Development of the Person becomes the Development both of the species and society. Personal Empowerment leads to Citizen Democracy and the replacement of Big Business by small business, self-employment, and world trade. In turn, the Paranormal becomes the Normal because personal empowerment leads to the expansion of the Psyche.

Dennis Bushnell, NASA's chief research scientist at their Langley Center has written: "Humans are now responsible for the evolution of nearly everything, including themselves. . . . The ultimate impacts of all this upon human society will be massive and could "tip" in several directions." (Speech at World Futurist Society's Annual Conference July 8, 2010.)

Extra-Biological Body: An alternate name for the Astral Body.

Extra-sensory Perception (ESP): The knowledge of, or response to, events, conditions, and situations independently of known sensory mechanisms or processes. See telepathy, clairvoyance, and precognition.

An important "facilitator" for ESP is the realization that most Telepathy and Clairvoyance is perceived simply as an impression rather than something arriving with "bells and whistles" blaring. In other words, psychic senses are primarily experienced as extensions of normal sensory perception. Yes, they can be deliberately activated through various procedures, one of which is well described in Chapter Two of this book. The more developed are the psychic senses the more they become a "normal" part of perception.

Fifth Dimension: It may be a challenging concept, but each cosmic plane "upward" from the physical adds another dimension. Thus the Physical has 3 dimensions, the Astral 4, and the Mental 5. See Chart of Seven Planes and Seven Bodies at the end of the Introduction.

Flowing Sand Strategy: A strategy based on the empowering effects of a handful of sand flowing through the fingers.

Galactic Alignment: The alignment of the December solstice Sun with the Galactic equator of the Milky Way occurs once every 25,800 years. Due to the width of the Sun, this stretches over an 18 year span from 1980 to 2016 and includes the end of the Mayan calendar Long Count in 2012. The belief is that this period is associated with the start of a series of cataclysmic and transformative events leading towards "the end of the world as it has been" and a spiritual rebirthing to a Global Civilization. The cataclysmic events would seem to include Extreme Weather, Substantial Earth Movements and Volcanic Activity, Disease Eruptions, Massive Flooding, Man-made Water and Air Pollution, Threats of Religious War, etc. while the transformative activities include new Technologies, Space Exploration, Advancing Education, Universal Healthcare, Better Nutrition and Water Purification, Environmental Protection, Rule of Law, Trade-based Economic Development, and more.

Major Astronomical/Astrological events release critical energies that have both negative and positive potentials; it's up to humans to make the best out of them.

Garden Empowerment Strategy: A strategy designed to facilitate empowering interactions with plants in a garden setting. The Earth is our "Foundation," and its care has become an every-person responsibility as our population has greater impact. Gardening, planting, nurturing, home-grown food, and more connect us with our Source—physically, emotionally, mentally, and spiritually. It's healing both to the planet and the "care giver."

Great Work: The path of self-directed spiritual growth and development. This is the object of your incarnation and the meaning of your life. The Great Work is the program of growth to become all that you can be—which is the realization that you are a "god in the making." Within your being there is the seed of Divinity, and your job is to grow that into the Whole Person that is a "Child of God." It is a process that has continued from "the Beginning" and may have no ending but it is your purpose in life. It is that which gives meaning to your being.

In this new age, you are both teacher and student and you must accept responsibility for your own destiny. *Time is of the essence!* Older methods give way to new ones because the entire process of growth and self-development has to be accelerated. Humanity has created a *time bomb* that's ticking away, and only our own higher consciousness can save us from self-destruction. But—have faith and do the Great Work for it is all part of a Great Plan.

The Great Work is not denial and restriction but fulfillment. There's not just one narrow Path, but many paths—one for each of us.

Incarnating personally: After death, the familiar personality that was the person we knew in life slowly moves "upward" through the Astral and Mental into the Causal levels while "letting go" of the previously accumulated non-essential memories and addictions (chemical and otherwise) to become its "essential" self. It is at the causal level that all the lessons of the past life are extracted and the remaining new personality is shaped with a plan for the next life. The new personality, with only a few "unfinished" memories of its previous lives, incarnates in a new body.

In a recent Boston University study published online January 2014 in the Journal of Child Development shows that up to age seven children often have a strong sense of their own existence extending back long before their birth into this life. Some children at this early age have memories of previous lives and others recognize persons known in a previous life.

Suggested Reading:

Newton, Michael: *Destiny of Souls, New Case Studies of Life Between Lives*, Llewellyn, 2000.

Newton, Michael: *Journey of Souls, Case Studies of Life Between Lives*, Llewellyn, 2002.

Newton, Michael: *Life Between Lives, Hypnotherapy for Spiritual Regression*, Llewellyn, 2004.

Newton, Michael: *Memories of the Afterlife—Life-Between Lives Stories of Personal Transformation*, Llewellyn, 2009.

Slate, Joe H., and Carl Llewellyn Weschcke: *Doors to Past Lives*, Llewellyn, 2011.

Innate Powers: A common phrase for our natural, inborn, powersand talents in contrast to those gained from external learned or developed powers.

Instrument of Nature: A potentially empowering element or object found in nature that is receptive to human interaction.

Intention: Acting with a goal in mind. However, "Intention" has become a key word in applied Quantum Theory where it is demonstrated that directed thought and image can effect changes in the Universal Field at the foundation of physical reality. In other words, forcefully expressed and goal-directed intention can become experienced Reality.

Interactive Effect: The resultant increase in effectiveness when two or more strategies or resources are combined.

Kali Yuga: The Hindu concept of current cycle as an Age of Darkness, Pain, and Evil that began February 17, 3102 BCE when the five visible planets of Mercury, Venus, Mars, Jupiter, and Saturn were aligned at 0 degree Aries. This Dark Age will end in 2025 CE with a 300 year transition to bring a new cycle of Enlightenment.

According to the Hindu tradition, the transitional periods between the Yugas bring a collapse of world civilization amidst environmental and social catastrophes. The current increase in earth movements and the increase in extreme weather may lead the way into a period of volatile earth changes. This is a call to be aware of these greater cycles of time that affect both world climate and civilization.

However, forewarned can bring correctional opportunities.

Kundalini: The Life Force rising from the base of the spine, the *Muladhara* chakra, and animating the body, our sexuality, the etheric body, and passing through the chakras to join with its opposite force descending through the *Sahasrara* chakra to open our higher consciousness.

Kundalini manifests as a transforming force centered in the Base Chakra and operating within the body, driving evolution, desire, sex drive, growth and individual development. It exists on all planes in seven degrees of force.

Bringing astral experiences into conscious (physical brain) awareness requires some arousal of Kundalini and its movement through other chakras whether spontaneously aroused or consciously directed in yogic ad magickal practice.

Suggested Reading:

Mumford, Jonn: *A Chakra and Kundalini Workbook, Psycho-Spiritual Techniques for Health, Rejuvenation, Psychic Powers and Spiritual Realization*, Llewellyn, 2002.

Lab Research: While the phrase may bring images of test tubes and glass retorts, a "Lab" is really a controlled environment equipped for specific scientific applications and/or dedicated research.

Laws of Nature: The orderly principles of nature that apply to all of us.

Life-between-lifetimes: One's existence in the spirit realm between one's lifetimes in physical incarnation. It is believed there is a period between the previous life and the next life during which the past life is reviewed and the next life planned.

Suggested Reading:

Newton, Michael: *Destiny of Souls, New Case Studies of Life Between Lives*, Llewellyn, 2000.

Newton, Michael: *Journey of Souls, Case Studies of Life Between Lives*, Llewellyn, 2002.

Newton, Michael: *Life Between Lives, Hypnotherapy for Spiritual Regression*, Llewellyn, 2004.

Newton, Michael: *Memories of the Afterlife—Life-Between Lives Stories of Personal Transformation*, Llewellyn, 2009.

Slate, Joe H., and Carl Llewellyn Weschcke: *Doors to Past Lives*, Llewellyn, 2011.

Longevity Research: Major research work being undertaken by diverse academic, scientific, and commercial organizations seeking to reverse aging factors, and improve and extend human life. "Live long enough and you can live forever."

Lower Astral: The lower sub-planes of the Astral Plane with vibrations close to the physical level. It is the realm of ghosts, hauntings, and poltergeist phenomena.

Lower Self: The conscious mind and the subconscious mind, together, are the Lower Self.

Mass Hypnosis: A relatively common experience in which large groups of people experience a unity of consciousness resulting from of trance-inducing music, mass entertainment, sports mania, religious ecstasy, or a charismatic speaker. Under such conditions, a mass of people experience mass hysteria, engage in destructive riots and killings, produce mayhem, and more. Likewise, crowd chanting, singing of gospel songs, and great speeches can lead to love and good actions.

Materialist Science: Physical sciences leaving no room for any non-materialist explanations of observed phenomena.

Mental Body: The fourth body. The mental body "thinks" in abstract rather than emotional form. The lower mental body unites with the astral and etheric bodies as the personality for the current incarnation. The higher mental body is home to the Soul between incarnations.

Middle consciousness: An alternate name for the Conscious Mind.

Mind of Man and Mind of God: The transcending unity of human and Divine Consciousness.

Mind over Matter: Recognition that Mind can produce physical phenomena such as psychokinesis, energy healing, and even poltergeist activity.

Movement is Life—Life is Movement: All spontaneous movement indicates life.

Natural Psychic: A person with innate paranormal skills.

Near-Death Experience (NDE): People near death, and sometimes those who have been resuscitated after dying, report common experiences of peacefulness followed by separation from the body. At first there is darkness then seeing a source of light and moving into the light, sometimes through a tunnel. At this point, many turn or are turned to move back into the body. Sometimes they see family and friends, and other times a "presence," who advise that it will not yet the time for the person to pass over. Other times there may be a review of the lifetime and a decision made by the person to return to complete unfinished business. It is nearly always a very positive and transformative experience, giving the person a much greater appreciation of life.

New Age: A phrase adapted by certain occult writers to describe 1) A belief in a new level of consciousness coincident with the Aquarian Age. 2) A social movement of diverse spiritual and political elements directed toward the transformation of individuals and society through heightened spiritual awareness obtained through practices of meditation, yoga, ritual and channeling. 3) A cultural phenomenon often associated with the psychedelic and mind-altering substances widely available in the nineteen sixties.

It is an ideal of harmony and progress that includes feminist, ecological, holistic and organic principles expressed through an alternative lifestyle that developed its own music, fashions, communal living, open sexuality, and political activism.

It became a commercial category, particularly in the book trade, which brought together subjects related to self-understanding, self-transformation, and self-development including acupuncture, alchemy, ancient civilizations, angels, anthroposophy, aromatherapy, astral projection, astrology, Atlantis, auras, bio-feedback, Buddhism, channeling, chanting, chakras, Chinese medicine, complementary healing, creative visualization, crystals, divination, dream interpretation, Egyptology, energy healing, ESP, extra-terrestrial life, ghosts, Gnosticism, handwriting analysis, herbalism, hypnosis, Kabbalah, magick, martial arts, meditation, natural foods, numerology, occult-ism, organic gardening, Paganism, palmistry, paranormal phenom-ena, past lives, psychic healing, psychic powers, reiki, reincarnation, runes, self-hypnosis, sex magick, shamanism, spiritual healing, Spiri-tualism, Tantra, Tarot, Theosophy, UFOs, Wicca, witchcraft, yoga, Zen, etc.

The New Age movement is inclusive of a resurgent paganism and rejection of formalistic religion in favor of Nature Mysti-cism and personal spirituality. While it generally includes roles for ministers and spiritual counselors along with those for priest and priestess as in Wicca, the religious aspect is participatory rather than hierarchical, ecstatic rather than puritanical, initiatory rather than theological, and inner-directed rather than outer. Divinity is found both within the person and in Nature, directly experienced rather than requiring an intermediary, and self-responsible rather than authoritarian.

While there are numerous organizations and groups, they are mostly informal, usually centered around lectures and workshops, and non-restrictive.

New Science of the Paranormal: The scientific study of the paranor-mal includes psychic skills *and* phenomena, and sees the people involved in real life applications. Replacing, or expanding upon the old science of parapsychology, this new science has grown out of the advanced and humanistic research led by Dr. Joe H. Slate at Athens (Alabama) State University and furthered under the in-fluence of the Parapsychology Research Institute and Foundation (PRIF). Aside from laboratory-based research programs, reports of paranormal experiences outside the lab were given equal respects and scientific analysis. Common, everyday paranormal experiences are given equal recognition as "real" and have resulted in new de-velopmental methods and new applications of psychic skills and tools.

Many of these technologies make use of self-hypnosis, thus enabling an individual to have full control of the development and the application of paranormal skills in everyday life.

Next Step: Advancement, growth, development, expansion all comes about when we are willing to take the "next step" out of self-imposed and societal limitations. Whether we are concerned with advancements in career, education, innovations in science and technology, or other worldly success, or projecting into the astral world, aura reading, psychic development, or spiritual growth, we have to jump over the fence, get out of the rut, breakthrough the walls.

Evolution results from the series of next steps that societies and individuals have taken and will take—for evolution is not just the past but even more the future. Without growth, without evolution, we are passé, in fact doomed like dinosaurs. *What does this have to do with you?* It is you, the individual, who is the vehicle of evolution. Unless you take the next step in your own life, growing in consciousness and psychic powers, you fail to lend your strength to our better future.

Psychic Powers and Spirit Communication are not just incidental to our evolutionary advancement; rather they are essential to the process. Undertaking their conscious development accelerates personal growth at a most critical time in world history.

Astral Projection is a vital contribution to this acceleration and to our ability to meet the challenges of this moment. Astral experiences *ignite* psychic development and the expansion of consciousness necessary for new knowledge and understanding of the cosmic adventure that is our origin and our destiny. The experience of astral consciousness is one of the dynamic "next steps" necessary to move forward, to make the transition into the real New Age that will be a reality for those willing to commit themselves *to becoming more than they are.*

Suggested Reading:

Slate, Joe H., and Carl Llewellyn Weschcke: *Astral Projection for Psychic Empowerment,* Llewellyn, 2012.

Slate, Joe H., and Carl Llewellyn Weschcke: *Clairvoyance for Psychic Empowerment*, Llewellyn, 2013.

Slate, Joe H., and Carl Llewellyn Weschcke: *The Llewellyn Complete Book of Psychic Development*, Llewellyn, 2011.

Slate, Joe H., and Carl Llewellyn Weschcke: *Psychic Empowerment for Everyone*, Llewellyn, 2009.

Numerology: (Divination) The study of the psychic significance of numbers, often based on numerical values assigned to the letters of a name or to the birthdate. In depth numerology can be studied in the Kabbalah.

Objectology: The study and use of tangible objects in relation to their paranormal functions as receivers and holders of psychic impressions and energies. Also, those objects used in active divination and magic, including psychic and ritual tools, and their relationships to psychic events and processes.

Occult: That which is, at least temporarily, hidden from our perception. In astronomy it refers to the passing of one body in front of another as when the Moon passes in front of the Sun (an eclipse). In the common culture it has been used as a category for "hidden" knowledge, i.e. those subjects and technologies functioning to manifest psychic and spiritual faculties.

Suggested Reading:

Greer, John Michael: *The New Encyclopedia of the Occult*, Llewellyn, 2003.

Operating System: Inside every computer there is a software package providing the instructions for the hardware to carry out the work requested by application software packages like Microsoft Word and Excel. The operating system is the interface between the computer hardware and the outer world, while the application packages are like the skills and training we learn by study and experience. Like every other computer the human brain requires an operating system that interfaces with the world and filters our perceptions to correspond to what we are conditioned to expect through parental guidance, our life experiences, education, training, and interaction with authority figures, social expectations, and to a far lesser extent by our genetic heritage and past-life memories. This operating system also conditions and directs the way we respond to external stimuli. Much of this operating system functions in the subconscious mind. Like computers, the operating system can be modified, up-dated, changed and even replaced. Self-understanding is learning about our operating system; self-improvement is about modifying and changing our operating system; self-transformation is about up-dating and largely replacing our operating system. It is a vital next step for every conscious person to undertake, again and again.

Ouija™ Board: A simple board with the alphabet printed on it along with "yes" and "no," and a planchette or easily moveable device used to communicate with spirits. The users, usually two people of opposite gender, rest fingers on the planchette which slides quickly to the various letters to spell out answers to questions. To use the Ouija™ the partners must relax and let the Unconscious Mind operate the planchette. It is helpful to have a formal starting and ending of the session—as simply as speaking "Please, if any spirits wish to speak through Ouija™, say YES." To end the session, simply say "Thank you, and goodbye for now," and put the Ouija™ away. Do not just leave it on a table but restore it to a box or drawer where it rests undisturbed and unobserved. A spirit or spirits may operate through the Unconscious but cannot until you "let go" of your conscious objective faculty. It's sort of like "Closing Down" one aspect of your consciousness in order to "Open Up" the other which can then act as a doorway to other units of consciousness—your own or spirit entities. Have questions prepared, speak them slowly and allow the planchette to move from one letter to another to spell out the answers.

Out-of-Body Experiences: (OBEs): States of awareness in which one's extrabiological part as a conscious, intelligent entity disengages from one's physiology to experience reality independent of the biological body. See astral projection.

Reports of the out-of-body experience (OBE) commonly describe the phenomenon as *enlightening, profound, spectacular,* and *empowering.* Out-of-body experiences—also called "astral projections" or "astral travels"—are states of awareness encompassing a conscious awareness of being in a spatial location away from the physical body. The out-of-body concept assumes a duality of human nature, and the existence of an extra-biological consciousness or astral double. OBEs further assume the capacity of the extra-biological to disengage the physical body, and in that disengaged or out-of-body state, to travel consciously to experience distant or other dimensional realities.

OBEs can occur both in the normal state of awareness and in altered states such as sleep, hypnosis, and meditation. The out-of-body state itself could be considered an altered state distinctly unlike other states of consciousness in that it is usually accompanied by a profound awareness of separateness from the physical body. Although sometimes described as dreamlike, OBEs appear to be expressions of the disengaged extra-biological state rather than simply the products of sleep. Furthermore, the OBE subject often chooses a destination and brings back clear, conscious recall of the experience.

Out-of-Body Skills: Skills develop with experience, and in response to pre-determined goals. What do you want to learn, where do you want to go, what do you want to do—are all typical questions but not particularly related to the potentials of this unique state of consciousness. Remember, you are in the astral world and be specific as to that "dimension."

Parallel Universe: The concept of one or more physical universes existing dimensionally parallel to our own. The difficulty with them being "physical" yet invisible to us. As soon as the idea of their existence in some other dimension or vibratory scheme enters into the discussion, then we are necessarily speaking in esoteric terms—astral, mental, spiritual, etc.—that are unacceptable to materialist science.

From the *esoteric* perspective, the astral world is some kind of parallel universe with astral imagery replicating physical structures.

Paranormal: Parallel to the normal. Phenomena that is beyond the understanding of material science. While the paranormal is mostly confined to psychic-type events and experiences, it also includes certain physical phenomena for which we do not as yet have an explanation.

Paranormal vs. Supernatural: The study of the Paranormal does not deal with anything called "Supernatural," but considers all phenomena as natural even if currently not as yet explainable.

Parapsychology: Also called PSI, the broad category that includes the study of such subjects as paranormal phenomena, clairvoyance, distant or remote viewing, out-of-body experience, precognition, psychokinesis (PK), telepathy, and others—all involving non-sensory perception.

Dr. Joe H. Slate (*Psychic Phenomena,* 1988, McFarland, Jefferson, NC) writes "Parapsychology is the study of extra-sensory perception (ESP), psychokinesis (PK), and related topics. As a science, it pushes back the borders of human experience and offers new ways to understand ourselves and the universe. Contemporary parapsychology focuses on two major goals: first, to engage scientific research to discover new knowledge and second, to liberate and optimize the development of human potential. Both goals are based on the premise that undiscovered knowledge and underdeveloped human potential do exist in forms, which can be reached through the application of parapsychological concepts and techniques."

"Through its emphasis on mental faculties and phenomena beyond recognizable physical explanations and causes, parapsychology reveals new possibilities for acquiring knowledge and for explaining higher mental processes. The challenge facing parapsychology . . . is the discovery and understanding of the complex parapsychological processes underlying human behavior, the mastery of the techniques of personal unfoldment, and the productive application of parapsychological skills. Because parapsychological concepts and techniques are not limited by the boundaries of physical perception and experience, they suggest new and more efficient ways to increase awareness and expand the human capacity for new knowledge and understanding."

Parapsychology challenges conventional thinking about life and death, the known and unknown, human potential and personal achievement, the nature of mind and body, known reality and perceived reality, and the meaning of our existence. All these age-old questions have been asked before with many different answers depending on conflicting ancient religious teachings.

In place of religious answers Parapsychology explores paranormal phenomena—including direct revelation by psychic technologies.

Despite it's apparent newness, Parapsychology explores the unknown through two age-old approaches: 1) the use of particular physical objects, some with associated symbols, and 2) particular mental disciplines. The first includes such objects as gazing crystals, dowsing rods, pendulums, tea leaves, as well as Runes, the I Ching, Tarot, Geomancy, etc.—all involving some form of physical contact and manipulation with degrees of mental focus and extended awareness. The second includes the use of hypnosis (more often self-hypnosis), active and passive forms of meditation, dream analysis, and the out-of-body state. In both approaches, the goal is two-fold: To gain particular information, often in response to precise questions; and to grow in psychic skills and the fulfillment of innate potentials, and thus to "become more than we are."

Modern parapsychology places an increased emphasis on practical applications by means of information not otherwise available through sensory channels. Examples include precognition, telepathy, clairvoyance, dowsing, remote viewing, reading the aura, past-life regression, spirit communication, and meditation.

Parapsychology Research Institute and Foundation (PRIF): Established at Athens State University in 1970 by Joe H. Slate, Ph.D., (first as the International Parapsychology Research Foundation), this foundation is committed to the study of parapsychology and related topics. It has conducted extensive research and established student scholarships in perpetuity at Athens State University and the University of Alabama.

Past Life Memories: Certain memories from previous lives continue from on in the current life much as a childhood trauma can continue into adulthood. This should not be confused with the continuation from the past into the present of certain talents and interests. While we say that nothing is ever truly lost, it can be ignored and put aside.

Pebble and Pail Strategy: An adaptation of the Pebble and Pool Strategy in which a pail of water is used as a substitute for a pool. See Pebble and Pool Strategy.

Pebble and Pool Strategy: A goal-directed strategy in which a pebble dropped into a pool is used to deepen one's resolve to achieve designated goals.

Pebble of Commitment and Vessel of Faith: A procedure in which a pebble dropped into a vessel of water as a symbolic representation of commitment and faith, particularly in goals related to spiritual efforts.

Pendulum: Simply a weight on the end of a string somewhat shorter than the length of the forearm. The string is held by the fingers so that the weight can freely swing over a simple chart or map, or sometimes an object, and revealing by the direction of the swing answers to specific questions framed mostly for yes/no response. By-passing conscious control, the subconscious provides the answers. Some people believe that spirits may move the pendulum similar to the movement of the planchette on the Ouija™ Board. Pendulums are also used in dowsing, often over a map with a sample of ore held in one hand or in a hollow cavity in the pendulum that serves as a "witness" to find a body of the same ore in the geographic location indicated by the pendulum over the map.

Working with a pendulum is a desirable practice developing psychic sensitivity and extended awareness. It is a valuable means to communication with the subconscious mind.

Suggested Reading:

Ghiuselev and Astanassov: *Pendulum Power Magic Kit.* Brass pendulum, book and Full Color Layout Sheet to develop extra-sensory faculties, Lo Scarabeo, 2005.

Slate, Joe H., and Carl Llewellyn Weschcke: *Psychic Empowerment: Tools and Techniques,* Llewellyn, 2011.

Personality: The immediate vehicle of personal consciousness we believe to be ourselves. It is a temporary complex drawn from the etheric, astral, and mental bodies containing current life memories, and the current operating system. It is the relatively enduring complex of attitudes, interests, behavioral patterns, emotional responses, social roles, and other individual traits. Each individual's personality is an aggregate conglomeration of decisions made throughout life. There are inherent natural, genetic, and environmental factors that contribute to the development of the personality. According to the process of socialization, "personality also colors our values, beliefs, and expectations . . . Hereditary factors that contribute to personality development do so as a result of interactions with the particular social environment in which people live."

The Personality is only one chapter in the full biography of the evolving Soul. And each chapter is analyzed and abstracted to secure the essential lessons and experiences of the entire lifetime, while the memories of that lifetime flow into the Subconscious Mind and become part of the Universal Consciousness providing a complete history of the Soul's many lifetimes. In between lives, the Soul absorbs lessons from the many successive personalities and thus evolves. From his now greater perspective, the Soul outlines a new chapter and sends part of his essence into incarnation to gain new experiences that will become new lessons for the evolving Soul. It is somewhat as if a mature adult could have planned the years of his childhood to get the right experiences and education for the professional life he has chosen.

Phantom Leaf Effect: In electrophotography, a phenomenon in which the energy pattern enveloping a full leaf remains intact after a part of the leaf is removed.

PK: See psychokinesis.

Planetary and Zodiacal Cycles: Planetary bodies and astronomical/astrological positions move in cycles that are mostly regular and predictable. As all are connected in varying degrees with life and matter, the cyclical influences cause and influence recognizable phenomena.

Poltergeist: Literally, a mischievous spirit. A presence or energy, sometimes confined to a single room but more often associated with a particular person, that creates unintentional disturbances such as knocking over vases, clocks, mirrors, knick-knacks, and other small but generally favorite objects. At one time, it was believed that the activity was the result of unstable emotional energies, often repressed, and unconsciously projected by adolescents during puberty.

Suggested Reading

Righi, Brian: *Ghosts, Apparitions and Poltergeists, An Exploration of the Supernatural Through History,* Llewellyn, 2008.

Power of Belief Can Change Reality: Beliefs establish conditions in which action and reaction take place, thus affecting perceived reality.

Prana (Chi, the Force, the Power): The universal life-force flowing throughout the universe, and locally emanating from the sun as vitality absorbed from the air we breathe and the food we eat. It can be visualized as flowing into the body as you inhale, and then distributed throughout the body as you exhale.

Prana is also considered as one of the "seven elements:" Prana, Manas (mind), Ether, Fire, Air, Water and Earth, corresponding to seven regions of the universe. In Hebrew Kabbalism, Nephesh (the Psyche) is Prana combined with Kama (Love), together making the vital spark that is the "breath of life." Prana is comparable to Chi (Chinese), Ki (Japanese), vitality globules (Theosophical), Nous (Rosicrucian), Orgone (Wilhelm Reich), animal magnetism (Mesmer), Quintessence (Alchemical), and Mana (Hawaii priests).

Precognition: The psychic awareness of the future, including knowledge of events, trends, and conditions. Like other mental faculties, the ability to perceive the future independently of presently known predictive circumstances exists to some degree in everyone.

Some believe that events yet to occur already exist in a fixed, unalterable form. Another view assumes that the future exists only in varying degrees of probabilities, ever dependent on past and present realities including human intervention.

Each view related to the fixedness of the future assumes the existence of time as an energy dimension within a continuum of the past, present, and future. From that perspective, personal consciousness, likewise an energy phenomenon, is endowed with the capacity to interact with that dimension to generate a *mind/future interaction* that not only perceives the future but influences it as well. In today's complex world, the precognitive challenge thus becomes twofold: to develop our precognitive powers to their peaks and use them to bring forth desired change.

By developing our capacity to interact with the continuum of time, we become empowered not only to access the future through precognition but also to dip into the past through retrocognition. While the past exists in unalterable or fixed form, increased knowledge of that dimension can alter our perceptions of the present and empower us to more effectively shape the future.

Dr. Joe Slate writes: "For instance, personal growth blockages including phobias and conflicts of past-life origin can be resolved, often instantly, through the retrocognitive retrieval of relevant past-life experiences. On a broader scale, awareness of the sources of global problems ranging from disease to environmental pollution can be essential to the correction of causative conditions. Once you're attuned to the continuum of time, your retrocognitive and precognitive potentials will become activated to work hand-in-hand to empower you as never before to increase the quality of your life while contributing to a better world." (Slate, Joe H., and Carl Llewellyn Weschcke: *Psychic Empowerment: Tools and Techniques,* Llewellyn, 2011.)

Accepting this interdependent view of time opens considerable speculation regarding as *interdimensional interaction* through our psychic faculties such as *telepathy* with its capacity to send and receive thought messages with relevance to future happenings. An even more challenging possibility is the capacity to actually influence distant causative happenings through *psychokinesis* (PK).

Precognition, as an enriched extension of sensory perception, is an expression of our innate ability to perceive the future psychically. In its voluntarily induced form, precognitive awareness is activated deliberately through certain procedures and techniques, some of which were developed in the controlled laboratory setting at Athens State University under the auspices of the International Parapsychology Research Foundation. (See Slate, Joe H., and Carl Llewellyn Weschcke: *The Llewellyn Complete Book of Psychic Empowerment,* Llewellyn, 2011.)

Precognition and Psychic Empowerment: Precognition provides such an extensive range of information and insight that hardly an individual or organization could fail to benefit from the experience. Here's a summary of the empowering possibilities of precognitive knowledge:

- Precognition can awaken and place in a state of readiness the inner faculties required to more effectively meet the demands of the present and future alike.
- Precognition can expand our awareness of the consequences of present actions and our capacity to shape the future by taking command of present situations. It can provide the lead time essential in preparing for disquieting or formidable events.

- Precognition along with retrocognition can attune us to the continuum of time and thereby manifest the continuity of our existence as evolving souls.
- Precognition and retrocognition together can generate a state of inner balance and self-enlightenment that empowers us to reach beyond the limitations of the present.
- Precognition can increase our sense of personal worth and wellbeing by connecting us to the psychic nature of our being.
- Precognition can expand our awareness of the afterlife and provide confirmation of our existence beyond death.
- Precognition can increase our effectiveness in making personal decisions, including but not limited to those related to careers, relationships, and finances.
- Precognition can stimulate problem solving and creativity.
- Precognitive awareness of future possibilities can build a powerful success-expectancy effect that increases motivation, generates self-confidence and gives the winning edge to future performance.
- Precognition and retrocognition can together validate the expansive nature of consciousness and bi-directional endlessness of our existence.

Source:

Slate, Joe H., and Carl Llewellyn Weschcke: *The Llewellyn Complete Book of Psychic Empowerment*, Llewellyn, 2011.

Precognition and the Subconscious: While precognition can be seen as the extra-sensory capacity of consciousness to perceive the future, there is evidence that the subconscious can function as both a channel and storehouse for precognitive knowledge. Once perceived at a subconscious level, awareness of a future happening can be retained in the subconscious motivating changes in behavior or conveyed to the conscious mind either directly or indirectly through dreams, déjà vu, slips of the tongue or pen, vague premonitions, and enigmatic emotions that can provide awareness of a future event.

Precognitive reality slip: A spontaneous cue that becomes a signal instantly activating the mind's precognitive faculty, particularly in danger-related situations. Rather than simple coincidences such slips as these seem to be designed by the subconscious to command our attention and promote preparation or prevention of a future event. A key feature of such slips is that they tend to linger in the conscious mind, often in vivid detail, until either preventive measures are undertaken or the predicted event occurs.

Precognitive Role of the Subconscious: (1) Subconscious energies interact with the continuum of time to gain extra-sensory awareness of the future; (2) the subconscious interacts with consciousness to facilitate a direct or indirect transfer of precognitive information; and (3) the conscious/subconscious interaction becomes a motivational force that promotes the productive application of precognitive knowledge.

Slate, Joe H., and Carl Llewellyn Weschcke: *The Llewellyn Complete Book of Psychic Empowerment*, Llewellyn, 2011.

Preexistence: One's existence before one's first embodiment on earth.

Suggested Reading:

Slate, Joe H.: *Beyond Reincarnation*, Llewellyn, 2005.

Psychic Empowerment: Generally the following of a specific plan or program, sometimes involving self-hypnosis and meditation, for the development of innate psychic powers into dependable skills. With empowerment, the psychic or spiritual bodies can be integrated into the Whole Person.

Psychic empowerment, rather than a theoretical possibility, is a measurable though complex process of personal evolvement. Using the traditional and newer tools and techniques you can accelerate that process by accessing your dormant inner potentials and activate them to enrich the quality of your life. Beyond that, you can become the master builder of an endless *tower of power* to the great beyond, a tower that connects you to the far reaches of the cosmos and the entire powers underling it. Built of the finest materials—those found in your own being— the tower of power

can become your empowerment connection to the boundless resources of the great beyond. It's a tower that brings you into balance with and in constant attunement to the universe.

Suggested Reading:

Slate, Joe H., and Carl Llewellyn Weschcke: *Psychic Empowerment for
Everyone*, Llewellyn, 2009.

Psychic Empowerment Hierarchy: When we are psychically empowered, our multiple faculties function in a dynamic hierarchy that is
constantly evolving and rearranging itself. Those abilities required
for immediate coping spontaneously rise within the hierarchy to
assume an appropriate place of prominence, thereby meeting our
empowerment needs of the moment. Those abilities not in immediate demand descend in the hierarchy, but remain in reserve for
future use as needed. In other words, our inner faculties are placed
"on line" within a psychic system that is responsive to our empowerment needs, even those we do not consciously anticipate. This
precognitive feature of the hierarchical system is a major characteristic of the psychically empowered individual.

Psychic Imagery: It is your ability to effectively visualize that turns
your imagination into a "psychic power tool" for use in psychic
work, active meditation, astral travel, remote viewing, the development of clairvoyance, activating archetypal powers, the assumption
of god forms, entering mythic worlds, Qabalistic path working,
symbolic "doorways" to access specific areas of the astral world,
as well as in all forms of magical application, and much more. In
each of these applications, visualization is a process of moving psychic energies along particular symbolic pathways. This includes
techniques involving the Chakra System and is used to actually
stimulate neural pathways in the physical body and brain. Visual-
izations of persons, living or deceased can be used to make communications more accurate and more powerful. The visualization
of a Spirit Entity or a God-Form can be employed in Evocation or
Invocation and in "conversation" with such beings to access Knowl-

edge or specific Powers. Effective visualization is the key to empowering your imagination to "make real the unreal."

Psychic Sand Reading: The use of the imprint of the hand in a tray of sand as a point of focus to stimulate paranormal functions.

Psychokinesis (PK): The ability of the mind to influence objects, events, and processes in the apparent absence of intervening physical energy or intermediary instrumentation. An extended definition of PK includes its capacity to influence internal biological systems. The movement of objects without physical contact.

Psychological and Esoteric Models of the Whole Self: Words such as Soul, Higher Self, Spirit, Psyche, Inner Self, the *Atman,* the Whole Personality, Causal Self, *Chiah, Neshamah,* Higher Manas, Higher Ego, Holy Guardian Angel, Spiritual Soul, Intuitional Self, *Buddhi,* Higher Causal Self, Super Conscious Mind, and many more in all languages and cultures have been used variously with little definition other than a presumed meaning of "other than physical consciousness," "that which survives physical death," and "that which is immortal."

In modern psychological and esoteric terminology these same words and related concepts have been associated with the Personal Unconscious, the Collective Unconscious, the Archetypal Mind, the Subtle Bodies making up the complex structure of the whole person, and more.

For our purposes here, we see a basic psychological model that parallels a similar esoteric model as follows:

The Psychological Model and the
Esoteric Model of the Whole Person

PSYHOLOGICAL MODEL	ESOTERIC MODEL
Lower Self, aka Sub-Conscious Mind	Astral Body and Consciousness (Self)
Middle Self, aka Conscious Mind	Mental Body and Consciousness (Self)
Higher Self, aka Super-Conscious Mind	Causal Body and Consciousness (Self)

In both models, at each level, there is more complexity than shown. Generally, and in relation to their multiple functions, each level in both models is further divided into seven sub-levels. Our focus is on the highest sub-level of Level 3, simply called the Higher Self and the Causal Self. Essentially, they are the same, but because our focus in this book is magickal and esoteric, we will target the Causal Self.

The Causal Self is not the Soul, nor is it the Spirit, but it is magickally called the "Holy Guardian Angel" and is the highest aspect of <u>personal</u> consciousness in *the incarnating personality*. Understand that *the Soul, itself, does not incarnate,* but abstracts the life lessons from the incarnated personality through the Causal Self, which then "dies" along with that personality. The Soul then creates a new "Causal Seed" with the abstracted memories of many life times and a new life plan which generates a new incarnating personality, step-by-step, following the Esoteric Model into physical incarnation from which new levels of psychological consciousness develop as the physical body grows and matures to work side-by-side with the esoteric selves through a new life time.

It is the Higher Self communicating with the Causal Self that is our aspiration in what we call the "Knowledge and Conversation with the Holy Guardian Angel" which is the goal of all High Magick, the purpose of all Self-Development, the ultimate accomplishment of all Meditation. It is the fulfillment of this process that fully transfers "command and control" of the entire personality from the reactive emotional-centered Lower Self and the more-or-less brain-centered mental Middle Self to the Spirit-centered Causal Higher Self. That the state of self-mastery we call "adepthood." (The chances of you encountering such an adept—whether in this world or the next—is very slight. No real adept will ask for your obedience, devotion, or your money—so don't give it!)

Purpose of Human Existence: Contrary to religious belief that Man is here to *worship* God, the only recognizable purpose for Life and Consciousness is continued Growth and Development.

Quantum: The minimum amount of any physical entity involved in an interaction. Beyond this, we see that a physical property may be "quantized." This means that the magnitude can take on only certain discrete values.

Quantum Theory, the "Bridge" between Physical and Esoteric Science. The new science of Quantum Theory tells us that the beginning is (not just was *but still is*) the Universal Field of Possibilities that manifests first as Energy/Matter under the guidance of packets of information/instruction. Thus we can see an analogy with a computer with its Operating Program and its Application Programs.

Reality: The personal world as seen through our belief system. While it mostly coincides with that of other people, self-analysis will show deviations and distortions reflecting the "feelings" of the person.

Rejuvenation PK: The term, *rejuvenation,* as used in psychic self-empowerment implies the deliberate restoration of youth and vigor through self-intervention into the aging process. Psychic rejuvenation recognizes the aging effects of an array of negative mental states, among them anxiety, depression, hostility, and insecurity. Even more importantly, psychic rejuvenation emphasizes the constructive effects of positive mental states, along with the empowering capacity of positives states to eliminate their negative opposites. Love, for instance, is one of the most empowering rejuvenation forces known. When present in the psyche, it neutralizes hate—its negative counterpart that is physically and mentally destructive and disempowering. Such positive states as self-confidence, self-esteem, and self-acceptance are both empowering and rejuvenating. They inject rejuvenating energies into the self system, eradicating those disempowering states, which contribute to aging.

The extension of PK to include rejuvenation suggests the possibility of living younger, longer, and better while literally reversing the physical signs of aging. An exercise called Rejuvenation PK is designed to activate the body's rejuvenation potentials and unblock the flow of rejuvenating energies from the inside out. Developed by Joe Slate and associates in the labs at Athens State University, the exercise involves empowering imagery and affirmations. Through Rejuvenation PK, physical functions, including those considered autonomic or involuntary, are linked to mental functions in a positive rejuvenating interaction. The results are actual and observable changes in the physical body.

Retrocognition: Psychic perceiving events that occurred in the past, often leading to a better understanding of present circumstances.

Sand Reading: A strategy in which a hand imprint made in a tray of sand provides a source of information. Also, **Automatic Sand Writing:** A procedure in which spontaneous, effortless writing on the smooth surface of sand becomes a source of relevant information or creative expression.

Self-Empowerment: A state of personal power originating within the self. A synthesis of Occultism, Psychology, and Self-improvement in a functional lifestyle that is both practical and spiritual. Its goal is the fulfillment of the innate potentials leading to the Whole Person. Through the use of self-hypnosis, it condenses traditional esoteric programs by activating the sub-conscious mind and drawing upon the collective unconscious.

The self-empowerment perspective recognizes the subconscious as an interactive phenomenon in which various subconscious processes work in concert with each other to promote our personal empowerment. The self-empowerment perspective focuses on your capacity alone to experience the subconscious, activate its powers, and focus them on self-designed goals. That's what self-empowerment is all about!

It follows that our personal empowerment depends largely on our capacity to interact with the subconscious. Therapeutic techniques based on this view include hypnosis, dream analysis, free association, and various forms of meditation that focus on specific subconscious processes.

The self-empowerment view recognizes the subconscious as a storehouse of knowledge not yet manifest to conscious awareness. As we dive deeper into the subconscious, the more we learn about ourselves and the more empowered and balanced we become. Amazing though it may seem, complex bodies of new knowledge have been accessed and transferred to conscious awareness through appropriate empowerment programs, including self-hypnosis.

Self-Hypnosis: A system of self-programing. "Self-hypnosis can be best defined as a self-induced state of altered consciousness that gives direct access to the vast reserve of resources and under-developed potential existing in everyone. It's a strategy based on the premise that you alone are your best personal hypnotist and growth specialist." (from Slate and Weschcke: *Psychic Self-Empowerment for Everyone*)

The self-induction of hypnotic trance and the <u>**catalytic power of direct self-programming**</u> through simple but carefully developed affirmations mostly expressed as already accomplished "I AM" conditions, such as "I AM slim."

Suggested Reading:

Park, Lincoln: *Get Out of Your Way, Unlocking the Power of Your Mind to Get What You Want.* Includes audio CD of self-hypnosis programs, Llewellyn, 2007.

Slate, Joe H., and Carl Llewellyn Weschcke: *Self-Empowerment through Self-Hypnosis—Harnessing the Enormous Potential of the Mind,* Llewellyn, 2010.

Self-realization: Self-realization depends on becoming connected to the powers within and beyond. Belief in Self ignites the process of internal growth and connection. Self-unification and self-empowerment leads to growth and self-realization. Self-understanding, self-discipline, and the rejection of distortion and division from outside influences—mostly those with strong emotional impact distorting the self-empowering process.

Soul: *"You" are not your Soul.* The "You" you know is best understood as a partial and temporary manifestation of "Soul" that we call "personality." This personality is not the *whole* soul but one of many aspects of it incarnating life after life and occupying a series of temporary vehicles each composed of the substance of one dimension after the other. Then the essence of each life's lessons is abstracted and eventually "absorbed" and further refined into the soul until the soul itself is ready to move on into still higher spiritual dimensions. The soul continues on its journey through the Cosmos, learning and/or "working" on behalf of the *Great Plan* set in motion by the "Creator Source" of all that is—which is better realized as *Unity* when not given a defining and hence *limiting* name.

Soul Travel: See out-of-body experience (OBE).

Spirituality: The study and exploration of the spiritual nature of the person, of humanity and of the Cosmos itself. The study includes the foundations and nature of religion, the nature of man in relation to Creator, and the connections of Spirituality with metaphysical subjects. Spirituality is the *supreme force* that energizes your growth and gives quality to your existence from your endless pre-existence to present moment and beyond.

Star Gaze: A procedure that selects a star or group of stars as a point of focus to connect oneself to the life force within and beyond.

Stream of Success: A procedure utilizing imagery of a stream of water to promote physical relaxation and a positive state of mind.

Subconscious, AKA the Subconscious Mind and the Personal Unconscious: The vast inner region of experiences not ordinarily available to the conscious awareness. It is believed to be the repository of all past-life experiences. The term subconscious is used in many different contexts and has no single or precise definition. This greatly limits its significance as a definition-bearing concept, and in consequence the word tends to be avoided in academic and scientific settings.

In everyday speech and popular writing, however, the term is very commonly encountered as a layperson's replacement for the unconscious mind, which in Freud's opinion is a repository for socially unacceptable ideas, wishes or desires, traumatic memories, and painful emotions put out of mind by the mechanism of psychological repression. However, the contents do not necessarily have to be solely negative. In the psychoanalytic view, the unconscious is a force that can only be recognized by its effects—it expresses itself in the symptom. Unconscious thoughts are not directly accessible to ordinary introspection, but are supposed to be capable of being "tapped" and "interpreted" by special methods and techniques such as meditation, random association, dream analysis, and verbal slips (commonly known as a Freudian slip), examined and conducted during psychoanalysis.

Carl Jung developed the concept further. He divided the unconscious into two parts: the personal unconscious and the collective unconscious. The personal unconscious is a reservoir of material that was once conscious but has been forgotten or suppressed.

The idea of the "subconscious" as a powerful or potent agency has allowed the term to become prominent in the New Age and self-help literature, in which investigating or controlling its supposed knowledge or power is seen as advantageous. In the New Age community, techniques such as autosuggestion and affirmations are believed to harness the power of the subconscious to influence a person's life and real-world outcomes, even curing sickness.

Though laypersons commonly assume "subconscious" to be a psychoanalytic term, this is not in fact the case. Freud had explicitly condemned the word as long ago as 1915: "We shall also be right in rejecting the term "subconsciousness" as incorrect and misleading". In later publications his objections were made clear:

"If someone talks of subconsciousness, I cannot tell whether he means the term topographically—to indicate something lying in the mind beneath consciousness—or qualitatively—to indicate another consciousness, a subterranean one, as it were. He is probably not clear about any of it. The only trustworthy antithesis is between conscious and unconscious." As outlined above, psychologists and psychiatrists exclusively use the term "unconscious" in situations where many lay-writers, particularly such as those in metaphysical and New Age literature, usually use the term "subconscious." It should not, however, be inferred from this that the orthodox concept of the unconscious and the New Age concept of the subconscious are precisely equivalent. Psychologists and psychiatrists, unsurprisingly, take a much more limited view of the capabilities of the unconscious than are represented by the common New Age depiction of a transcendentally all-powerful "subconscious."

The Subconscious retains memories of everything through the feelings associated with that memory. In general, however, we are mostly concerned with childhood memories, fears, and misunderstandings that have been—often—repressed. As childish memories, they live on and may still influence our adult understanding and feelings erroneously and painfully. By recalling those memories, an adult perspective can replace the childish one and at the same time release energies tied up in those childish fears and misunderstandings.

The Subconscious Mind **is never asleep, always aware. It is the *Nephesh* on the Kabbalistic Tree of Life.** That part of the mind below the threshold of consciousness. Normally, unavailable to the conscious mind, it can be accessed through hypnosis and self-hypnosis, meditation, automatic writing, etc.

More importantly, in the studies of Joe H. Slate and Carl Llewellyn Weschcke, it is the *lower* part of the Personality which while containing forgotten and repressed feelings and memories and our emotional nature, it is also the fundamental Belief or Operating System that filters Reality, that collection of guilt feelings called the "Shadow," the "Anima" or "Animus" collection of feelings representing our idealization or fear and hatred of the opposite gender, the various Archetypes and Mythic images formed though the history of human experience, all of which can operate as doorways or gates to the astral world and connect to the higher or super consciousness. The subconscious is also home to our instincts and the autonomic system that cares for the body and its operation.

"The subconscious is not only a content domain but a dynamic constellation of processes and powers. It recognizes that the wealth of our subconscious resources is complementary to consciousness rather than counteractive. It's a powerful component of who we are and how we function." (from Slate and Weschcke: *Psychic Self-Empowerment for Everyone*, Llewellyn, 2009).

According to the self-empowerment perspective, the subconscious never sleeps—it's in continuous interaction with consciousness. It embraces the physical, spiritual, and psychical nature of our existence. Awareness of future events, telepathic communications, and clairvoyant insight are all among its powers. The subconscious, with communication to the Collective Unconscious and the Super-Consciousness has very nearly unlimited resources available to you through your Guide. Almost like a forgotten best friend or favorite mentor, the subconscious welcomes our probes and challenges us to use its powers.

The Sub-Conscious Mind has no ethics or morals; it is your Conscious Mind that must make choices and impose order on chaos, develop distinct channels to reliable resources, and otherwise understand and learn that your Sub-Conscious Mind is your key to the infinite resources of the Universe. Helping you to build the relationship between the Sub-Conscious Mind and the Conscious Mind is the purpose of Self-Empowering procedures. (see Slate, Joe H., and Carl Llewellyn Weschcke: *Self-Empowerment and the Sub-Conscious Mind*, Llewellyn, 2010).

But the major message we want to give you is that the Sub-Conscious Mind is an unlimited resource, not only of memories and information but also of powers and skills. It is the foundation and matrix to all we are and all that we will become. Our personal unit of consciousness is part of the Universal Consciousness so we have unlimited potential and have yet to discover any limits to our capacity or ability to use that potential. Our goal is to become adept at calling upon these powers and resources to match our needs and interests, and to keep "pushing the envelope" towards yet greater capacity and ability.

Aside from the integrative process, there's evidence suggesting that the subconscious can literally generate new potentials and growth energies independent of our conscious interactions through processes not yet fully understood, possibly through the synergistic or holistic results of the integrative process alone. What we need to understand is that the Sub-Conscious Mind is not a passive by-stander but always aware and always active. As you grow in consciousness and integrate more of your psychic and other powers into your Whole Person, the Sub-Conscious Mind grows and contributes more to the Whole Person you are becoming.

Understanding these creative processes of the subconscious mind is among our greatest challenges with potential for enormous benefit. The point here, as elsewhere, is always that the greater our understanding, the greater the benefit, but even as we face the continual challenges, the very attempt at understanding stimulates positive developments.

Contrary to some views, the subconscious is the "essential you," the essence of your being as an evolving soul. Without the subconscious, you would not exist at all. It's the vast totality of your existence: the "old you" of the past, the "dynamic you" of the present and the "infinite you" of the future.

There are a number of methods in use in the contemporary New Age and paranormal communities to try to directly affect the latter, such as Affirmations, Autosuggestion, Hypnosis and Self-Hypnosis, Meditation, Prayer, Pre-Sleep suggestions followed by Dream Analysis, Ritual, and various Shamanic techniques.

Suggested Reading:

Slate, Joe H., and Carl Llewellyn Weschcke: *Psychic Self-Empowerment for Everyone,* Llewellyn, 2009.

Slate, Joe H., and Carl Llewellyn Weschcke: *Self-Empowerment and the Sub-Conscious Mind,* Llewellyn, 2010.

Surviving Personality: For most people a "Spirit" is thought to be the person formerly living in a physical body and now living in a non-physical body or "vehicle" in "the Next World" also called the Spirit World. But for Occultists and an increasing number of psychologists and paranormal scientists, the entity called a "spirit" in séance and other Spiritualist phenomena is better understood as the "surviving personality" of a deceased person in transition to another dimension, temporarily occupying a vehicle composed of the substance of the currently occupied dimension.

In other words, the person (personality) we know in daily life does not become a "spirit" after death but continues as a *personality* surviving death and occupying an astral vehicle instead of the cast-off physical vehicle. At some point, it will abandon the astral vehicle and move into a mental-causal vehicle. This "surviving personality" is not the *Soul* but a partial projection of the Soul seeking learning and growth opportunities by means of incarnating through a series of personalities manifesting successively again and again through physical, astral, mental, and causal vehicles—all of which are absorbed into the Soul.

During each life the personality functions through all these vehicles (physical-etheric-astral-mental-casual-spiritual) simultaneously but with different levels of awareness and purpose. In this life, the primary focus of consciousness is through the physical *(biological)* vehicle. After death there is movement into the energy aspect of the physical known as the "Etheric Double" from which it quickly moves on to focus through progressive levels of the astral vehicle with degrees of *emotional* awareness to the mental and causal vehicles. It is an astral-mental-causal unity that is primarily focused through the astral vehicle that is generally called "spirit" in the séance and other forms of spirit communication.

Table-Tilting, Table Tipping, Table-Lifting, Table-Turning: The partial or complete lifting of a table in a group setting used as an intermediary device in communication (most in response to yes/no questions with one tilt or two) with spirits.

Suggested Reading:

Slate, Joe H., and Carl Llewellyn Weschcke: *The Llewellyn Complete Book of Psychic Empowerment—A Compendium of Tools and Techniques for Growth and Transformation—Includes Journey of a Lifetime, a Self-Directed Program of Developmental Actions to "Put it All To-gether,* Llewellyn, 2011.

Tarot: A vast system of Archetypal Knowledge condensed into a system of 78 images on cards that can be finger-manipulated and then laid out in systematic patterns to answer specific questions or provide guidance to the solution of problems. While it is a form of divination, it is one of the most sophisticated and carefully developed systems of images and relationships following the structure of the Kabbalah's Tree of Life. Going beyond divination, it is also a system to access the Unconscious, and to structure magical ritual. It's a powerful Western esoteric system comparable to the Eastern I Ching.

The concepts of the Tarot cards have kept pace with the evolution of advancing knowledge, with the concepts and psychology of the European peoples. This is a very important point for it is fairly unique among occult divinatory systems for such evolution to take place. While interpretations of such systems as the I Ching will have some evolutionary change, the system and its physical representation in the 64 Hexagrams has remained static. The Tarot, in contrast, has changed, been modified, and evolved in physical form and structure, and in interpretation and application.

And there is inter-change between the Tarot deck and the person using the deck, facilitated by the artwork that—in my opinion—provides a positive aspect no other system has. The reader is *invited* to communicate with the cards, and that's one among many reasons that there are so many Tarot decks—over a thousand—to choose from.

Suggested Reading :

Amber K., and Azrael Arynn K: *Heart of Tarot, an Intuitive Approach,* Llewellyn, 2002.

Ferguson, Anna: *The Llewellyn Tarot.* 78-card deck and 288 page book, Llewellyn, 2006.

Cicero, Chic, and Tabatha: *The New Golden Dawn Ritual Tarot—Keys to the Rituals, Symbolism, Magic and Divination,* Llewellyn, 1997.

Hollander, P. Scott: *Tarot for Beginners—An Easy Guide to Understanding and Interpreting the Tarot,* Llewellyn, 2002.

Kraig, Donald Michael: *Tarot and Magic—How to use the Tarot to do magic on a practical level, with Tarot Spells, Talismans, working on the Astral Plane, etc.,* Llewellyn, 2002.

Louis, Anthony: *Tarot Plain and Simple—A self-study program to do readings for yourself and others,* Llewellyn, 2002. Written by a psychiatrist, with a Jungian approach to understanding human nature and psychological conflict.

Slate, Joe H., and Carl Llewellyn Weschcke: *Psychic Empowerment—Tools and Techniques,* Llewellyn, 2011.

Sterling, Stephen: *Tarot Awareness, Exploring the Spiritual Path, Llewellyn—How the Tarot can be a gateway toward spiritual development by unlocking a vibrant communication with the divine,* Llewellyn, 2000.

Telepathy: Mind-to-mind communication of thoughts, ideas, images, feelings and messages through psychic means and generally categorized within extra-sensory perception. The communication may take the form of a mental image, voices, dreams, feelings of anxiety, or thoughts "out of the blue."

Telepathy is commonly recognized as a natural ability that can be developed through training and practice. Some people—as is the case with any natural ability—have a greater natural skill than others. Sometimes a temporary increase in ability is associated with shamanic practices and spiritualist phenomena. In other cases telepathy is spontaneous in times of crisis.

Telepathic communication can be deliberately induced under hypnosis (Telepathic Hypnosis), and Russian scientists, including L. L. Vasiliev in the mid-1920's, investigated manipulating behavior at a distance in persons through post-hypnotic suggestion *and* telepathic communication between hypnotist and subject. Through both hypnosis and self-hypnosis, telepathic ability and sensitivity is experienced during trance, and likewise in other trance experiences in séances and meditation.

There is some evidence that telepathic ability improves with age, with caffeine, and when the physical senses are impaired.

"Think Long" and **"Think Small:"** Both these admonitions are relative to the magnitude of the project under consideration, and our knowledge and understanding of the factors involved. "Think Long" contrasts to *Short Term* Planning and Measurement, both in business applications and in research studies. "Short term profits" negate the need for long term planning and investment, often leading to misjudgment of long term funding and viability.

"Think Small" encourages careful consideration and development of all the factors important to long term success. Thinking (and Planning) Long and Big become progressively important to maintaining the growth and development of successful projects. While avoiding the mistakes of Haste and Waste.

Thought Form: 1) An astral image created by concentrated thought intended to accomplish a specified objective. When reinforced with emotion and charged with etheric energy, it will become physically manifest. 2) A spontaneous image created in the imagination that is charged with emotional energy. Either is perceived by a clairvoyant and is felt by ordinary people with some degree of psychic sensitivity. A carefully constructed mental image that is charged with emotional energy can become a manipulative tool used in product marketing, political action, and religious domination.

Suggested Reading:

Ashcroft-Nowicki, D., and Brennan, J. H. *Magical Use of Thought Forms, a Proven System of Mental and Spiritual Empowerment,* Llewellyn, 2001.

Transitioning into the New Age, NOW!: While dating of when an Age ends and another begins is difficult and subject to debate, the fact of transition starts NOW and calls for forward thinking, analysis, and planning. *What are the foreseeable challenges? What do we need to do now and later?*

Tree Power Procedure: A procedure designed to facilitate an empowering interaction with a tree as an instrument of nature.

Triangle of Power: (Self-Hypnosis) A physical gesture used to generate a triangle with the hands by joining the thumbs to form its base and the right index fingers to form its peak. It is a multi-purposeful gesture which can be use dto facilitate induction of self-hypnosis as well as to view the human aura, including that of oneself and others alike. It can also be used as a post-hypnotic or post-script cue.

Vibration: Everything that exists "vibrates." Vibrations are the *motion* of physical and non-physical atoms within all matter and substance, and are measured by their frequency per second. Touch, sound, odor, taste and sight are each characterized by particular ranges of vibrations and all phenomena perceived by these senses occur within defined ranges of vibration.

Further it is in our sharing of consciousness with all things that we can be aware of that motion. More importantly, however, the nature of matter and of consciousness changes as the *rate* of vibration changes. As we consciously raise our own vibrations we perceive the matter at different levels, or "planes."

And our perceptions are uniquely *tuned in* to specific ranges of vibration that we sense with our appropriate organs—physical as well as psychic although these psychic organs are different in structure and nature than the physical ones. Nevertheless, some psychic perceptions combine the physical organ with one of the chakras—which we can call "psychic" or etheric organs.

"Vibration" refers to movement and vibrations are measured by their frequency per second.

The following table is scientific and speculative. It is also visibly incomplete and begs reader input. Its intention is to provide a structure for our understanding of the position of Whole Person within the Whole Universe inclusive of all that lies outside of our physical perception. Because of the size of some of the numbers, we are providing a table of the "meanings" of standard prefixes to terms used in measurements.

Frequency (approximate Vibrations or Beats or Waves or Cycles or Hertz (Hz) per Second)

Note: the meanings of prefixes—

nano- means **n** 10^{-9} or 0.000000001 (minus 8 zeros = milliardth)

micro-	**u** 10^{-6} or 0.000001 (minus 5 zeros = millionth)
milli-	**m** 10^{-3} or 0.001 (minus 2 zeros = thousandth)
centi-	**c** 10^{-2} or 0.01 (minus 1 zero = hundredth)
deci-	**d** 10^{-1} or 0.1 (no zeros—tenth)
	10^{0} or 1
Deca-	**D** 10^{1} or 1 zero = ten
Hector-	**H** 10^{2} or 100 (2 zeros = hundred)
Kilo-	**K** 10^{3} or 1,000 (3 zeros = thousand)
Mega-	**M** 10^{6} or 1,000,000 (6 zeros = million)
Giga-	**G** 10^{9} or 1,000,000,000 (9 zeros = billion)
Tera-	**T** 10^{12} or 1,000,000,000,000 (12 zeros = trillion)
Peta-	**P** 10^{15} or 1,000,000,000,000,000 (15 zeros)
Exa-	**E** 10^{18} or 1,000,000,000,000,000,000 (18 zeros)
Zeta-	**Z** 10^{21} (21 zeros)
Yotta-	**B** 10^{24} (24 zeros)

Infrasonic to Very Low Frequency (VLF)
Waves, Magnetism and Gravity:

(Measured in **G** Gauss (not a prefix) 10^{-2} or minus 2 zeros to 100 Hz)

Certain Paranormal senses and phenomena, including levitation.

.00000	.0000	.000	.00	0 gauss
ESP	Dowsing	Black	Gravity	Magnetic
	Field	Streams*	Field	Field

*Described as "harmful earth rays" studied by members of the Institute of Electrical and Electronics Engineers in John Keel's *The Eighth Tower*.

Physical Senses—in vibrations per second:

Touch	2 to 16
Hearing	(from 16 in infants) 20 to 28,000
	Infrasonic Base Treble Ultrasonic

Taste

Smell

Sight	370 THz	to	750 THz
	Infrared Red	*Violet*	*Ultraviolet*

Brain Waves in vibrations per second:

Delta	1 to 3
Theta	4 to 7
Alpha	8 to 13
Beta	14 to 28

Electromagnetic Spectrum, longer waves: in Hertz:

Electric Power and AC Motors	60 to 100
Very Low Frequency Radio	3 KHz to 300 KHz
Radio, AM	540 KHz to 1630 KHz
Radio, Shortwave Broadcast	5.95 MHz to 26.1 MHz
Very High Frequency (VHF)	30 MHz to 300 MHz
Television, Band I	54 MHz to 88 MHz
FM Radio, Band II	88 MHz to 174 MHz
Television, Band III	174 MHz to 216 MHz
Ultra High Frequency (UHF)	300 MHz to 3000 MHz

Television, Bands IV and V, Channels 14-70   470 MHz to 806 MHz

Super high frequencies (SHF)—Microwaves: 3 GHzto 30 GHz

Infrared, Heat   300 GHz to 430 GHz

Visible Light (visible to human, *physical,* sight:430 THz to 750 THz

Red	400 to 484 THz
Orange	484 to 508 THz
Yellow	508 to 526 THz
Green	526 to 606 THz
Cyan	606 to 630 THz
Blue	631 to 668 THz
Violet	668 to 789 THz

Ultraviolet	1.62 PHz to 30 PHz
Spirit Light (visible to human, *psychic,* sight)	300 GHz to 40 PHz
X-Ray	30 PHz to 30 EHz
Gamma Rays	30 EHz to 3000 EHz
Cosmic Rays	10^{20} to 10^{21}

Includes levels of Psychic Projections, and of Soul Essence

Vibration (of voice): When pronouncing a word or phrase for psychic effect it must be done 1) at a lower octave than normal; 2) louder than normal but without stress; 3) with a vibratory feeling—sort of a trembling or buzzing sensation throughout the body. With practice the effect should be noticeable wherever the words are projected inside or outside the body.

Vibrations: The *motion* of physical atoms within all matter. It further recognizes that in our sharing of consciousness with all things, we can be aware of that motion. More importantly, however, the nature of matter and of consciousness changes as the *rate* of vibration changes. As we consciously raise our own vibrations we perceive the matter at different levels, or "planes."

Water Gazing: A procedure in which gazing at a bowl of water is used to activate various psychic functions as well as promote creativity, problem solving, and a positive mental state.

Whole Person: In addition to the physical/etheric composite, the entire spirit manifested "whole-person" is made up of the astral, mental and causal vehicles. The chakras repeat in some manner through all levels, including the physical where they relate to the nerve complexes mainly located from the bottom to the top of the spinal column culminating with the brain. Each etheric chakra is a *channel* between the physical nerve plexi and the astral chakras.

Also, an expression to represent the entirety of our potential and inclusive of all the subtle bodies. In "becoming more than you are," you are fulfilling the innate potentials that you have. You are born a potentially whole and complete person, with undeveloped powers. The meaning of life is found in developing those powers, turning them into skills, and fulfilling all your potentials. That will make you a Whole Person and serves the purpose of Creation as we can know it.

"Ye are Gods in the making": While common in esoteric literature and teachings, old and new, East and West, it is a phrase said many times with many different meanings depending on the context. The most common interpretation is within the contexts of reincarnation and continued human biological and spiritual evolvement. A further concept includes that of continued cosmic evolution—of a universe starting with either a Big Bang or a Soft Whisper (who knows for sure!)—and evolving in continuous waves of expansion and complexity inclusive of all life and consciousness from the most minute to the most huge, and both visible and invisible. Still other concepts include a hierarchy of divine and semi-divine beings from "elementals" through angels, and then also of those Gods and Goddesses believed to have initiated with human thought forms nurtured by emotion, devotion, sacrifice, and prayer.

Another aspect of the concept is that of "Success Magick" (also known as "Creative Visualization") in which the trained human magician shapes his or her own destiny in the material environment.

REFERENCES

American Psychological Association. (Spring 2006). APA books and APA videos. 24.

Collier, R. (1926). The secret of the ages, Vol. 2. Robert Collier, Publisher. New York. 140.

Kierulff, S. (September/October 2005). Time changed author's beliefs. Columbus, Ohio: The national psychologist, Columbus, Ohio. 18.

Kirchheimer, S. (September/October 2005). Spark your "sixth" sense. AARP the magazine (p. 27). Washington, DC: AARP.

Miller, W. R. (1999). Integrating spirituality into treatment. Washington, DC: American Psychological Association.

Miller, W. and Delaney, H. (Eds.) (2005). Judeo-Christian perspectives on psychology. Washington, DC: American Psychological Association.

Richards, P. S., and Bergin, A. E. (2005). A spiritual strategy for counseling and psychotherapy (2nd ed.). Washington, DC: American Psychological Association.

———. (2004). Casebook for a spiritual strategy in counseling and psychotherapy. Washington, DC: American Psychological Association.

———. (2000). Handbook of psychotherapy and religious diversity. Washington, DC: American Psychological Association.

Sperry, L., and Shafranske, E. P. (Eds.) (2005). Spiritually oriented psychotherapy. Washington, DC: American Psychological Association.

INDEX
IF YOU DON'T KNOW WHAT YOU ARE LOOKING FOR,
YOU PROBABLY WON'T FIND IT!

TO WRITE TO THE AUTHORS

If you wish to contact the author or would like more information about this book, please write to the author in care of Llewellyn Worldwide Ltd., and we will forward your request. Both the author and publisher appreciate hearing from you and learning of your enjoyment of this book and how it has helped you. Llewellyn Worldwide Ltd. cannot guarantee that every letter written to the author can be answered, but all will be forwarded. Please write to:

Llewellyn's New Worlds of Mind and Spirit
2143 Wooddale Drive, Woodbury, MN 55125-2989
Please enclose a self-addressed, stamped envelope for reply, or $1.00 to cover costs. If outside USA, enclose international postal reply coupon.

FREE CATALOG FROM LLEWELLYN

For more than one hundred years Llewellyn has brought its readers knowledge in the fields of metaphysics and human potential. Learn about the newest books in spiritual guidance, natural healing, astrology, occult philosophy, and more. Enjoy book reviews, New Age articles, a calendar of events, plus current advertised products and services. To get your free copy of Llewellyn's *New Worlds*, send your name and address to:

Llewellyn's New Worlds of Mind and Spirit
2143 Wooddale Drive, Woodbury, MN 55125-2989